JOURNAL FOR THE STUDY OF THE HISTORICAL JESUS
SUPPLEMENT SERIES

Executive Editor
Robert L. Webb

Editorial Board
Dale C. Allison, Jr., Scot McKnight, Mark Allan Powell

Published under
JOURNAL FOR THE STUDY OF THE NEW TESTAMENT
SUPPLEMENT SERIES
275

Editor
Mark Goodacre

Editorial Board
John M.G. Barclay, Craig Blomberg, Elizabeth A. Castelli,
Kathleen E. Corley, R. Alan Culpepper, James D.G. Dunn,
Craig A. Evans, Stephen Fowl, Robert Fowler, Simon J. Gathercole,
Michael Labahn, Robert Wall, Robert L. Webb, Catrin H. Williams

Apocalypticism, Anti-Semitism and the Historical Jesus

Subtexts in Criticism

Edited by
John S. Kloppenborg
with
John W. Marshall

T & T CLARK INTERNATIONAL
A Continuum imprint
LONDON • NEW YORK

Copyright © John S. Kloppenborg with John W. Marshall and the
contributors, 2005
A Continuum imprint

Published by T&T Clark International
The Tower Building, 11 York Road, London SE1 7NX
15 East 26th Street, Suite 1703, New York, NY 10010

www.tandtclark.com

British Library Cataloguing-in-Publication Data
A catalogue record for this book is available from the British Library

ISBN 0567084280   (hardback)

Typeset by Data Standards Ltd, Frome, Somerset, BA11 1RE
Printed on acid-free paper in Great Britain by Antony Rowe Ltd,
Chippenham, Wilts.

CONTENTS

The essays in this volume originated as the fruit of a symposium, held on March 7, 2003 under the generous patronage of the Chancellor Jackman Program for the Arts at the University of Toronto, on the topic 'Apocalypticism, Anti-Semitism, and the Historical Jesus: Subtexts in Criticism'. The point of the symposium and the volume which came from it was not to debate, yet again, whether the historical Jesus ought to be thought of as an apocalypticist of some variety, or to discuss the particular location within Second Temple Judaism that he and his immediate followers occupied. Instead, it was to ask why these issues are seen to matter as topics of intellectual inquiry and matter so acutely. For these two topics have come to mark the fault lines in much of the recent scholarly literature on the historical Jesus.

The burden of historical-Jesus scholarship for the last few decades has been to distinguish between core historical memories and later trans-formations, accretions and distortions and to arrive at a responsible and defensible reconstruction of the historical Jesus. Virtually all agree that apocalyptic beliefs and millenarianism formed at least part of the matrix of the culture in first-century Jewish Palestine. There is a sharp disagree-ment, however, concerning the extent to which Jesus shared apocalyptic and millenarian beliefs. The possibility of arriving at a consensus appears rather slight at the moment, due to disagreements in the evaluation of the historical worth of some of the primary sources available (Mark, Q, the *Gospel of Thomas* and a few other sources), disagreements concerning the application of the so-called 'criteria of authenticity', disagreements about how to define the specific intellectual and cultural environment(s) in which Jesus lived, and a few other methodological disagreements.

Although much ink has been spilled in defending or opposing an 'apocalyptic Jesus', almost nothing has been said on the questions of what, from the standpoint of modern historiography on Jesus, is *at stake* in the issue of whether or not he was an apocalypticist or a millenarian prophet, and what is at stake in insisting that his alleged apocalypticism is a central and defining characteristic or, alternatively, a secondary or even incidental feature. These questions have less to do with the quantity and character of the available ancient evidence than they do with the ways in which the modern critic assembles evidence into a coherent picture, and with the conceptual and theological subtexts of historical Jesus scholarship. Scholars of Christian origins have been exceedingly slow to inquire into the ideological location of their own work as scholars or to be forthright about what conceptual 'work' is done by a particular historical reconstruction or by a particular privileging of one set of data over another. But such questioning is crucial in achieving a critical self-awareness of the larger entailments of historical scholarship on Jesus and the early Jesus movement.

A second focus of the symposium, and this volume, has to do with the 'Jewishness' of Jesus. Since the end of the Second World War, Jesus' 'Jewishness' has been variously acknowledged. Yet ironically, it *appears* to be one of the most controverted issues of scholarship on Christian origins. This is so for several reasons: twentieth-century scholarship on Judaism of the Second Temple period has shown that a great plurality in beliefs and practices existed, and that there was nothing approaching an 'orthodoxy'. Thus one way of framing the question is to inquire into the *kind* of first-century Judaism that Jesus best represents. Again, the primary evidence from the gospels and Q is susceptible to a variety of evaluations and several partly incompatible reconstructions have been advanced, including Jesus as a liberal Pharisee, a *hasid*, a Jewish peasant, a reformist prophet, an advocate of village reconstruction, an apocalyptic prophet, a visionary, a sage, and a Jewish cynic. This list could be expanded and, of course, various combinations are also possible.

While there is sharp disagreement concerning the kind of Judaism(s) represented by Jesus, there has been far less discussion of why the question matters and what is at stake in promoting Jesus' 'Jewishness' over other possibly defining characteristics. It is obvious that in the wake of the Shoah and the awareness in Western scholarship of the role that supersessionism in Christianity played in creating ideological conditions in which anti-Semitism could flourish, a careful recovery of Jesus' Jewishness was a desideratum, both from the standpoint of responsible historical scholarship and from that of the *Wirkungsgeschichte* of de-Judaized images of Jesus. Now, however, we find ourselves faced with several competing versions of a *Jewish* Jesus without much clarity on what is at stake historiographically or theoretically in such portraits. And the argument over what sort of Judaism Jesus represented appears at times to be an argument about what constitutes *authentic* Judaism.

The guiding question for this symposium is not whether, at the level of evidence and argument, the Jesus of history should be regarded as an apocalypticist and what sort of Judaism he represented, but instead what is at stake in these questions. In asking about stakes, we do not have in mind an exercise in amateur psychologizing about colleagues' motivations. Such speculations are both idle (since they are normally proffered without any real evidentiary foundation or professional psychotherapeutic competence) and ineffective (since such accusations are *ad hominem* and are inevitably dismissed as vacuous by those attacked and by intelligent readers). The stakes that we seek to lay out have to do rather with the conceptual 'work' that is done by certain ways of posing questions. It should be obvious in hindsight that the pronounced shift in the agenda of scholarship on Christian origins that occurred in the early 1970s, from a preoccupation with theological *ideas* to explorations of the *social world* of the early Jesus movement – its implicit and explicit political postures, the influence of Hellenistic and Roman social practices upon the movement, and the movement's role as an agent of social innovation – had very much to do with social and political questions that had arisen in Western society as a result of the Viet Nam War, Kent State, the Democratic National Convention, and the 1968 student demonstrations in Europe. These and other events put into sharp relief the tensions that existed between churches and synagogues and governments, between citizens and their leaders. It energized scholars of Christian origins to raise analogous questions about the politics, social location, and economics of the Jesus movement. This is not necessarily a matter of reading modern problems into antiquity, though, if done in an undisciplined and reckless fashion, it might be. Rather, it is to acknowledge that the questions that we raise as scholars are not innocent, 'neutral' questions, but belong in part to conceptual frameworks that *we* bring to our work as scholars.

Although our colleagues in the field have been remarkably reticent to lay out what they see as the intellectual stakes in contemporary Jesus scholarship – with the consequence that there is practically no serious body of literature from which to begin a discussion – a few publications were read by all of the panelists and, whether or not they appear in the essays that follow, served as a general orientation to this complex topic. This were:

> Dale C. Allison, *Jesus of Nazareth: Millenarian Prophet* (Minneapolis: Fortress, 1998).
>
> John Dominic Crossan, *The Birth of Christianity: Discovering What Happened in the Years Immediately After the Execution of Jesus* (San Francisco: HarperSanFrancisco, 1998), 575–86.
>
> Paula Fredriksen, *Jesus of Nazareth, King of the Jews: A Jewish Life and the Emergence of Christianity* (New York: Alfred Knopf, 1999), 261–70.
>
> John S. Kloppenborg, 'A Dog Among the Pigeons: The "Cynic Hypothesis" as a Theological Problem', in *From Quest to Quelle: Festschrift James M. Robinson* (ed. Jon Asgeirsson, Kristin de Troyer and Marvin W. Meyer; BETL, 146; Leuven: Uitgeverij Peeters, 1999), 77–117.
>
> Amy-Jill Levine, 'Second Temple Judaism, Jesus and Women: Yeast of Eden', *Biblical Interpretation* 2.1 (1994): 8–33.
>
> Robert J. Miller (ed.), *The Apocalyptic Jesus: A Debate* (Santa Rosa, CA: Polebridge, 2001).

The organizers of the conference and editors would like to thank the Chancellor Jackman Program for the Arts, Trinity College at the University of Toronto, the Department for the Study of Religion and its chair, James DiCenso, and the Jewish Studies Program and its chair, Derek Penslar. The organizers are also grateful to Polebridge Press, David Penner, Peter Richardson, Colleen Shantz and Junko Chodos for various kindnesses.

JSK

ABBREVIATIONS

BETL	Bibliotheca ephemeridum theologicarum lovaniensium
Bib	*Biblica*
BZNW	Beihefte zur die *Zeitschrift für die neutestamentliche Wissenschaft*
ESCJ	Studies in Christianity and Judaism/Études sur le christianisme et le judaïsme
HTKNT	Herders theologischer Kommentar zum Neuen Testament
HTR	*Harvard Theological Review*
ICC	International Critical Commentary
Int	*Interpretation*
JBL	*Journal of Biblical Literature*
JECS	*Journal of Early Christian Studies*
JSHJ	*Journal for the Study of the Historical Jesus*
JTS	*Journal of Theological Studies*
NovT	*Novum Testamentum*
NTS	*New Testament Studies*
PVTG	Pseudepigrapha Veteris Testamenti Graece
RevQ	*Revue de Qumrân*
SBT	Studies in Biblical Theology
SJLA	Studies in Judaism in Late Antiquity
TF	Theologische Forschung
TS	*Theological Studies*
VC	*Vigiliae christianae*
WUNT	Wissenschaftliche Untersuchungen zum Neuen Testament
ZTK	*Zeitschrift für Theologie und Kirche*

As One Unknown, Without a Name?
Co-opting the Apocalyptic Jesus

John S. Kloppenborg

University of Toronto

The goal of this volume is to attempt to make some sense of two features of recent discussions of the historical Jesus. The first feature has to do with the way in which apocalypticism and beliefs about the future have come to occupy a central position in the debate concerning the reconstruction of Jesus' views and significance – probably *the* central position in Jesus research. Did Jesus expect God to intervene in cosmic affairs in the imminent future to bring about the Kingdom of God, the resurrection of the dead, and the judgment of the wicked? Or should the futuristic language and metaphors found in the Jesus tradition be treated either as secondary, apocalypticizing accretions, or as language that comments on the present rather than the future? Scholars are aligned generally in two camps, viewing basically the same set of primary sources and arriving at diametrically opposed conclusions.

To settle this issue is far beyond the scope of a volume of this nature. Instead, our goal is more modest: to ask why this question *matters* in the first place and why it has achieved such a central and defining place in scholarship. For it is my working assumption that in humanistic scholarship the general framework within which specific questions are posed and the intellectual constructs that flow from these frameworks are rarely innocent but serve, explicitly or implicitly, deeper theoretical goals. It will not solve the initial question to understand what those theoretical goals might be, but it may well make it possible to conduct the debate at a greater level of self-consciousness.

Nowhere is this more important than in regard to the second topic of this volume: the Jewishness of Jesus. As William Arnal recently observed, a curious state of affairs now exists in contemporary Jesus scholarship:

'No one denies Jesus' Judaism, yet it is bitterly contested'.[1] Ever since Géza Vermès' *Jesus the Jew* and E.P. Sanders' *Jesus and Judaism*,[2] there has been a concerted and self-conscious effort to escape the theological supersessionism and lurking anti-Semitism that infected previous generations of scholarship on Jesus, which programmatically opposed Jesus to 'Judaism', the 'Torah', and 'Jewish religion', denigrating – even demonizing – these in the process. At least part of the impetus for the renewed effort to situate Jesus *within* Second Temple Judaism is clear: the realization, however belated, of how Christian anti-Semitism fuelled the murder of Jews before and during the Shoah and how it disinclined Christians from rendering aid and refuge to the victims of the Shoah. Along with this realization comes the imperative to rid Jesus scholarship of this toxic waste.

This only makes the current situation more perplexing, since Jesus' Jewishness is affirmed by virtually all involved in the debate. So why is it still a matter of bitter polemics? It seems obvious that at one level the debate is in fact about the *kind of Jew* that Jesus was. But this way of framing the question disguises another debate, about what defines Second Temple Judaism. Since the discovery of the Dead Sea Scrolls and the intensive analysis of other writings of the Second Temple period, it is agreed by almost all that Second Temple Judaism was highly varied in its complexion. The question has now become, what kinds of diversity are imaginable and what are the limits of 'Judaism'? This issue is seen most acutely in the criticism leveled at Burton Mack and John Dominic Crossan for their characterizations of Jesus as a 'Jewish cynic' – criticism that appears often to rest on an unargued, indeed probably unarguable, assertion that 'Jewish' and 'cynic' are mutually exclusive conceptual categories.[3] Or again, E.P. Sanders' contention that the synoptic Sabbath

---

1.   William E. Arnal, 'Making and Re-Making the Jesus-Sign: Contemporary Markings on the Body of Christ', in *Whose Historical Jesus?* (ed. William E. Arnal and Michel Desjardins; ESCJ, 7; Waterloo, Ont.: Canadian Corporation for Studies in Religion/ Corporation canadienne des sciences religieuses by Wilfrid Laurier University Press, 1997), 308–19, at p. 309.

2.   Géza Vermès, *Jesus the Jew: A Historian's Reading of the Gospels* (London: SCM; Philadelphia: Fortress, 2nd edn, 1983 [1973]); E. P. Sanders, *Jesus and Judaism* (London: SCM, 1985).

3.   N.T. Wright (*Christian Origins and the Question of God. Volume 2: Jesus and the Victory of God* [Minneapolis: Fortress; London: SPCK, 1996], 79 n. 233) makes the invidious insinuation that those who propose a cynic analogy belong to the legacy of the Nazi scholarship. 'Have the New Questers, and the advocates of the Cynic Jesus, come to terms with the politically problematic analogy between themselves and those German scholars who, in the 1920s and 1930s, reduced almost to nil the specific Jewishness of Jesus and his message?' For a careful analysis of the polemical use of Nazi scholarship in the current debate, see Peter M. Head, 'The Nazi Quest for an Aryan Jesus', *JSHJ* 2.1 (2004): 55–89.

controversies and Mark 7.15, understood strictly as a saying about *kashrut*, are inauthentic because they represent views too radical to ascribe to a first-century Jew, point to a deeper question of the degree of nonconformity with common Second Temple Jewish practices that can be tolerated in a figure or movement that is called 'Jewish'. An earlier generation of scholars influenced by neo-orthodoxy happily pronounced Jesus to have transcended and superseded 'Judaism', to have 'broken free' of it (as if Jews generally believed themselves to be enslaved). Such a view, besides being unduly misled by the Pauline polemic in Galatians, generally assumed an exceedingly narrow, not to say inaccurate, definition of what constituted 'Judaism'. Ironically, the more recent wave of Jesus scholarship, which variously concedes important diversities in practice and belief in Judaism, often holds the historical Jesus to a higher standard of conformity with a 'common Judaism' than that allowed for other Second Temple groups and persons.[4] Thus the debate about the historical Jesus has become a debate about 'historical Judaism', rather like Séan Freyne's quip that the debate about the historical Jesus has become a debate about the historical Galilee.

Albert Schweitzer and Jesus' Apocalypticism

The title of this essay (minus the question mark) is taken from the final paragraph of Albert Schweitzer's *The Quest of the Historical Jesus*, published in 1906: 'He comes to us as one unknown, without a name, [just] as of old, by the lakeside, he came to those men who knew him not'.[5] Schweitzer's statement served as a shorthand for the argument developed in his book, that for the historical Jesus the term 'kingdom of God' had nothing to do with the realization in human history of state of moral enlightenment through the inculcation of rational and humane values – a view strongly promoted by the preceding decades of German Protestant Jesus scholarship, nurtured by seventeenth-century rationalism, and

4. On 'common Judaism', see Martin Hengel and Roland Deines, 'E.P. Sanders' "Common Judaism", Jesus, and the Pharisees', *JTS* 46 (1995): 1–70.

5. Albert Schweitzer, *Von Reimarus zu Wrede: Eine Geschichte der Leben Jesu Forschung* [Tübingen: J.C.B. Mohr (Paul Siebeck), 1906]; ET: *The Quest of the Historical Jesus: A Critical Study of Its Progress from Reimarus to Wrede*, preface by F.C. Burkitt (New York: Macmillan & Co., 1910), 403; *Geschichte der Leben-Jesu-Forschung*, 2. Aufl. des Werkes *Von Reimarus zu Wrede* (Tübingen: J.C.B. Mohr [Paul Siebeck], 1913); *idem, The Quest of the Historical Jesus* (ed. John Bowden, foreword Dennis Nineham; Minneapolis: Fortress, 1st complete edn, 2001), 487.

epitomized in H.J. Holtzmann's sketch of a life of Jesus in 1863.[6] Instead, the Jesus of history breathed the strange and foreign air of Second Temple Jewish apocalypticism, with its belief in God's imminent intervention in the cosmos to bring about a new order of things: the destruction or subjugation of the forces of evil and impiety, the resurrection of the dead, and the judgment of the wicked and the reward of the pious.[7] Two consequences followed from this: first, and most obvious was the fact that Jesus was mistaken in his belief that cosmic transformation was

6. See the 'Portrait of Jesus' Life according to the "A" Source' in Heinrich Julius Holtzmann, *Die synoptischen Evangelien: Ihr Ursprung und geschichtlicher Charakter* (Leipzig: Wilhelm Engelmann, 1863), 268–96. This view of the 'kingdom of God' as essentially moral in nature is of course much older than Holtzmann. Kant (*Religion Within the Limits of Reason Alone* [trans. Theodore M. Greene and Hoyt H. Hudson; New York: Harper, 1960], 125–26), commenting on Luke 17.21–22 (which he rendered 'the kingdom of God is within you [*in euch*]'), argued Jesus 'revealed to his disciples the kingdom of God on earth only in its glorious, soul-elevating moral aspect, namely, in terms of the value of citizenship in a divine state, and to this end he informed them of what they had to do, not only to achieve it themselves but to unite with all others of the same mind and, so far as possible, with the entire human race'. In respect to beliefs in the Antichrist, the millennium, and the End, Kant declared: 'all these can take on, before reason, their right symbolic meaning; and to represent the last of these as an event not to be seen in advance (like the end of life, be it far or near) admirably expresses the necessity of standing ready at all times for the end and indeed . . . really to consider ourselves always chosen citizens of a divine (ethical) state'. Schweitzer's answer to this is clear: 'the Jesus of Nazareth who came forward publicly as the Messiah, who preached the ethic of the kingdom of God, who founded the kingdom of heaven on earth, and died to give his work its final consecration, never existed. He is a figure designed by rationalism, endowed with life by liberalism, and clothed by modern theology in a historical garb' (*Quest* [1913/2001], 478).

7.   Dale Allison has rightly pointed out to me (*per litt.*) that Schweitzer (and Johannes Weiss, in *Die Predigt Jesu vom Reiche Gottes* [Göttingen: Vandenhoeck & Ruprecht, 1892]) were not the first to emphasize the apocalypticism of Jesus, as indeed Schweitzer's own survey of prior scholarship makes clear. The fact that scholars such as Timothée Colani (*Jésus-Christ et les croyances messianiques de son temps* [Strasbourg: Treuttel et Wurtz, 2nd rev. and exp. edn, 1864]) so strenuously argued against the authenticity of Mark 13 and other apocalyptic elements in the Jesus tradition indicates that there were some who upheld these elements as constitutive of a portrait of the historical Jesus. Allison points out further (and rightly), and Schweitzer's contemporary Oskar Holtzmann (*The Life of Jesus* [London: A. & C. Black, 1904], 160 note) independently of Schweitzer held that 'the starting point of Jesus' preaching is . . . to be found in its eschatology: "The end of the existing world is immediately at hand, therefore repent ye". In that case we must regard the eschatological discourses in the preaching of Jesus as being (to use a metaphor) not merely accidental offshoots, but the roots which support the trunk of the tree. It was, we cannot doubt, with eschatological discourses that Jesus came forward in the first instance.' Nevertheless, it is also true that in the period between the 1860s and 1900s, the advocates of an apocalyptic Jesus were far less influential than the voices of Ritschl and Holtzmann and their successors.

imminent.[8] And second, Jesus' ethical teachings did not represent a program for the gradual realization of God's kingdom in history; rather, they were 'interim ethics'.[9]

This Jesus was indeed a stranger to the culture of pre-World War I Germany, with its *Kulturoptimismus* and its confidence in the imperative of European Christian culture to produce by moral exertion a truly enlightened and humane society through colonialist extension, even in 'darkest Africa', where Schweitzer himself had served as a medical missionary. As a missionary, Schweitzer's cultural sympathies lay with the European Enlightenment, not with an apocalyptic Jesus. He described European missionary activities in the 'heathen world' as the province of two competing groups: on the one hand, the pietists and orthodox, concentrating on 'saving souls' and preaching a 'faith that was in fetters to dogmatism'; and on the other, liberal Christianity, in whose company he includes himself, whose aim 'was to set the Gospel working primarily as a force for the restoration of mankind and the conditions of human society in the heathen world'.[10] As a modern man, Schweitzer's 'gospel' was not the strange gospel of the historical Jesus, but the moralizing gospel of Kant and Holtzmann.

Two related aspects of Schweitzer's argument about the historical Jesus have caught the attention of recent scholars of the historical Jesus. The first is his conclusion that Jesus believed himself to be the Messiah and that God's kingdom would be realized dramatically in the imminent future – this, in spite of the fact that Schweitzer personally was not at all sympathetic to such apocalyptic beliefs. This has been taken as a measure of Schweitzer's objectivity as a scholar. Second is his argument that the previous forty years of Jesus scholarship, in promoting a non-eschatological, ethical and transformationist view of the Kingdom, had confused

---

8.   Schweitzer, *Quest* [1913/2001], 327–29. Similarly, Oskar Holtzmann, *Jesus*, 501: 'The passing away of Jesus' contemporaries not only proved that he had been mistaken in certain of his sayings; it proved more than this, because the motive force of his preaching had been the thought of the speedy coming of the judgment, of the nearness of the kingdom of God. The expectation had been the determining factor in his own preaching of repentance, as well as that of his apostles.'

9.   Albert Schweitzer, *The Mystery of the Kingdom of God: The Secret of Jesus' Messiahship and Passion* (New York: Dodd, Mead, 1914), 101–103: '[T]here is no place for a morality of the Kingdom of God or for a development of the Kingdom – it lies beyond the borders of good and evil; it will be brought about by a cosmic catastrophe through which evil is to be completely overcome. Hence all moral criteria are to be abolished. *The Kingdom of God is super-moral*.'

10.   Albert Schweitzer, *Out of My Life and Thought: An Autobiography* (trans. C. T. Campion; New York: Holt, 1933), 95.

its own theological outlook with that of Jesus, whose own ethical views were inextricably connected to his apocalypticism.[11] Schweitzer opined:

> The Jesus of Nazareth who came forward publicly as the Messiah, who preaching the ethic of the kingdom of God, who founded the kingdom of heaven upon earth, and died to give his work its final consecration, never existed. He is a figure designed by rationalism, endowed with life by liberalism, and clothed by modern theology in a historical garb.[12]

Thus Schweitzer has been viewed as a signal example of the scholar of religion who resisted the urge to make Jesus a spokesperson for his or her own beliefs, and one who relentlessly exposed those who did. The enduring legacy of Schweitzer's two points is that any reconstruction of the historical Jesus which neglects or minimizes apocalyptic features is immediately liable to be treated as a self-serving effort to modernize Jesus.[13] Those who stress Jesus' apocalypticism are taken to be immune from such a criticism. In this paper I will suggest that, since Schweitzer's day, apocalypticism has also achieved important *theological* functions in contemporary Christian theology, such that the charge of ideological modernization is more generally applicable to *all* efforts to produce a portrait of the historical Jesus.

In recent discussion and polemics Schweitzer's originally *conceptual* point – that certain portraits of the historical Jesus betray the theological interests of German liberalism – has often been misconstrued as psychological or sociological commentary. Thus, for example, Ben Witherington opines that the Jesus of the Jesus Seminar 'tells us more about various members of the Jesus seminar than about Jesus',[14] although he provides no evidence whatsoever that he has direct knowledge of any of the personal beliefs of any of its members or that he is competent to pronounce on their personal motivations and beliefs. N.T. Wright, who

11. Schweitzer, *Out of My Life and Thought*, 53: 'We must reconcile ourselves to the fact that Jesus' religion of love made its appearance as part of a system of thought that anticipated a speedy end of the world. We cannot make it our own through the concepts in which he proclaimed it but must rather translate it into those of our modern view of the world.'

12. Schweitzer, *Quest* [1906/1910], 398; *Quest* [1913/2001], 478.

13. See already Martin Kähler, *The So-Called Historical Jesus and the Historic Biblical Christ* (ed., trans. and introduction by Carl E. Braaten; Philadelphia: Fortress, 1964), 55–56 who argues, first, that the process of historical reconstruction typically operates from 'the analogy [of the biographer's] own life and of human life in general' (55), and second, that the biography is usually guided 'by a preconceived view of religious and ethical matters. In other words, the biographer who portrays Jesus is always something of a dogmatician in the derogatory sense of the word' (56).

14. Ben Witherington, *The Jesus Quest: The Third Search for the Jew of Nazareth* (Downers Grove, IL: InterVarsity, 1995), 57.

expressly claims to be reviving Schweitzer's legacy,[15] comes closer to making a conceptual or perhaps sociological (rather than psychological) claim when he avers that Burton Mack's work is more about 'twentieth-century American religion' than about a first-century Galilean.[16] But since Wright never tells us what he thinks is constituted by 'American religion' – is he thinking about the legacy of American pragmatism and its impact on American religiosity, or does he have in view the impact of 'civil religion', or the social gospel, or fundamentalism?[17] – or how Mack might exemplify such a 'religion', Wright's use of the term 'American' appears little more than an instance of negative labeling. The work of the Jesus Seminar is routinely dismissed with the observation that it is 'California-based', as if Californians and those who associate with Californians represent a discrete social or psychological type with clearly demarked attitudes and beliefs.[18] Luke Timothy Johnson declares that 'many contemporary questers' of the historical Jesus suffer under an inner compulsion to overcome their fundamentalist pasts.[19] Insofar as some of those who engage in historical scholarship on Jesus are Christian, and insofar as some of those might have had a fundamentalist upbringing – I would not dare to venture any statistics, since I simply do not know – Johnson's claim could well be correct for certain individuals. Johnson himself makes no attempt whatsoever to document his claim. The incoherence in Johnson's assertion, however, lies in the fact that it provides neither a necessary nor a sufficient account of the views of the historical Jesus he wishes to explain. For he offers no reasonable basis for believing that there is a necessary link between a scholar's upbringing or current beliefs and his or her conclusions as a historian, and *a fortiori*, no

15. Wright, *Jesus*, 81.

16. Wright, *Jesus*, 43.

17. See William Baird, *History of New Testament Research. Volume 2: From Jonathan Edwards to Rudolf Bultmann* (Minneapolis: Fortress, 2003), 3–53, 288–360 for a nuanced treatment of the variety of trends in American New Testament criticism in the nineteenth and early twentieth centuries.

18. E.g., Gerd Theissen and Annette Merz, *The Historical Jesus: A Comprehensive Guide* (trans. John Bowden; London: SCM; Minneapolis: Fortress, 1998), 11. See Robert Miller's discussion of the attacks on the Jesus Seminar by Richard Hays, Luke Timothy Johnson, Howard C. Kee, Birger Pearson and Ben Witherington in *The Jesus Seminar and Its Critics* (Santa Rosa, CA: Polebridge, 1999), 67–77, where he chronicles the near-hysterical reactions to the Seminar and the numerous misrepresentations of its work.

19. Luke Timothy Johnson, 'The Humanity of Jesus: What's at Stake in the Quest for the Historical Jesus?' in John Dominic Crossan, Luke Timothy Johnson and Werner H. Kelber, *The Jesus Controversy: Perspectives in Context* (Harrisburg, PA: Trinity Press International, 1999), 59–60. Johnson refers to Robert Funk's autobiographical comments in *Honest to Jesus: Jesus for a New Millennium* (San Francisco: HarperSanFrancisco, 1996), 3–10, and apparently generalizes these to larger circles of historical Jesus scholars.

grounds for supposing that the collective personal histories of groups of scholars is a sufficient basis for evaluating their work.

I think it best to avoid such amateur psychological or sociological *ad hominem* speculations, which are whimsical at best and fatuous at worst, and instead concentrate on what was Schweitzer's interest, the theological or conceptual 'work' done by certain portraits of the historical Jesus.

For Schweitzer, Jesus' apocalyptic *beliefs* did no conceptual work as such in Schweitzer's world, since he regarded them as belonging to an outdated and 'world-denying' worldview.[20] Or at least, he concluded that in spite of Jesus' debt to the earlier Israelite beliefs in the fundamental goodness of creation, his ethics amounted to

> a renunciation of the present imperfect world in comparison with the perfect world to come. It is not a total, but only provisional, denial of life and the world.... Jesus...is in a position to call for active ethical behaviour toward our fellow men, even if he too must renounce systematic ethical activity as being really meaningful.[21]

This worldview was in sharp contrast to Schweitzer's own liberal theological convictions about what was needed in Western culture, languishing from its lack of a constructive worldview that could affirm human potential and contribute to material and spiritual progress.[22]

One might have expected Schweitzer simply to declare that the Jesus of history lacked any contemporary theological or conceptual relevance. Indeed some of Schweitzer's statements in the first edition of *Quest* point in this direction,[23] where he denied the possibility of arriving at an enduringly valid ethics of Jesus by stripping away its outer apocalyptic

---

20. Albert Schweitzer, *Indian Thought and Its Development* (trans. Mrs. Charles E.B. Russell; Boston, MA: Beacon, 1936), 1–2: 'World and life affirmation consists in this: that man regards existence as he experiences it in himself and as it has developed in the world as something of value *per se* and accordingly strives to let it reach perfection in himself, whilst within his own sphere of influence he endeavours to preserve and further it.

'World and life negation on the other hand consists in his regarding existence as he experiences it in himself and as it developed in the world as something meaningless and sorrowful, and he resolves accordingly (a) to bring life to a standstill in himself by mortifying his will-to-live, and (b) to renounce all activity which aims at improvement of conditions of life in this world.'

21. Albert Schweitzer, *The Kingdom of God and Primitive Christianity* (ed. Ulrich Neuenschwander; London: A. & C. Black, 1968 [posthumously published]), 99, 100.

22. Albert Schweitzer, *Civilization and Ethics*. II. *The Philosophy of Civilization* (London: A. & C. Black, 1923), 6–9.

23. Schweitzer, *Quest* [1906/1910], 398; *Quest* [1913/2001], 478–79.

dress.[24] The apocalyptic context was just too integrally connected with Jesus' ethics to be so easily removed. In the second (1913) edition of *Quest*, Schweitzer still denied that it was possible to isolate elements in Jesus' *beliefs* that are timeless, but now he argued that what was timeless was what he called Jesus' *will*. This 'will' is seen in

> the qualities of enthusiasm and heroism which arise out of the longing for the kingdom of God and belief in it, and which are not lessened but heightened by the limits within which such a world-view must exist. It is the strength and vehemence of belief in the kingdom of God which governs the level of understanding of the historical Jesus in a religion.[25]

Though the *content* of Jesus' ethics was wholly determined by his world-denying apocalyptic worldview, Jesus also manifested the 'inner freedom' of one who dared to meet the challenges of his world. 'The truth is', Schweitzer argued, 'that he cannot be an authority for us at the level of understanding but only at the level of the will.'[26] One sees here a certain parallel between Schweitzer's view and that of existential theology's distinction between the *content* of Jesus' and/or early Christian preaching – mythological in its cast and therefore irrelevant to post-Enlightenment Christians – and the self-understanding of the human subject before God, which came to expression in that preaching. Where Schweitzer, who wrote his doctoral dissertation on Kant, focused on ethical will, existential theology, influenced by Heidegger, spoke of *Existenzverständnis*.

Later, Schweitzer would comment on the 'magnificent paradox' of a

---

24. Schweitzer, *Quest* [1906/1910], 401: 'It is not given to history to disengage that which is abiding and eternal in the being of Jesus from the historical forms in which it worked itself out, and to introduce it into our world as a living influence.' Compare Schweitzer's later formulation in *Out of My Life and Thought* (above, n. 11), where he speaks of reclothing the religious truth of Jesus. (I owe this latter reference to Dale Allison, *per litt.*)

25. Schweitzer, *Quest* [1913/2001], 484: This view is already partially anticipated in the first edition: 'But the truth is, it is not Jesus as historically known, but Jesus as spiritually arisen within men, who is significant for our time and can help it. Not the historical Jesus, but the spirit which goes forth from him and in the spirits of men strives for new influence and rule, is that which overcomes the world' (*Quest* [1906/1910], 401).

26. Schweitzer, *Quest* [1913/2001], 482. There is also a gesture in the direction of this formulation in the first edition of *Quest* [1906/1910], 402: 'But in reality that which is eternal in the words of Jesus is due to the very fact that they are based on an eschatological worldview, and contain the expression of a mind for which the contemporary world with its historical and social circumstances no longer had any existence. They are appropriate, therefore, to any world, for in every world they raise the man who dares to meet their challenge, and does not turn and twist them into meaningless, above his world and his time, making him inwardly free, so that he is fitted to be, in his own world and in his own time, a simple channel of the power of Jesus.'

world-affirming ethical will existing in a world-denying worldview;[27] it is this world-affirming ethical will that was consistent with Schweitzer's own conviction of the necessity of an ethic that would permit civilization to survive and to make possible material and spiritual progress. Thus in the end, while the content of Jesus' apocalypticism was irrelevant to Schweitzer and did no conceptual work for him, Jesus turned out not to be entirely a stranger at the level of world-affirming will and in this context Schweitzer even spoke of the possibility of a mystical relationship with Jesus.[28] In his autobiography, Schweitzer ventured,

> even if that liberal Christianity has to give up identifying its belief with the teachings of Jesus in the way it used to think possible, it still has the spirit of Jesus not against it but on its side. Jesus no doubt fits his teaching into the late Jewish Messianic dogma. But he does not think dogmatically... Nowhere does he demand of his hearers that they shall sacrifice thinking to believing. Quite the contrary!... In the Sermon on the Mount he lets ethics, as the essence of religion, flood their hearts, leading them to judge the value of piety by what it makes of a man from the ethical point of view. Within the Messianic hopes which his hearers carry in their hearts, he kindles the fire of an ethical faith. Thus the Sermon on the Mount becomes the incontestable charter of liberal Christianity. The truth that the ethical is the essence of religion is firmly established on the authority of Jesus.[29]

Thus Schweitzer manages to retrieve a positive, world-affirming ethical will from Jesus' world-denying apocalypticism, while relegating Jesus' belief that he was the Messiah to the 'background'. With the eclipsing of Jesus' apocalypticism, 'we are now at liberty to let the religion of Jesus become a living force in our thought, as its purely spiritual and ethical nature demands'.[30]

There are several problems with Schweitzer's views. One is his rather obscure distinction between Jesus' culture-bound ethics and the ethical will that was somehow not culture-bound. In his autobiography, Schweitzer recalled his early dissatisfaction with the way his teacher

27. Schweitzer, *Civilization and Ethics*, 65–67. See the helpful discussion by Gregory W. Dawes, *The Historical Jesus Question: The Challenge of History to Religious Authority* (Louisville: Westminster/John Knox, 2001), 150.

28. Schweitzer, *Quest* [1913/2001], 486: 'Our relationship to Jesus is ultimately of a mystical kind. No personality of the past can be transported alive into the present by means of historical observation of by discursive thought about his authoritative significance. We can achieve a relation to such a personality only when we become united with him in the knowledge of a shared aspiration, when we feel that our will is clarified, enriched and enlivened by his will and when we rediscover ourselves through him. In this sense absolutely any deeper relationship is of a mystical kind. Our religion, insofar as it proves to be specifically Christian, is therefore not so much a Jesus-cult as a Jesus-mysticism.'

29. Schweitzer, *Out of My Life and Thought*, 58.

30. Schweitzer, *Out of My Life and Thought*, 59.

Holtzmann and Adolf von Harnack had 'spiritualized' eschatology. As Schweitzer saw matters, there were only two options:

> either to recognize and admit that Jesus did really live with a belief in the ideas of late Jewish eschatology, or assert that only those sayings are genuine in which He speaks in a truly spiritual way of the Messiah and the Messianic Kingdom, the remainder having been attributed to him by a primitive Christianity which had fallen back into the realistic views of late Judaism.[31]

William Wrede had taken the latter route, arguing that Messianic consciousness had been ascribed to Jesus by his followers.[32] Schweitzer's choice was the opposite, arguing that Jesus belonged firmly in the world of 'late Jewish eschatology', and that Jesus indeed believed himself to be the Messiah, even though his fate indicated that this was a false belief. But this decision, as his autobiography indicates, brought with it a deluge of questions from his contemporaries, inquiring what possible relevance an apocalyptic Jesus could have for the modern Christian. Schweitzer's answer appears to be little different from the 'spiritualizing' solutions he had rejected, for he ends up by reclaiming a useful 'essence' that had been clothed in strange apocalyptic clothing.[33]

A second problem is his notion of 'civilization' and its imperative of making material and spiritual progress. It was Schweitzer's nineteenth-century liberal confidence in the capacity of the human spirit to make progress and to establish 'civilization' – European civilization, that is – throughout the world that ran into direct conflict with (what he saw as) the world-denying pessimism of Jesus' apocalypticism. But Schweitzer's view of 'civilization' and its imperatives were scarcely an objective, rational construct, but reflected instead the cultural optimism of late-nineteenth-century beliefs – beliefs that were shattered by the horrors of the First World War. The progress of human society was not as ineluctable as Schweitzer's generation had thought, and the veneer of humane values revealed itself as much thinner than it had wanted to imagine. If the mechanized killing and the use of poison gas at Ypres and the Somme in World War I had not made this lesson clear enough, the horrors of the *Blitzkrieg*, the fire-bombing of Köln, and the ovens of Auschwitz would drive the point home three decades later for those who wished to see it.

---

31. Schweitzer, *Out of My Life and Thought*, 47.

32. William Wrede, *Das Messiasgeheimnis in den Evangelien* (Göttingen: Vandenhoeck & Ruprecht, 1901), ET *The Messianic Secret*, foreword by James M. Robinson (Greenwood, SC: Attic, 1971).

33. Schweitzer, *Out of My Life and Thought*, 55: 'The essence of Christianity is an affirmation of the world that has passed through a rejection of the world. Within a system of thought that rejects the world and anticipates its end Jesus sets up the ethic of active love.'

The Apocalyptic Jesus after Schweitzer

After Schweitzer the role of apocalyptic in constructions of the historical Jesus changed in two significant and seemingly opposed ways. On the one hand Schweitzer's view, that Jesus expected the Kingdom to be realized in the imminent future, was progressively qualified and eroded. It is not only the case with scholars such as C.H. Dodd, who denied apocalyptic eschatology altogether as constitutive of Jesus' outlook, but also among those who ostensibly embraced an apocalyptic Jesus, but who regularly reinterpreted futuristic language as 'really' meaning something else, as Dale Allison has pointed out.[34] But on the other hand, apocalyptic was embraced as an increasingly important *theological* category in a way that was quite foreign to Schweitzer.

Even though he was skeptical about the possibility of substantial knowledge of the historical Jesus and denied that historical knowledge constituted a basis for Christian faith, Rudolf Bultmann in 1926 accepted Schweitzer's conclusion that Jesus was a Messianic prophet, indeed perhaps 'more than is even apparent from the tradition'.[35] Jesus shared with other Jews of his day the expectation of a 'tremendous eschatological drama', including the resurrection of the dead, judgment, the punishment of the wicked, and the reward of the faithful.[36] Thus the Kingdom of God was not liberal theology's 'highest good', which can be pursued by human will and action; instead it was a 'miracle' wrought solely by God and as

34. See Dale C. Allison, *Jesus of Nazareth: Millenarian Prophet* (Minneapolis: Fortress, 1998), 152–71, who criticizes the approach of G. B. Caird (*The Language and Imagery of the Bible* [London: Duckworth, 1980], 243–71) and Wright (*Jesus*, 280–338), who argue that Jesus' futuristic language is really metaphorical. Wright, for example, declares that '[t]he "coming of the son of man" is. . .good first century metaphorical language for two things: the defeat of the enemies of the true people of God, and the vindication of the true people themselves. . . [T]he imagery of Mark 13,24–5, 27 can be easily understood. These verses, as Caird urged, are not "flat and literal prose." They do not speak of the collapse or end of the space-time universe. They are, as we have seen from the passages in Isaiah and Jeremiah quoted above [Isa 13.6, 9–11; 14.4, 12–15; 34.3–4; Jer 50.6, 8, 28; 15.6–10, 45–46, 50–51, 57], typical Jewish imagery for events within the present order that are felt and perceived as "cosmic" or, as we should say, as "earth-shattering".' Witherington, *The Jesus Quest*, 128 tries to avoid explicit futuristic language by arguing that Jesus did not *necessarily* expect the imminent end, only that it was *possible*. For a critique, see Robert J. Miller, 'Can the Historical Jesus be Made Safe for Orthodoxy? A Critique of *The Jesus Quest* by Ben Witherington III', *Journal of Higher Criticism* 4.1 (1997): 120–37.

35. Rudolf K. Bultmann, *Jesus* (Berlin: Deutsche Bibliothek, 1926); *idem, Jesus and the Word* (New York: Charles Scribner's Sons; London: I. Nicholson, 1934), 124.

36. Bultmann, *Jesus*, 38–39 qualifies Jesus' apocalypticism by observing that it contained no elaborate depictions of punishment or reward: 'In fact he absolutely repudiates all representations of the Kingdom which human imagination can create'. . . and he 'rejects the whole content of apocalyptic speculation, as he rejects also the calculation of the time and the watching for signs' (p. 39).

such 'wholly other'.[37] Thus far Bultmann is one with Schweitzer. But far from declaring apocalypticism to be strange and foreign, Bultmann embraced it with an existential interpretation:

> The real significance of the 'Kingdom of God' for the message of Jesus does not in any sense depend on the dramatic events attending its coming, nor on any circumstances which the imagination can conceive. It interests him not at all as a describable state of existence, but rather as the transcendent event, which signifies for man the ultimate Either-Or, which constrains him to decision.[38]

Although Kingdom language is wholly futuristic, its significance and power lay in determining the present:

> The coming of the Kingdom of God is therefore not really an event in the course of time, which is due to occur sometime and toward which man can either take a definite attitude or hold himself neutral... If men are standing in the crisis of decision, and if precisely this crisis is the essential characteristic of their humanity, then every hour is the last hour and we can understand that for Jesus the whole contemporary mythology is pressed into the service of this conception of human existence.[39]

Apocalypticism, thus stripped of its *actual* content of beliefs about the future and its mythological overcoat, was pressed into the service of Bultmann's philosophy of existence borrowed from Heidegger. It is clear why the liberal depiction of Jesus as a moralist would not serve Bultmann's theological purposes, since Jesus as a teacher of humankind's 'highest good' could scarcely be regarded as confronting humankind with an absolute Either-Or decision about existence itself, the key element in Bultmann's existential theology. Where Schweitzer ultimately sought to liberate Jesus' world-affirming ethical will from its apocalyptic conceptual content, Bultmann insisted that Jesus' ethical teachings, which he noted hardly constituted a complete or adequate lexicon of moral beliefs, had meaning only in their eschatological setting, as calls to treat the present as the moment of decision: 'Just this is what we found to be the final significance of the eschatological message', Bultmann writes, 'that man *now* stands under the necessity of decision, that his "Now" is always for him the final hour, in which his decision against the world and for God is demanded, in which every claim of his own is to be silenced'.[40] The cost of this existential interpretation is high: apocalyptic beliefs are stripped of their particularity and reduced to the confrontation of the individual with

---

37. Bultmann, *Jesus*, 35–37.
38. Bultmann, *Jesus*, 41.
39. Bultmann, *Jesus*, 51–52.
40. Bultmann, *Jesus*, 131 (emphasis original).

her own finitude and with the sovereignty of God's demand; and ethical beliefs, robbed of all specific content, become instances of the subject apprehending herself as a subject before God, no longer at her own disposal but as a subject in God's world and serving God's ends.

Apocalypticism, as Bultmann interpreted its inner demythologized sense, thus became a cipher of the *finality* towards which human existence is oriented and served to exemplify the twin Reformation doctrines of God's absolute sovereignty over humankind and the necessity of creaturely decision and obedience. Apocalypticism in its classical, Second Temple form was no more congenial to Bultmann than it had been to Schweitzer. Read 'existentially', however, it did conceptual work that Schweitzer had not thought possible.

The paradox mentioned above, of apocalyptic views being progressively manipulated and reduced through reinterpretation, and of apocalyptic increasingly becoming a central theological category is illustrated in the work of Ernst Käsemann and Martin Hengel. In Käsemann's famous 1953 address to fellow students of Bultmann, he was no more sanguine than his teacher about the ability of critical scholarship to produce a biography of Jesus. But he famously argued that the structure of early Christian preaching had a vested interest in the life of Jesus – so much so that the early Jesus movement felt the need to create a history where it was lacking. Its commitment to history is demonstrated by the fact that it never allowed myth to replace history.[41] This provided the authorization for contemporary scholars to ask about the historical Jesus. It is in this context that Käsemann developed the so-called criterion of double dissimilarity, according to which sayings or traditions might be recognized as authentic

> when there are no grounds either for deriving a tradition from Judaism or for ascribing it to primitive Christianity, and especially when Jewish Christianity has mitigated or modified the received tradition, as having found it too bold for its taste.[42]

Käsemann's point of entry into the Jesus tradition is the *egō de legō hymin* formula of the Matthaean antitheses (Mt. 5.21–48), which he declares to

---

41. The 1953 address to the 'Old Marburgers' was published as 'Das Problem des historischen Jesus', *ZTK* 51 (1954): 125–53, ET 'The Problem of the Historical Jesus', in *Essays on New Testament Themes* (SBT, 41; London: SCM, 1964), 15–47, at p. 25. He continues: '[Early Christians] were agreed only in one judgment: namely, that the life history of Jesus was constitutive for faith, because the earthly and the exalted Lord are identical. The Easter faith was the foundation of the Christian kerygma but was not the first or only source of its content. Rather, it was the Easter faith which took cognizance of the fact that God acted before we became believers, and which testifies to this fact by encapsulating the earthly history of Jesus in its proclamation' (33–34).

42. Käsemann, 'Problem', 37.

be indubitably authentic on the grounds that their claim to a Moses-like authority is unparalleled in Second Temple Judaism, and irrelevant to post Easter Christians. (I leave aside, of course, the issue of whether Käsemann's historical conclusions are in fact justified). Käsemann finds the same authoritative voice in Mark's saying, 'the Sabbath was made for humanity not humanity for the Sabbath' (Mk. 2.27) and the saying about the sources of defilement (Mk. 7.15). This Jesus is said to have '"shattered" the framework of Jewish piety and the letter of the law'.[43]

This brought Käsemann immediately to the nature of Jesus' authority and it is here that he invoked apocalyptic expectations. Although Käsemann's criterion of double dissimilarity might have disqualified as inauthentic anything that was too much in agreement with Second Temple apocalyptic beliefs, he concluded that Jesus in fact embraced the apocalyptic expectation of the imminent coming of God's kingdom. What was distinctive, however, was Jesus' peculiar connecting of apocalyptic beliefs with his own actions: 'the *basileia* breaks through on earth in the word of Jesus, setting men in its presence and facing them with the decision between obedience and disobedience'.[44] Later he would sharpen the distinction between Jesus' beliefs and apocalyptic:

> Jesus admittedly made the apocalyptically determined message of John his point of departure; his own preaching, however, did not bear a fundamentally apocalyptic stamp but proclaimed the immediacy of God who was near at hand. I am convinced that no one who took this step can have been prepared to wait for the coming of the Son of Man, the restoration of the Twelve Tribes in the Messianic kingdom and the dawning of the Parousia (which was tied up with this) in order to experience the near presence of God... The historical and hermeneutical problem seems to me to become meaningful and urgent only when we see how Easter and the reception of the Spirit caused primitive Christianity to respond to the preaching of Jesus about the God at hand and, in a certain sense, to replace it with a new apocalyptic.[45]

It was in this sense that apocalyptic, not fundamental to Jesus' own preaching, became 'the mother of all Christian theology'.[46]

Two features of Käsemann's understanding are noteworthy. His statement 'the *basileia* breaks through on earth in the word of Jesus, setting men in its presence and facing them with the decision between obedience and disobedience' is remarkable for its affinities with Bultmann's dialectical theology: like his teacher, Käsemann understood

---

43. Käsemann, 'Problem', 37–39.
44. Käsemann, 'Problem', 44.
45. Ernst Käsemann, 'The Beginnings of Christian Theology', in *idem, New Testament Questions of Today* (London: SCM, 1969), 82–107, at pp. 101–102.
46. Käsemann, 'Beginnings', 102.

Jesus' message ultimately to be about existential decision. But in the first part of the statement, Käsemann moved well beyond Bultmann by claiming that Jesus believed that the Kingdom was being realized in his very words. It is this harnessing of apocalyptic that served christological interests, despite the fact that Käsemann argued that none of the titles later given to Jesus – prophet, Messiah, Son of Man – was authentic. Käsemann's manoeuvre not only posited a 'Jesus' who stood over against his culture as one who 'shatters' its values, but also laid the groundwork for the claim that Jesus was absolutely unique and incommensurable insofar as he escaped the framework of 'Judaism':

> To this there are no Jewish parallels, nor indeed can there be. For the Jew who does what is done here [in the Matthaean antitheses] has cut himself off from the community of Judaism – or else he brings the Messianic Torah and is therefore the Messiah.[47]

In seeking a basis for Christian christological claims, Käsemann here comes perilously close to the supersessionism that lay at the heart of anti-Jewish interpretations of the figure of Jesus.

The apogee of the use of apocalyptic to shore up claims to uniqueness can be seen in Martin Hengel's *The Charismatic Leader and his Followers* (1968, ET 1981).[48] Beginning with Q 9.59–60, Jesus' injunction to follow him and 'let the dead bury the dead', Hengel asks whether the kind of personal authority implicit in the saying is comparable with the prophetic call of Elisha by Elijah, or the call of a 'charismatic' figure to join in battle, or the call of Cynics to abandon family and stable society, or the call of 'apocalyptic-zealot' prophets, or the rabbis' call to devote oneself to Torah. After reading a few pages it becomes clear that Hengel will disqualify each of these models, repeatedly citing Jesus' 'eschatological-charismatic' orientation as the decisive feature that distinguished him from all others. In the case of the 'apocalyptic-zealot prophets' with whom Jesus did share an apocalyptic outlook, it is Jesus' (allegedly) apolitical orientation that distinguishes him from the Zealots. Thus, concludes Hengel, 'Jesus stood outside *any discoverable uniform teaching tradition of Judaism*'.[49] Instead of employing the available ancient categories of leadership – sage, scribe, prophet, bandit, priestly Messiah, royal Messiah, prophet-like-Moses, Elijah *redivivus*, rabbi – Hengel invents the category of 'eschatological charismatic' for Jesus. But even that is not enough:

---

47. Käsemann, 'Problem', 37.

48. Martin Hengel, *Nachfolge und Charisma: Eine exegetisch-religionsgeschichtliche Studie zu Mt. 8, 21f. und Jesu Ruf in die Nachfolge* (BZNW, 34; Berlin: Walter de Gruyter, 1968); ET Martin Hengel, *The Charismatic Leader and His Followers* (Edinburgh: T. & T. Clark; New York: Crossroad, 1981).

49. Hengel, *Charismatic Leader*, 49 (emphasis original).

Even within the characterization we have preferred, of an 'eschatological charismatic', he remains in the last resort incommensurable, and so basically confounds every attempt to fit him into the categories suggested by the phenomonology or sociology of religion. Consequently, the centrality, in recent discussion, of the phenomenon of the underivable nature of *Jesus' authority*, is fully justified. One can find no better adjective than 'messianic' to describe it.[50]

The key element in Hengel's argument is the invocation of Jesus' apocalyptic beliefs: his call of disciples 'is to be explained only on the basis of his unique authority as a proclaimer of the *imminent Kingdom of God*'.[51]

If one were to compare Schweitzer's characterization of apocalyptic beliefs, which included an imminent cosmic transformation, resurrection, judgment of the wicked, and the reward of the faithful, with what appears implicit in Käsemann's or Hengel's uses of the term 'apocalyptic', it seems that for Käsemann and Hengel much less is involved. The constellation of apocalyptic beliefs that were embraced by Schweitzer's Jesus has been compressed into the belief in the imminent appearance of the Kingdom of God, which is itself strangely devoid of any real content. The real function of this 'Kingdom' is negative. For it is Jesus' embracing of the Kingdom and his belief that the Kingdom is somehow present in his own actions that 'shatters' the letter of the Torah (Käsemann) and renders Jesus utterly incomparable (Hengel).

Käsemann and Hengel use the category of apocalypticism, sharply reduced in its scope and richness, not simply in the discourse of finality and ultimacy in which Bultmann engaged, but in order to characterize Jesus as unique, unsurpassable, incommensurable. The conceptual work done by apocalypticism now had everything to do with Christology and the claims of Christians to uniqueness among the religions of the world.[52] As Dieter Georgi shrewdly observed, this process was already set in motion by Bultmann who

---

50. Hengel, *Charismatic Leader*, 69 (emphasis original).

51. Hengel, *Charismatic Leader*, 15 (emphasis original).

52. The importance of the connection between eschatology and christology is underscored by John Galvin (' "I Believe... in Jesus Christ, His Only Son, Our Lord": The Earthly Jesus and the Christ of Faith', *Int* 50 [1996]: 373–82, at p. 375). Commenting on the historical Jesus as reconstructed by John P. Meier (*A Marginal Jew: Rethinking the Historical Jesus. Volume II: Mentor, Message, and Miracles* [Anchor Bible Reference Library; New York: Doubleday, 1994]) and Joachim Gnilka (*Jesus von Nazaret: Botschaft und Geschichte* [HTKNT Supplementband, 3; Freiburg im Breisgau; Basel; Wien: Herder, 1990]), Galvin observes that both balance the futuristic and present aspects of Jesus' expectations and both provide sufficient purchase for the idea Jesus saw his own activities as part of the eschatological events he proclaimed. Thereby these portraits allow traditional christological affirmations to be seen 'as a plausible, though not rationally compelling, interpretation of Jesus and of the events of his public ministry'.

opposes what he calls the relativism of the history-of-religions school. Again I need to mention the term 'eschatological'. It works for Bultmann and for many New Testament scholars and systematic theologians ever since as a magic wand. Whereas for the history-of-religions school the term 'eschatological' described the foreignness of Jesus and of the early church – together with Jewish apocalypticism and other comparable ancient eschatologies – for Bultmann...the term 'eschatological' stands for the novelty of Christianity, its incomparable superiority, the uniqueness of the victorious religion, deservedly victorious. Wherever a comparison is ventured, wherever analogies lift their head, wherever challenges are heard from other religious options but the canonical ones, the invocation of the 'eschatological' is made, and the demons, the shadows have to disappear.[53]

Among scholars of Christian origins, Seán Freyne is uncharacteristically forthright on this point. His insistence on the eschatological nature of Jesus' career, he says,

arises from my concern regarding the claims of ultimacy that Christian faith makes in terms of Jesus... In the absence of an eschatological dimension to Jesus' utterances it would be impossible to see how any christological claims could be grounded in his earthly life, which is precisely the issue that gave rise to the quest for the historical Jesus in the first place as both an ecclesial and academic exercise.[54]

The related point has been made trenchantly by Frances Young, who argues that in the contemporary theological debate about the exclusivity of Christian claims about Jesus, it is not the doctrine of the incarnation that accounts for such exclusivity, but rather 'the Christian insistence upon the finality of Christ'. The claim to finality is in turn related to the motif of fulfilment, found throughout writings of the early Jesus movement.

Christ's *finality*, in so far as the New Testament writers were convinced of it, was related to this fulfilment-theme, rather than to any coherently

53.   Dieter Georgi, 'Rudolf Bultmann's *Theology of the New Testament* Revisited', in Edward C. Hobbs (ed.), *Bultmann, Retrospect, and Prospect: The Centenary Symposium at Wellesley* (Harvard Theological Studies, 35; Philadelphia: Fortress, 1985), 75–87, at p. 82.

54.   Seán Freyne, 'Galilean Questions to Crossan's Mediterranean Jesus', in William E. Arnal and Michel Desjardins (eds.), *Whose Historical Jesus?* [Studies in Christianity and Judaism/Études sur le christianisme et le judaïsme, 7; Waterloo, Ont.: Canadian Corporation for Studies in Religion/Corporation canadienne des sciences religieuses by Wilfrid Laurier University Press, 1997], 61–91, at p. 90). Galvin ('I Believe') expresses a similar view is expressed apropos of Crossan's Jesus.

framed idea of his divine nature. In other words, it is *eschatology*, not incarnation, which makes Christ final in the New Testament.[55]

Although Young does not address the issue of the historical Jesus' investment in eschatological beliefs, it is clear that weighty conceptual work related to Christology is done by eschatology: it allowed the early Jesus movement to identify Jesus with the coming Judge (rather than selecting Enoch or Melchisedek or Michael) and, hence, with finality in history and in personal and corporate existence; and it permitted Christians to resolve tensions between present beliefs and future expectations by positing a Christ in whom eschatological fulfilment was already complete. Yet she raises some doubts as to whether the current penchant for stressing eschatology as a means of underscoring Jesus' finality will last.

> [I]t is doubtful whether the eschatological version of the claim to Christ's finality, linked as it is to the cultural conditions of the ancient world Jewish and Hellenistic, can now be revitalized outside rather specialist theological circles. The 'fulfilment of prophecy' cuts no ice as an argument in the current intellectual climate and present expectations of a cataclysmic End of the World are grounded not on hope in God's intervention but on secular pessimism. The 'penal substitution' theory of atonement continues to have evangelical appeal; but for many inside and outside the church it has proved increasingly unacceptable, if not positively offensive. If now the objections to incarnational belief prove valid, the classic grounds on which claims to Christ's finality have rested [i.e., eschatology] may all prove shaky. Yet in one form or other Christianity has clung to its convictions that Jesus Christ is in some sense final, that he has a unique and central role in theological understanding... Ultimately the question at issue is one of Christian identity – hence the emotive reaction to anything which suggests doubts or questions.[56]

Young has put her finger on the problem. One of the remarkable features of theological scholarship in the post World War II era is the dramatically increased attention paid to eschatology and apocalyptic. This is in part due to discoveries such as the Dead Sea Scrolls, which underscored the importance of apocalyptic beliefs in Jewish Palestine in the first century BCE. But it also has to do with the fact that after the War eschatology was elevated to a central *theological* category by such major Protestant theologians as Wolfhart Pannenberg and Jürgen Moltmann. The historical Jesus' announcement of an imminent and decisive transformation of

55. Frances Young, 'The Finality of Christ', in Michael Goulder (ed.), *Incarnation and Myth: The Debate Continued* (Grand Rapids, MI: Eerdmans, 1979), 174–86, at p. 174 (emphasis added).

56. Young, 'Finality', 185.

human reality thus happily coincided with what was now seen to be at the heart of the Christian theological project itself. Christology, the unique status of Christianity among the religions of the world, and the basic contours of a salvation history that embraced the history of Israel and reached to the ends of the world, could be seen to flow from Jesus' eschatological beliefs. Pannenberg argues:

> In fact, Jesus' emphasis on the anticipatory presence of God's kingdom in his own activity (Lk 11,20) involved his own person in a way that essentially implies what later on was explicated by incarnational language and by titles like Son of God. But then, the uniqueness attributed to Jesus by the incarnational theology of the church was already characteristic of his own eschatological message and activity... The Christian claim to uniqueness is not based on any Christian experience. If this were so, it would be fair to argue that there are other experiences of uniqueness within world religions. But *the claim to uniqueness concerning the person of Jesus is bound up with his own eschatological message, especially the eschatological finality of God's kingdom as becoming present in his activity.*[57]

I must underscore at this point that my intent in this paper is not to dismiss apocalyptic constructions of the historical Jesus simply because they were in fact harnessed to serve certain conceptual (christological and theological) goals. I have not indeed considered any of the relevant primary evidence nor made any argument as to whether, given the evidence, the apocalyptic Jesus is a reasonable construct. Nor am I suggesting that Bultmann or Pannenberg preferred an apocalyptic Jesus disingenuously, or that Käsemann and Hengel posited Jesus' transformation and adaptation of apocalyptic beliefs as a way of smuggling in theological notions of finality, ultimacy, uniqueness and incommensurability. I have no access to their motives and intentions, and in fact their personal motivations would be of no intellectual interest to anyone but their therapists. I have access only to their exegetical and historical arguments and recognize these as, for the most part, reflecting the methodological habits and assumptions typical of their day. I see no disingenuousness or scholarly sleight of hand. Instead, my point is to underscore the *conceptual work* that is done by the ascription of apocalyptic beliefs to Jesus given the broader intellectual context of Bultmann's dialectical theology or the theology of hope that developed after the Second World War. And I wish to underscore the wide gulf between Schweitzer's view of apocalypticism and that of exegetes after

---

57. Wolfhart Pannenberg, 'Religious Pluralism and Conflicting Truth Claims: The Problem of a Theology of the World Religions', in Gavin D'Costa (ed.), *Christian Uniqueness Reconsidered: The Myth of a Pluralistic Theology of Religions* (Maryknoll, NY: Orbis Books, 1990), 96–106, at pp. 100–101 (emphasis added).

Bultmann, for whom apocalypticism, ironically, did not distance Jesus from modern Christian sensibilities, but rather served Christian interests in articulating what was unique about Jesus and, by extension, Christian claims. This is especially the case if it could be argued that Jesus not only held apocalyptic beliefs about the kingdom but uniquely associated his own activities with its realization in history, for in that case there was a material connection between Jesus' self-consciousness and the messianic claims that his followers would later make.

Conclusion

While significant conceptual work has been done by apocalyptic constructions of the historical Jesus in grounding discourses on finality, ultimacy, uniqueness and Christology, it should be obvious that none of these is a necessary consequence of apocalyptic constructions. Nothing requires the Jesus of history to do any conceptual work at all for modern believers, still less for Jews or atheists. He could well remain an interesting figure of the past and no more. One might insist, as Paula Fredriksen has done, on a sharp distinction between historical reconstruction and conceptual relevance:

> In the end, the person we seek stands with his back turned toward us, his face toward the others of his own generation. For Jesus of Nazareth, as any person, lived intact and entirely within his own culture and period, innocent of what the future held.[58]

Rejecting 'the false familiarity proffered by the dark angels of Relevance and Anachronism', Fredriksen quotes the closing sentence of Schweitzer's book and settles for seeing in 'Jesus, his contemporaries, and perhaps even ourselves, more clearly in our common humanity',[59] a position that comes perhaps the closest to Schweitzer's own view of things of a century ago.

Yet the interest in harnessing Jesus' apocalypticism remains high. Let me close by pointing to two possible tendencies:

First, apocalyptic constellations, insofar as they affirm God's control of history and imagine the eventual and dramatic triumph of justice, piety and goodness over their opposites, secure these same values for the present. That is, one's commitment to a just and humane society can be seen to stand fast in the embrace of apocalyptic beliefs. The relationship between an apocalyptic Jesus and the securing of humane values is recognized by Dale Allison when he writes:

---

58. Paula Fredriksen, *Jesus of Nazareth, King of the Jews: A Jewish Life and the Emergence of Christianity* (New York: Alfred Knopf, 1999), 268–69.

59. Fredriksen, *Jesus of Nazareth*, 270.

> In [Jesus'] imagination, he does not just look forward, from the present to the consummation – he also looks backward, from the consummation to the present. He engrosses himself in the unadulterated will of God as it will be lived in the kingdom, when Torah will be done on earth as it is in heaven. Moreover, this ideal will is not for him just a dream about the future but it is equally a demand for the present: eschatology is an imperative... [A]n eschatological worldview that judges the transient in terms of the transcendent has the great virtue of moving us some distance from, and so giving us much-needed perspective on, the contingencies that we misinterpret as necessities.[60]

Of course it must be said that one hardly need Jesus to have been an apocalypticist to hold such beliefs. As a Jew I might look forward to the Torah being done on earth without holding any particular views about the historical Jesus at all or, additionally, without framing my beliefs in apocalyptic garb. Nevertheless, it is fair to say that the powerful drama of cosmic and human transformation that apocalyptic scenarios imagine provides a compelling narrative in which certain moral values stand fast and resist the erosion or corrosion of modernity.

Second, while the narrative of God's control of history and the fantasy of the eventual restoration of justice can be seen to hold certain current values fast, it is also the case that, historically, apocalyptic narratives were also employed to *destabilize* the present, precisely by placing it under threat of dissolution, thereby 'clearing a space' for alternate moral practices in the present. As Allison details, millenarian movements frequently engage in social experimentation and alternate behaviours, believed to be anticipations of the future state of things.[61] But if this is so, and it surely is, then it is all the more peculiar that many of those advocating an apocalyptic Jesus – I take E.P. Sanders and John Meier as examples – arrive at a Jesus who has pronounced beliefs about the future but practically nothing to say about the present.[62] Meier's reading of the Q beatitudes, for example, is futuristic and borders on being anti-Pelagian: God alone 'acts in the end time to establish his kingdom...; humans can only wait for it'. The kingdom will indeed reverse the plights of the poor and downtrodden, but this reversal will be God's gratuitous act. The proclamation of the kingdom does not imply any program of social or political resistance.[63]

It is this silence which I find curious, for it seems that apocalyptic's

60. Dale C. Allison, 'Jesus was an Apocalyptic Prophet', in Robert J. Miller (ed.), *The Apocalyptic Jesus: A Debate* (Santa Rosa, CA: Polebridge, 2001), 149.

61. Allison, 'Apocalyptic Prophet', 78–94.

62. Allison, 'Apocalyptic Prophet', 89–91, by contrast, allows for Jesus being both an apocalyptic prophet and a social prophet, though appears still to stop short of claiming that apocalyptic beliefs funded a form of countercultural experimentation in the present.

63. Meier, *Marginal Jew II*, 330–31.

conceptual potential for undergirding certain moral and theological convictions is celebrated, but its potential as a destabilizing, threatening and subversive discourse that clears room for alternative social practices is conspicuously ignored. This too might suggest, no less, that Bultmann's apocalyptic Jesus, or Käsemann's Jesus-in-whom-the-kingdom-had-broken-through, or Hengel's eschatological charismatic Jesus, the current incarnations of the apocalyptic Jesus, are still busy at work, functioning not as one unknown, but as one well known, and quite congenial with contemporary christological and theological beliefs.

As I have already indicated, my purpose in this paper is not to support or attack the proposition that Jesus held apocalyptic beliefs, but rather to respond to the insinuation, frequently encountered in debates about the historical Jesus, that while those espousing a non-apocalyptic Jesus are presenting a portrait torqued by their own ideological interests, the apocalyptic Jesus, as foreign and strange to the twentieth, and now the twenty-first century, is somehow less susceptible to such co-optations. This claim is demonstrably false. After Schweitzer, apocalypticism has become a category highly serviceable to a number of conceptual claims. While none of them follows necessarily from an apocalyptic image of Jesus, it is important to recognize how various images of Jesus are put to work, and to learn to engage in practices of historical reconstruction that are self-conscious and forthright about what conceptually is at stake in particular reconstructions.

The Cipher 'Judaism' in Contemporary Historical Jesus Scholarship

William Arnal

University of Regina

The topic around which this collection of essays centers is the *agenda* that lurks beneath controversies in historical Jesus scholarship and the *subtexts* that seem to be animating current work, including the acrimony that sometimes characterizes scholarly exchanges over Jesus. I would begin any discussion of the Judaism of the historical Jesus by stressing that anti-Semitic or even anti-Jewish scholarship, at least in the 'mainstream', contemporary, and Western study of ancient Christianity, is simply not a problem today.[1] Anyone who reads the work of genuine anti-Semites from the past or present, and compares them to any and all of the Western European and North American scholarship on Christian origins today will see immediately that we are dealing with *completely* different entities, with completely different agenda. The specter of anti-Judaism, at least, was still an aspect of a great deal of New Testament scholarship from even the 1950s, 1960s and 1970s, and various forms of actual anti-Semitism remain with us today. But it is simply not the case that current scholarly work on early Christianity is animated by such an agenda.

Nonetheless, even though *no* contemporary New Testament scholar

---

1. The caveat that such an issue is not controversial specifically in Western and 'mainstream' scholarship is probably necessary. Amy-Jill Levine has informed me (personal communication) that a surprising amount of biblical scholarship coming out of 'third world' countries is guilty of some of the anti-Jewish slurs that Anglophone and German scholarship left behind decades ago. Levine's (rather materialist) explanation for this odd phenomenon is perfectly satisfying. At least one source of scholarly writings on early Christianity in impoverished parts of the world are bequests of personal libraries from the wills of European and North American pastors. Since the bulk of these libraries is comprised of works composed and published decades ago, many third-world scholars are relying on work which reflects the assumptions and biases of the past. I wish to thank Professor Levine both for drawing this phenomenon to my attention and for offering such a lucid explanation of it. [Ed. note: see Amy-Jill Levine, 'Lilies of the Field and Wandering Jews: Biblical Scholarship, Women's Roles, and Social Location', in Ingrid Rosa Kitzberger (ed.), *Transformative Encounters: Jesus and Women Re-Viewed* (Leiden: E.J. Brill, 2000), 329–52.]

contests that Jesus was a Jew, for about the last ten years we have encountered the spectacle of accusations, sometimes quite vicious, that certain historical Jesus scholars – often John Dominic Crossan, Robert Funk or Burton Mack – are reconstructing a 'non-Jewish' Jesus. Consider, for instance, the comments of Birger Pearson about the Jesus Seminar:

> The Jesus of the Jesus Seminar is a non-Jewish Jesus. To put it metaphorically, the Seminar has performed a forcible epispasm on the historical Jesus, a surgical procedure for removing the marks of circumcision. The result might arouse some disquiet in the minds of people who know the history of the 30's and 40's of our century. But the Jesus of the Jesus Seminar is much too banal to cause us to think that the ideology producing him is like that which produced the 'Aryan Jesus' of the 1930's.[2]

Pearson's comments are extreme, but not unique: we encounter similar accusations from scholars such as E.P. Sanders and John P. Meier as well.[3] In addition, we have also been faced in the last ten years with an

---

2. Birger A. Pearson, 'The Gospel According to the Jesus Seminar', *Occasional Papers of the Institute for Antiquity and Christianity* 35 (Claremont: The Claremont Graduate School, 1996), 42; repr. 'The Gospel According to the Jesus Seminar', *Religion* 25 (1995): 317–38.

3. E.P. Sanders, 'Jesus, Ancient Judaism, and Modern Christianity: The Quest Continues', in Paula Frediksen and Adele Reinhartz (eds.), *Jesus, Judaism, and Christian Anti-Judaism: Reading the New Testament after the Holocaust,* (Louisville, KY and London: Westminster John Knox, 2002), 31–55 at p. 34, for instance, writes: 'What is common to all the questers, whether early or recent, is the view that some of the material in the Gospels is "authentic" and represents the real historical Jesus, who should be followed, while other material should be rejected... Not infrequently, the parts of the Gospels that some people regard as silly and obviously bad, and which they wish not to attribute to Jesus, come from ancient Judaism. This gives an anti-Jewish bias to the separation of wheat from chaff.' Similarly, John P. Meier, *A Marginal Jew: Rethinking the Historical Jesus,* Volume III: *Companions and Competitors* (Anchor Bible Reference Library; New York: Doubleday, 2001), 3–4, writes: 'Yet, especially among certain authors now or formerly connected with the Jesus Seminar, emphasis on the Jewishness of Jesus is hardly a central concern. Whether one looks at the more serious works of writers like John Dominic Crossan and Burton L. Mack or the sensationalistic popular works of authors like Robert W. Funk, one finds Jesus the Cynic philosopher or Jesus the generic Mediterranean peasant or Jesus the social revolutionary or Jesus the religious iconoclast largely overshadowing if not obliterating the specific 1st-century Palestinian Jew named Jesus. To be sure, words like "Jew" and "Jewish" often adorn titles or subtitles of such works, and politically correct comments are made on the importance of Jesus' Jewishness. But in most of these books, one searches in vain for detailed treatments of various religious movements competing for influence in first-century Palestine (e.g., the Pharisees, Sadducees, and Essenes) and of the ways in which Jesus the Jew interacted with or reacted to them as he debated questions of Jewish practice and belief.' Meier's comments are more temperate (and accurate) in 'The Present State of the "Third Quest" for the Historical Jesus: Loss and Gain', *Biblica* 80 (1999): 459–86, esp. 484–85.

increasingly *shrill* insistence on Jesus' Judaism.[4] If no one denies that Jesus was Jewish, why this constant reiteration – in book titles and in scholarly discourse in general – of a known, agreed upon and uncontroversial fact?

A related issue is the way in which some scholars have attempted to promote their own particular historical reconstruction of Jesus – often a reconstruction approached by applying generalizations about ancient Judaism to Jesus – as *the* Jewish Jesus. Both the technique and the rhetoric seem misplaced. Here we find the assumptions both that a portrait of ancient Judaism in general is a good way to get at who Jesus was, specifically; and the assumption that any other approach to or characterization of Jesus is somehow *non*-Jewish. Neither of these two assumptions is valid.[5]

So why the continued insistence on a point everyone accepts? What is behind the shrill reiteration of Jesus having been Jewish? What agenda is served by accusing contemporary scholars – with no evidence whatsoever[6] – of an anti-Jewish animus, or by offering sly insinuations to this effect? Why the invocation of the specter of the Third Reich? – particularly now, when it seems that this aspect of our scholarly past has been decisively left behind. I can only conclude that the issue is somehow overdetermined; that it is a screen onto which other, more current, and unresolved matters are being projected. It is a manufactured controversy serving to express other problems, theological and secular, in a covert or implicit manner.

---

4. This shrill insistence on Jesus' Judaism is especially evident in the *titles* of many recent books on the historical Jesus. Examples include: Géza Vermès, *Jesus the Jew: A Historian's Reading of the Gospels* (Philadelphia: Fortress, 1973); E. P. Sanders, *Jesus and Judaism* (Philadelphia: Fortress; London: SCM, 1985); Meier, *A Marginal Jew III*; John Dominic Crossan, *The Historical Jesus: The Life of a Mediterranean Jewish Peasant* (New York: HarperCollins, 1991); Géza Vermès, *The Religion of Jesus the Jew* (Philadelphia: Fortress, 1993); Paula Fredriksen, *Jesus of Nazareth, King of the Jews: A Jewish Life and the Emergence of Christianity* (New York: Alfred Knopf, 1999).

5. The first assumption is not valid because, as everyone knows, statistical probabilities cannot be used to infer the features of individuals. The second assumption is invalid because it assumes a stable identity for 'Judaism'. On this latter point, and the difficulties involved in any effort to define ancient Judaism, see especially Jonathan Z. Smith, 'Fences and Neighbors: Some Contours of Early Judaism', in *idem, Imagining Religion: From Babylon to Jonestown* (Chicago: University of Chicago Press, 1982), 1–18.

6. Indeed, the scholars most frequently accused of producing a 'non-Jewish' Jesus – John Dominic Crossan, Robert Funk and Burton Mack – have all quite explicitly repudiated anti-Judaism in print, and have aligned themselves with efforts to remove this specter from historical scholarship. See, for instance, John Dominic Crossan, *Who Killed Jesus? Exposing the Roots of Anti-Semitism in the Gospel Story of the Death of Jesus* (San Francisco: HarperSanFrancisco, 1995), 35; Robert W. Funk and the Jesus Seminar, *The Acts of Jesus: What did Jesus Really Do?* (San Francisco: HarperSanFrancisco, 1998), 153; Burton L. Mack, *A Myth of Innocence: Mark and Christian Origins* (Philadelphia: Fortress Press, 1988).

The invocation of a Jewish Jesus and the 'debate' around this figure appears to me to be less about Jesus himself, and much more about our own *identities*: political, religious and cultural. I will try to explore each of these aspects briefly – space does not permit the exhaustive treatment each deserves.

A caveat needs to be noted from the start, however. An endeavor such as this is necessarily speculative: I do not have direct access to the inner motives behind scholarly assertions about the past. I must stress, then, that in what follows I am not especially concerned with the personal and individual motives of the scholars advancing the views I discuss. Rather, my concern is with the ideological resonance of those views; their implications; their effect on the way we view certain broad issues (and vice versa); their correlation with important perspectival issues; and the cultural *work* that they do, regardless of individual intentions. In general, I do not want to get deeply involved in questions of cause and effect. For example, if scholarship focusing on Jesus as a religious devotee of (a normative) Judaism shares certain key assumptions with, say, contemporary efforts to entrench the boundaries of religious traditions, this *need* not mean (a) that the scholar in question intended this correspondence; (b) that the contemporary trend caused the historical conclusion; or (c) that the historical conclusion must influence the contemporary trend. Any one, or for that matter all, of these conclusions *may* be true, but the simple correspondence between scholarly claims and present issues does not *require* any of them. My intent in what follows is to point to the correspondences I see, without necessarily imputing specific motivations to individual authors, unless the evidence seems to allow it.

Saving our Political Souls

The most obvious undercurrent in contemporary historical Jesus scholarship and the 'controversy' over a Jewish Jesus is political in nature. A great many of the works that emphasize the 'Jewish Jesus', and especially that criticize scholars such as Crossan or Mack for producing an allegedly 'non-Jewish' Jesus, make *explicit* reference to anti-Semitism, and to the great anti-Semitic event of the twentieth century, the Shoah. Seán Freyne, for instance, is very straightforward and open about this connection.[7] So

---

7. See especially Seán Freyne, 'Galilean Questions to Crossan's Mediterranean Jesus', in *Whose Historical Jesus?* (ed. William E. Arnal and Michel Desjardins; Studies in Christianity and Judaism/Études sur le christianisme et le judaïsme, 7; Waterloo, Ontario: Wilfrid Laurier University Press, 1997), 63–91, at p. 91.

are others.[8] What is especially interesting is that this connection will be made even when their authors explicitly disavow any anti-Semitic motivation in those they criticize. Thus Pearson's critique of the Jesus Seminar, quoted above, invokes the genuinely anti-Semitic scholarship of the Nazi period and surmises that the Seminar's 'non-Jewish' Jesus 'might arouse some disquiet in the minds of people who know the history of the 30's and 40's of our century'.[9] But immediately he volunteers that 'the Jesus of the Jesus Seminar is much too banal to cause us to think that the ideology producing him is like that which produced the "Aryan Jesus" of the 1930's'.[10] Likewise Sanders, who asserts that 'genuine anti-Judaism . . . has been a feature of many scholarly descriptions of Jesus',[11] nonetheless believes that the unspecified scholars who promote this anti-Judaism do not do so out of any specific anti-Semitic animus but from a general distaste for ancient religiosity.[12] That such a concern – whether with Nazi ideology or with generalized anti-Semitism and anti-Judaism – is invoked, only immediately to deny its applicability, is a strong indication that it rests heavily in the minds of the scholars who mention it. The discourse of our field is attempting to establish a distance from the Germany of Adolf Hitler, and indeed the culpable anti-Judaism of our scholarly forebears.

What is at issue here, at the political level, is a scholarly, narrative and symbolic repudiation of anti-Semitism among those researchers who insist on a Jesus whose Judaism is identifiable *as* Judaism even today. Crossan's Jesus is a Jew; as is Mack's, Vaage's,[13] and the Jesus Seminar's.[14] But Jesus the Jew in *these* avatars is not easily identifiable with or conformable to the Jews of today, the Jews of modern Israel, or especially the Jews of Eastern Europe, the primary victims of Hitler's genocide. Conversely, Jesus the Jew who is concerned with the Temple, with the city of Jerusalem,[15] with Torah; a Jesus proximate to but segregated from his

---

8.   See, among others, Vermès, *Religion of Jesus the Jew*, 213–15. And note the subtitle to Paula Fredriksen and Adele Reinhartz, *Jesus, Judaism, and Christian Anti-Judaism*, namely: 'Reading the New Testament after the Holocaust'.

9.   Pearson, 'Gospel According to the Jesus Seminar', 42.

10.   Pearson, 'Gospel According to the Jesus Seminar', 42.

11.   Sanders, 'Jesus, Ancient Judaism, and Modern Christianity', 54.

12.   Sanders, 'Jesus, Ancient Judaism, and Modern Christianity', 34–35.

13.   Vaage argues that the earliest Jesus-traditions were Cynic-like in both their ethos and their representation of Jesus and John the Baptist. See Leif E. Vaage, *Galilean Upstarts: Jesus' First Followers According to Q* (Valley Forge, PA: Trinity Press International, 1994).

14.   Again, I mention these scholars in particular because they are most often accused of having produced a 'non-Jewish' Jesus.

15.   Even after 70 CE, the Temple and Jerusalem have been potent symbols of an 'exiled' Jewry. There may also be a link between these alleged concerns on Jesus' part and attitudes toward political Zionism.

Gentile neighbors;[16] a Jesus who was circumcised, who had a recognizably Jewish name,[17] who wore distinctively Jewish clothing and religious paraphernalia; and so on[18] – *this* Jesus shows enough similarity and continuity to the type of the nineteenth to twentieth-century European Jew as to stand in for this later historical figure.[19]

The Eastern European Jew is the very image of anti-Semitic stereotype; he or she is 'the eternal Jew' of Hitlerian propaganda. The figure who resists assimilation, is segregated, obeys distinctive ancestral law, speaks in an incomprehensible and 'foreign' language written in an incomprehensible and 'mystical' alphabet, eats differently, dresses differently – such a figure can stand in easily as a target for any xenophobia whatsoever. Who is the outsider lurking within? Who is the yeast that leavens the whole loaf? The subversive? The communist? The usurer? Why, of course, the Jew; who else could it be? And how do we know? Because 'the Jew' self-presents as an outsider in his or her whole way of life. Thus a particularly segregated Jewish subculture, that of central and eastern European Ashkenazi Jews, comes to symbolize Judaism in general, and, at the same time, to be the quintessential target for intolerance, racism, and religious and socio-cultural prejudice emanating from European (and subsequently, too, North American) Gentiles.

The fact that the very distinguishability of Eastern European Jewry is what it seems most to share with the Jewish Jesus of recent scholarship – language, law, clothing, distinctive practice, lack of assimilation, segregation – suggests to me that Jesus himself is being made to conform to a

16.   Galilee was ringed with Gentile cities, but the 'Jewish Jesus' advocates insist that he understood his mission as devoted exclusively to Jews. This is interesting in light of the situation of European Jews in the recent past: surrounded by Gentiles, but segregated.

17.   I.e., Yehoshua or Yeshua. Note that this name is nowhere attested for Jesus in any of the New Testament literature. If multiple attestation tells us anything, it is that Jesus' name was, in fact, *Jesus*.

18.   Note especially the characterization of Bruce D. Chilton, *A Galilean Rabbi and His Bible: Jesus' Use of the Interpreted Scripture of His Time* (Wilmington, DL: Michael Glazier, 1984), as, precisely, a Rabbi. The Gospels use this term from time to time, of course, but as a respectful address (the term occurs 15 times in the entire NT, but only in Mark, Matthew, and [pre-eminently] John). Chilton, using the term the way he does, implies a clerical role, one associated, of course, with modern Judaism.

19.   Nowhere is this clearer than the cover of Fredriksen's *Jesus of Nazareth*, which features a painting by Marc Chagall of a crucified Jesus surrounded by figures in Eastern European garb ('White Crucifixion', 1938). Chagall can be forgiven his artistic license: this is a painter, after all, who presents us with naked figures riding giant roosters, faces in the sky, and floating buildings. But Chagall's amazing vision is not history. The cover of a book is not necessarily an indication of the scholarship inside the book, and in some instances cover art is beyond the author's control. But in this case, whether the cover art was chosen by Fredriksen or not, I believe it tells us something about the conceptualization of both Jesus and of Judaism that one finds in this book, and even hints at some of the reasons for these conceptualizations.

stereotype of Judaism that was anti-Semitic in its inception. But this, I suspect, is no irony: it is precisely the point. The very center of traditional (anti-Jewish and, at times, anti-Semitic) European culture has been the figure of Jesus. The historically dominant religion(s) of Europe have revolved around this Jesus; its art has portrayed him ceaselessly; its architecture has been offered to his greater glory; its literature has aimed at exegeting his importance or explaining him to the masses. How better, then, to repudiate the anti-Semitism that springs from xenophobia than by making this center of European culture himself one of the recognizable 'outsiders'? A Jesus who is not obviously one of 'those' Jews, who is not a Jew who looks, even today, just like 'we' expect a Jew to look, cannot serve this purpose. A Jesus who does, however, performs a massive act of inversion and subversion of a sordid European history: a final Christian assimilation and appropriation of the 'other'; or the final victory of the 'other' by claiming its central place in the culture that repudiated it. In either case – and I am not sure which, if either, is the accurate characterization – the Jewish Jesus of modern scholarship accomplishes, or at least implies, the repositioning of the quintessential outsider as, in fact, in the end, the center and pinnacle of the dominant culture. 'The very stone which the builders rejected has become the head of the corner; this was the Lord's doing, and it is marvelous in our eyes' (Mark 12.10–11).

The agenda here has two facets. It offers a way to respond to the Holocaust, *and*, simultaneously, a rejoinder to contemporary anti-Semitism. In terms of the former, the travesty of the Holocaust is underscored by insisting on its *irony*. No, the 'eternal Jew', as it happens, was not a *threat* to European civilization (and its North American spin-offs), but its *basis*. The Holocaust was thus not only a crime against humanity, but a crime against the very values that were invoked to promote it. Moreover – and it is here that my sympathy with this agenda begins to wane – Jesus the Jew serves as a way to reclaim Christianity from complicity in the Holocaust; even to insulate it from this complicity. Intrinsically, then, Jesus – standing in for the whole of the 'true' and 'proper' Christian religion[20] – shows that what Christianity is not, at its core, is anti-Jewish or anti-Semitic. How could it be, when its founder was a Jew? And not simply a Jew, but, apparently, a religious and identifiable Jew, a Jew of comparable kind to the Jews who have been so savagely persecuted in the last few centuries by Christians themselves?

The figure of Jesus has often been a device for recasting Christianity,

---

20. This, it seems to me, is much of the gist of Fredriksen and Reinhartz, *Jesus, Judaism, and Christian Anti-Judaism*. The book does offer some very critical essays which expose the anti-Jewish roots of Christianity, but the overall thrust of the text appears to me as an effort to deny the anti-Jewish origins of the Christian religion, and so to explain (later) Christian anti-Judaism as an aberration or deviation.

sometimes polemically, in such a way that whatever present features are
deemed to be unattractive are eliminated as late accretions, and the 'true
essence' of Christianity recaptured and revived by appeal to Jesus himself.
In short, much Jesus scholarship has just been Gospel writing done anew.
Is Christianity too dogmatic? It did not used to be; that was a later
accretion at the hands of 'early catholicism'. Is it too supernaturally-
oriented? Well, Jesus would have no truck with that nonsense. And so,
too, was it complicit in centuries upon centuries of inhumanity to Jews,
culminating in the 'final solution'? Only through the sheerest perversity of
those Christians who failed to understand that their religion was created
by, and revolves around, the very kind of figure they were abusing. Jesus
the Jew, then, stands as the clearest possible indication that Christianity is
not anti-Jewish, properly, and so is not implicated in the Holocaust.
Christian justifications for and participation in the Nazi movement were
perversions – not expressions of what Christianity genuinely and
essentially is. Thus Christian anti-Judaism of both the past and present
is condemned; thus the responsibility of *contemporary* Christians for the
Holocaust is lessened; and thus, especially, are the doors opened to
Jewish-Christian interfaith dialogue now that this messy business of anti-
Judaism has been dispensed with.[21]

I do not wish to imply that the less-recognizable Jew reconstructed in
the historical work of Mack, Crossan, the Jesus Seminar, and others, is a
function of a lack of interest in contemporary anti-Semitism or the
Holocaust. Both are critical issues, invested with passion, for all of these
scholars. But if so, why do they present us with a Jesus who does not –
cannot – stand in for the persecuted, identifiable Jew of modernity? My
own hunch is that these scholars view anti-Semitism as more about
ideology than ancient history; perhaps even more, that historical reconstruction itself is neither the cause nor the cure for anti-Semitism. To put it
as graphically as possible, what if 'the Jews' *were* responsible for the death
of Jesus? What if Jesus really *did* call 'the Jews' children of the devil (John

21. This latter point seems to be of special and explicit concern to several authors. See,
e.g., the introduction to Fredriksen and Reinhartz, *Jesus, Judaism, and Christian Anti-
Judaism*, 5 (emphasis added):
'Our hope is that this volume will contribute in positive ways to the efforts of lay readers to
understand the historical circumstances of early Christianity. By making this effort, such
readers will be able to see how anti-Judaism *entered* Christian theology at a formative stage
of its development...determining the church's interpretation of foundational New
Testament texts. We also hope this book will help readers to see that we have other
interpretive possibilities and available readings when, with historical understanding, we
approach the Christian scriptures. Readings that neither distort history nor encourage
prejudice... As scholars of ancient Christianity *who are committed to interfaith dialogue*, we
assemble these essays for you to think with as you study the New Testament.'
This particular concern with current Jewish-Christian relations is present, and obvious,
throughout much of the book.

8.44)? What if Matthew's words, 'his blood be on us and on our children' (Mt. 27.25) *were* really, historically, spoken? Would such *historical* conclusions justify the Holocaust? Would they make it a good thing, after all? Would they imply that Christians really should hate Jews? Emphatically, no. These alleged events are from the distant past, and, for thinking people today, have, or ought to have, no bearing at all on today's interpersonal or inter-religious relations: those must be determined by present attitudes and circumstances, not obscure historical reconstructions.

And so, it seems to me, the Macks and Crossans and Funks of contemporary scholarship, in their avoidance of the particular kind of recognizable 'religious Jew' promoted by other scholars, are not at all allying themselves with anti-Semitism or approving of the Holocaust; they are, instead, seeking to address anti-Semitism in other ways. We are all, it seems, trying to save our souls, politically speaking, from anti-Semitism and its consequences; but the paths taken differ. In the case of scholars such as Crossan and Funk, there *is* an effort to use ancient history to comment on Jewish-Christian relations today. But the history that *they* focus on is that of characterizations of Jews in the ancient Christian writings. Crossan, for instance, goes to great lengths to deny 'Jewish' responsibility for the crucifixion; Funk emphatically denies the historicity of Mt. 27.25.[22] The focus is shifted away from Jesus himself.

But if they share similar concerns, why would Crossan or Funk not join Sanders, Fredriksen, Chilton, Freyne, and the like in casting Jesus in distinctively 'Jewish' garb? I would suggest that at least some of their motivation is precisely to *avoid* the fixed stereotype of 'the eternal Jew' used to such great effect by their scholarly rivals. There are always at least two ways to attack stereotypes, especially racial stereotypes. One is to embrace them, reclaim them and force them to the center of the discourse.[23] The other, of course, is to deny them emphatically, to show that the hated *image* need not correspond to the reality of actual people and the ways they lead their lives. Thus it seems to me that the contribution of those scholars who give us a 'non-Jewish' Jesus is precisely to demonstrate the ways in which *being* a Jew are as multiple and open to possibility as being anything or anyone else. Here the stereotype is attacked by discarding it. In this way, then, both the allegedly 'non-

---

22. Crossan, *Who Killed Jesus?* 35; Funk and the Jesus Seminar, *Acts of Jesus*, 153.

23. As I suggest may be happening with 'Jewish Jesus' scholarship. As for other, contemporary, examples, they are numerous and obvious: the appropriation, reclamation and refiguring of words such as 'nigger' by blacks; of 'dyke' by lesbians; and especially of all *kinds* of misogynist terminology by Mary Daly (see especially her *Webster's First New Intergalactic Wickedary of the English Language* [in cahoots with Jane Caputi; Boston: Beacon Press, 1987]).

Jewish' Jesus and the 'Jewish Jesus' advocates are pursuing essentially the same agenda, albeit in different ways.

Burton Mack goes even further: he quite properly, in my view, rejects the salience of actual historical events (very few of which he regards as residing behind the gospels anyway), and instead associates both anti-Judaism and American triumphalism with contemporary promotions of the gospels' ideologies, particularly that of the Gospel of Mark.[24] The issue here is not whether or how the events recounted in gospel stories intersect with actual historical events; rather, the issue is the overall effect of the story itself on attitudes and conceptions of the self and others. And this, I think, is exactly right. What a small handful of people living in Jerusalem in the year 30 CE or so might have said or done is really of little import; but what is said and implied in canonical writings and in their normative interpretations is of tremendous import. These documents do have a huge impact on contemporary attitudes, precisely because they are canonical. And so Jews today who wish to relate congenially with Christians must somehow address Talmudic slanders against Jesus, just as Christians today must address the much more extensive and dangerous slanders against 'the Jews' in their own holy books.[25]

The obvious corollary here is that, ultimately, academic historical conclusions, if they cannot disprove Christian doctrine, cannot improve it either. We may have shifts among many Christians in their understanding of the historical development of their faith, but I would submit that these shifts are a function of theological changes imposing themselves on sacred history; not of an assimilation of academic history to such a point that basic theological beliefs are actually altered. And so, it seems to me, *any* efforts – whether those of Crossan and Funk, or those of their critics – to reconstruct a *history* of Jesus and ancient Christianity that would both serve to separate Christianity from the Holocaust, and to make further Christian anti-Judaism impossible, are doomed to failure because they are addressing the wrong issues. The right issues are attitudes; to be sure, attitudes engendered by the canonical texts of Christianity and by much subsequent Christian theology. But the source of those attitudes is not anything that 'the Jews' said or did, nor is it the extent to which Jesus may or may not have agreed with the religious or other cultural practices of his contemporaries. It resides, rather, in the techniques that the emerging Christian religion used, and has continued to use, to define itself over against its parent religion and to maintain its *raison d'être* as a *superior* religion which exists precisely because it expropriated the function of its

---

24. Especially, Mack, *Myth of Innocence*, 375.
25. Similarly, Sanders, 'Jesus, Ancient Judaism, and Modern Christianity', 32, notes that Christian beliefs will not be much affected by historical scholarship.

parent. Until and unless Christianity is able to find a mode of self-definition that does not require a supercessionist theology or a strong contradistinction to Judaism, it will never be able to shed its intrinsic tendency to anti-Judaism. We will not – cannot – save our souls from anti-Semitism, nor assuage our guilt, by making the supposed founder of Christianity into an honorary Jew.

Saving our Religious Souls

Of course, the figure of Jesus is also important precisely because of his *religious* centrality; he was never a political leader, or a military general, but rather is imagined to have founded a religion. We should expect, then, that the manufactured debate over the 'Jewish Jesus' should reflect religious anxieties and agenda as well. Again, I want to stress that since no one in contemporary scholarship *denies* that Jesus was a Jew, the debated issue is really *what kind* of Jew he was. In effect, then, the rhetoric sometimes being employed – better scholars produce a Jewish Jesus, while inferior scholars produce a non-Jewish Jesus – suggests that there are certain ways of behaving that *make* one non-Jewish, that *exclude* one from Jewish identity. In short, what we have here is a construction of and debate about what constitutes a 'true' Jew.

Of course, the stage onto which this agenda is projected is antiquity, not the present, and so advocates of the peculiarly reified and rigidly Jewish Jesus can deny the applicability of their models of Judaism to the present, and to questions of Jewish identity today. But the fact is that critics such as Pearson, Hays,[26] Meier and Sanders are claiming that some modern scholars are producing a non-Jewish Jesus even when those scholars specifically assert that their Jesuses *are* Jewish; and scholars such as Fredriksen, Chilton and Wright feel fairly confident in making inferences from the fact of Jesus' Judaism to the character of his behavior and teaching. What this implies is that all of these scholars have a clear idea of what 'Judaism', as a religious entity, *must* be, and are using that idea as a template for reconstructing who Jesus, therefore, *must have* (or can*not* have) been. In short, we are here in the presence of a *normative* definition of Judaism.

The 'real' form of Judaism that is being advocated here is, as I noted above, one that tends to have significant affinities with certain forms of contemporary, albeit traditional, Judaism. In the Judaism of the Jewish Jesus, there tends to be a focus on Torah, the interpretation thereof and obedience thereto. The Temple figures significantly, as does, at times,

---

26. Richard Hays, 'The Corrected Jesus', *First Things* (May 1994): 43–48, at p. 47.

eschatological expectation. So too does concern with the holy land of God's promise, Israel, and the native Semitic speech of the inhabitants. Jesus is a rabbi and debates with rabbis; he is attendant at festivals and honors the sabbath; he is circumcised.

The question that arises here is precisely why, if indeed this construction of Judaism is intended to be normative, any of these scholars would care at all about the current construction of the Jewish religion, especially since very few of them are themselves Jewish. As Marianne Sawicki incisively notes:

> How can a meaningful Jewish identity today and tomorrow be secured through claiming certain people, places, and practices of the past as the antecedents and sources of one's own Jewishness? This question I respectfully leave for Jews to address; a Christian has no business trying to tell Jews how to be who they are.[27]

Without actually knowing anything about which historical Jesus scholars might themselves be religious Jews, if any, I can nonetheless surmise that the reconstructions of antique Judaism, and Jesus with them, that employ the normative definition discussed above may very well, as Sawicki implies, be offered in the service of 'claiming certain people, places, and practices of the past as the antecedents and sources of one's own Jewishness'. Such claims not only may serve a particular 'insider' construction of contemporary Judaism, but, additionally, serve the purposes of intra-Jewish polemic, particularly useful against Reform Judaism. This last possibility would not even have occurred to me had Rodney Stark not suggested an explicit comparison between the marginalized Diaspora Judaism of antiquity and that of modern Europe. Stark claims:

> *People will attempt to escape or resolve a marginal position.* Some Jews in the nineteenth century tried to resolve their marginality by assimilation, including conversion to Christianity. Others attempted to resolve their marginality by becoming a new kind of Jew. Reform Judaism was designed to provide a nontribal, non-ethnic religion rooted in the Old Testament (and the Enlightenment), one that focused on theology and ethics rather than custom and practice... [It] is forthright in its attempt to strip ethnicity from theology.[28]

Stark is no historical Jesus scholar, and there is reason enough to doubt his reconstruction of an earliest Christianity marked by large-scale 'conversion' of Jews. But his comments here must draw our attention to

---

27. Marianne Sawicki, *Crossing Galilee: Architectures of Contact in the Occupied Land of Jesus* (Harrisburg, PA: Trinity Press International, 2000), 232.

28. Rodney Stark, *The Rise of Christianity: A Sociologist Reconsiders History* (Princeton, NJ: Princeton University Press, 1996), 52–53 (emphasis original).

the ways in which a denial that the figure reconstructed by Crossan, or Mack, or the Jesus Seminar is a 'real' Jew, implies with it a denial of the Jewish character of modern Reform Judaism. If Crossan's Jesus is no Jew, then neither was, say, Rabbi Samuel Holdheim.[29] Such a conclusion would, of course, be very congenial to many conservative religious Jews, who may indeed hold that, religiously speaking, Reform Judaism is no Judaism at all. Of course, I must stress again that I honestly do not know which, if *any*, of the 'Jewish Jesus' advocates are themselves Jewish or would for any reason be interested in such a campaign. But I cannot help but feel that, at the very least, the polemics of scholars such as Sanders, Meier, Pearson and Hays are congenial in their implication that there is essentially *one* way of being Jewish, and that those who fail to adhere to that narrow path are, simply, not Jewish at all.

One might additionally surmise that those Christian and other *non-Jewish* scholars (who constitute the majority in this field, I am certain) who are constructing such a rigid and fixed image of ancient Judaism are simply projecting onto antiquity their own beliefs about the key hallmarks of Judaism, and are reluctant enough to let go of these presumptions that they criticize any Jesus who does not conform to them as 'un-Jewish'. But I think much more is at issue here than simple fixed ideas about Judaism as a religion. Again, I would insist that a normative and prescriptive agenda lurks behind these characterizations, such that a claim is being made that a person who fails to accord to these (or similar) criteria is not simply unidentifiable as a religious Jew, but, whatever protestations to the contrary, is actually not a (proper) religious Jew.

As Sawicki reminds us, the Christian or any other non-Jew has no business telling Jews what they ought to believe and do, nor has any business at all in defining their religious traditions in any normative respect.[30] But it would not strike me as especially surprising, in light of the hubris of Christianity and its influence on those raised in its shadows, for Christians to do just this. After all, it must surely strike one as odd that all of the supposed definitional hallmarks of ancient Judaism are precisely the features that have been invoked in traditional anti-Jewish Christian polemic. Temple, Torah, the land of Israel, ethnic identity, circumcision – are these not precisely the features that Christians, historically, have grasped as the salient points of *their* distinction from Judaism? Should we not then worry that some Christian scholars are insisting on such an identity for Judaism precisely so that a distinctive Christian identity can be maintained? After all, if Jesus the Jew turns out to be defined mainly in

---

29. Cited by Stark, *Rise of Christianity*, 53, as the first Rabbi of Berlin's Reform congregation.

30. This is of course quite different from scholarly efforts at non-normative classification, as should be obvious.

terms of such things as, say, belief in God, interest in the prophetic scriptures, interest in ethical behavior, the prioritization of love of one's neighbor and one's personal duty over against the strictures of custom, and so on, then might it not turn out that Judaism could and can include and embrace everything that Christianity claims to be? And if so, why bother to be a Christian at all? So it seems to me that, perhaps, Christians, or Gentiles from a Christian background that may still mean something to them, do indeed have a vested interest in defining a normative Judaism, in order to define themselves.

But there is more still. The character of the Judaism imposed, as a discrete and fixed system, upon the figure of Jesus is one marked above all by its traditionalism and by claims to a common and rather standardized conformity to key distinctive behaviors and doctrines.[31] The specific content of these behaviors and doctrines, in at least one sense, hardly matters. What may be of more importance to non-Jews, and particularly to Christians, is the *identification* of a particular religion with the 'fundamentals', the observance of and adherence to its *traditional* identity. If, for instance, 'Jesus the Cynic' can be no Jew,[32] this implies that such a syncretistic, assimilatory, socially engaged or radical option can exist in *no* religious tradition; that, properly speaking, such traditions are and must be focused on their 'proper' objects and, to the extent that their adherents are *not* so oriented, they are no longer a part of the tradition to which they lay claim.

While I imagine that the main interest of those promoting such a view rests with Christianity (and Judaism to a more limited degree), the basic point can apply to just about any modern religion. Thus by identifying 'Jesus the Jew' as only conceivably meaning 'Jesus the Torah-observant, Semitic-speaking, circumcised, Temple-oriented, Sabbath-observant Jew' one speaks, again normatively, for a whole host of other traditions, and, more perniciously, *against* a whole host of contemporary religious options hanging by their fingernails at the peripheries of their traditions. If, for instance, Pearson is correct that Crossan's characterization of Jesus as a

31. This is necessarily a common feature of the Jewish Jesus reconstructions, because these reconstructions depend on a stable image of Judaism from which to make inferences about Jesus. It is essentially impossible to reconstruct a fluid, non-conformist, variegated Judaism from which to make inferences about Jesus' 'religiosity' for the simple reason that one would not know where, amidst this variety, to slot Jesus.

32. This is implied by, for instance, Paul Rhodes Eddy, 'Jesus as Diogenes? Reflections on the Cynic Jesus', *JBL* 115 (1996): 449–69, especially 460–61. Note too that the point of Vaage's or Mack's arguments is not that Jesus *was* a Cynic but that Jesus may be *compared* to a Cynic. Nonetheless I am here presenting the straw man that has been so often criticized, since it is the critique itself I am focusing on now, and not the original hypothesis.

Jewish Cynic is an oxymoron,[33] then we should similarly dismiss as oxymoronic such phenomena as Marxist Catholic priests, feminist Muslims, orthodox Jews who are atheists, homosexual Cree traditionalists, Communist Taoists, and so on. Of course, such phenomena *do* exist; wishing them out of existence is not the point. The point, rather, is denying them the legitimating links to the traditions they lay claim to. Feminist Muslims, for instance, may be decried by their opponents as no Muslims at all;[34] in short, they are oxymorons. A traditionalist view of Islam has no place for such an agenda at all, and so its proponents are cast outside of the tradition. Thus too, by offering up a definition of the boundaries of Judaism that excludes all but a traditionalist perspective from genuine belonging in the religion, the more rigid 'Jewish Jesus' scholars may be suggesting a similarly traditionalist definition of Christianity: one in which assent to the creeds, belief in God, veneration for God's word in the canonical Bible, and the general supernatural paraphernalia of orthodox Christian faith are the litmus test for whether one can, or cannot, claim to be a Christian at all.

Confirmation that this retrenchment of traditionalist Christian identity may be a subtext for at least some historical Jesus scholars may be found in an odd and interesting place: the theological agenda of their opponents. New Testament scholars such as John Dominic Crossan and Robert Funk make no secret at all of their interest in *reforming* a Christianity to which they are in some fashion committed. And for both of these scholars, and others besides,[35] this reform is oriented especially to a marginalization of the purely supernatural and dogmatic orientation of the religion, and an emphasis instead on its social and cultural effects. The Jesus of a Crossan or Funk is a Jesus who is quite clearly intended to inspire Christian followers of Jesus to become more engaged in this world, more socially active, and less rigid about or even concerned with dogmatic or creedal formulations. Funk, for instance, compares his own project with that of Galileo, shunting aside the gloomy clouds of dogma to free us from their slavery and open us to the truth.[36] So also Crossan, who reconstructs a Jesus who promoted 'a religious and economic egalitarianism that negated alike and at once the hierarchical and patronal normalcies of Jewish

---

33. Pearson, 'Gospel According to the Jesus Seminar', 12, referring to Crossan, *Historical Jesus*, 421.

34. See, e.g., Shahnaz Khan, *Aversion and Desire: Negotiating Muslim Female Identity in the Diaspora* (Toronto: Women's Press, 2002).

35. E.g., Marcus Borg, Stephen Patterson, and many of the participants in the Jesus Seminar.

36. See the comments in Robert W. Funk, Ray Hoover and the Jesus Seminar, *The Five Gospels: What did Jesus Really Say?* (New York: Macmillan, 1993), 1–4.

religion and Roman power'.[37] And lest we miss the ultimate import of these ciphers – 'normalcies of Jewish religion' as conservative Christianity, and 'Roman power' as especially American military hegemony over the world – Crossan introduces a contemporizing figure or two to his discussion. This Jesus who promoted the egalitarianism described by Crossan can be interpreted in terms of the Cynics, who 'were hippies in a world of Augustan yuppies'.[38] Moreover, says Crossan, historical reconstruction is at the very heart of Christianity,[39] and he laments that:

> Maybe, Christianity is an inevitable and absolutely necessary 'betrayal' of Jesus, else it might have died among the hills of Lower Galilee. But did that 'betrayal' have to happen so swiftly, succeed so fully, and be enjoyed so thoroughly? Might not a more even dialectic have been maintained between Jesus and Christ in Jesus Christ?[40]

Crossan, as much as Funk and much more clearly, is at least partly interested in a historical Jesus who will serve as a reforming model for modern Christianity, moving it away from a dogmatic focus and more toward a socially activist focus. Hence a reconstruction of Jesus who is not defined in terms of Jewish religiosity is a Jesus who offers a model for a type of Christianity that maintains its relevance in a secular world.

This last point is especially worth stressing. I do not suspect that either Funk's or Crossan's agenda is precisely to *secularize* Christianity simply because of some alleged desire to promote secularism.[41] Rather I suspect that, especially in the case of Crossan, the ultimate agenda is to *preserve* a place for Christianity within a world in which, say, the doctrine of the

---

37. Crossan, *Historical Jesus*, 422. See also his comments on apocalypticism, which, while they do not directly reflect on the 'Jewish' character of the historical Jesus, do indeed show us something about Crossan's religious orientation and agenda: 'You will recall that, in my first response to Dale [Allison] above, I noted that each of us had used that phrase "heaven on earth" for the historical Jesus. *On earth, as in heaven. Not, heaven instead of earth*' (Crossan, from Robert J. Miller [ed.], *The Apocalyptic Jesus: A Debate* [Santa Rosa, CA: Polebridge Press, 2001], 138, emphasis added).

And ... 'We are guilty of historical malpractice to go on using a phrase that can only misunderstand the past *and mislead the present. A millenarian seer or apocalyptic prophet announces the imminent transcendental change of a terribly evil world into a perfectly good one.* Say that clearly, and we might get somewhere. At least we might get to something *worth arguing about.* Go on talking about "the end of the world" and only misunderstanding and *irrelevance* are possible' (Crossan, from Miller, *Apocalyptic Jesus*, 138, some emphasis added).

38. Crossan, *Historical Jesus*, 421.

39. See especially Crossan, *Historical Jesus*, 423–26.

40. Crossan, *Historical Jesus*, 424.

41. Rather against the assessment of the Jesus Seminar's agenda in Pearson, 'Gospel According to the Jesus Seminar', 42–43.

Trinity or the rituals of the Mass appear to have less and less relevance.[42] The situation is quite different for Burton Mack, however. Here the agenda seems not only to be genuinely secularizing, but even anti-Christian (at least in its American forms). The last chapter of *A Myth of Innocence* makes it very clear that Mack believes that Christianity has, historically, had an undesirable (to say the least) impact on our attitudes and behaviors. And so I suspect that at least in part the 'non-religious' (and hence, for those who are using 'Jewish' as a cipher for 'religious', the 'non-Jewish') Jesus he constructs is intended to serve as a *poor*, even *impossible*, basis for a religion he regards as at least potentially harmful.

In any case, regardless of the ultimate motivations of Funk, Crossan, Mack, or others, I am suggesting that behind their lack of emphasis on the specifically *religious* features of Jesus' teaching and activity is neither an anti-Semitism nor an anti-Judaism, but a desire to minimize the doctrinal, creedal and supernaturalistic elements of Christianity. To my mind this serves as further indication that those who do precisely the opposite – that is, who stress the 'Judaism' of Jesus by stressing the 'religious' dimensions of his thought or actions – are likewise making a comment on contemporary Christianity, an assertion of the import of its traditional creedal, supernatural, 'religious' basis. Pearson's fulminations against the 'secular' Jesus reconstructed by the Jesus Seminar underscore and confirm this conclusion:

> The 'hidden agenda' in the work of the Jesus Seminar is clearly an ideology that drives it. So what is this ideology? An important clue is found in the frequency with which the word 'secular' appears in *The Five Gospels*... The ideology driving the Jesus Seminar is, I would argue, one of 'secularization'... What we have ... is an approach driven by an ideology of secularization, and a process of coloring the historical evidence to fit a secular ideal. Thus, in robbing Jesus of his Jewishness, the Jesus Seminar has finally robbed him of his *religion*.[43]

I do not offer this quotation as further evidence of a secularizing undercurrent behind the Jesus Seminar, but as evidence that the accusation that their (and others') reconstruction of Jesus is non-Jewish itself betrays the undercurrent of an *anti*-secularizing perception of religion on the part of their critics. It is not that Pearson, or other critics of the Jesus Seminar, necessarily think that Canada or the United States should be theocracies, of course. It is that they wish, apparently, to use Jesus as a model for insisting on traditional perceptions of religion and what it means to be religious. Thus, as noted, 'Jesus the Jew' may be

---

42. See Robert W. Funk, *Honest to Jesus: Jesus for a New Millennium* (San Francisco: HarperSanFrancisco, 1996), 298: 'If what we have to say about Jesus does not matter to those outside the precincts of traditional Christianity, it probably will not matter at all, at least not for the long term.'

43. Pearson, 'Gospel According to the Jesus Seminar', 42–43 (emphasis original).

offered in the service of such a prescriptive, normative understanding of religion. Indeed, Pearson himself links the two in the quotation above. Since I know nothing about Pearson's own religious views (or lack thereof), it is impossible for me to say that he is actively promoting political desecularization here. In fact, I very much doubt this is the case.[44] But what he is resisting is the secularization of *religion*: the figure of Jesus cannot be 'secular', for this would imply a definition of Christianity (or, in theory, any other religious tradition: Judaism, Islam, Buddhism, etc.) quite at odds with its traditional self-presentation.

Finally, an additional piece of evidence that the Jewish Jesus 'debate' is the manifest content of a latent engagement (positive or negative) with traditionalistic definitions of religion (usually, though not necessarily, Christianity) may be found in the differing treatment of each 'camp' of the debate over extra-canonical sources. This is most marked in the case of the *Gospel of Thomas*, and the differing assessments of its utility for historical Jesus research. Typically, those scholars who actively promote the traditionalistic and identifiable Jewish religiosity of the historical Jesus explicitly reject the *Gospel of Thomas* as having any utility for historical Jesus work, or simply ignore it as a potential source.[45] Conversely, those scholars who tend to be accused of producing a 'non-Jewish' Jesus *do* tend to make use of *Thomas* in their reconstructions of Jesus.[46]

Here is not the place to engage the debate about *Thomas*' date or

44.   Note that Pearson quite explicitly defends non-theological approaches to historical scholarship ('Gospel According to the Jesus Seminar', 43): 'Of course, one should expect that, in secular academic settings (such as a state university in the U.S.), a non-theological approach to historical evidence, including religious evidence, is standard. In my view, it ought to be the starting point even for theological historical research.'

45.   E.g., Sanders, Meier, Fredriksen, Pearson, etc. Meier offers explicit arguments for rejecting *Thomas* in *A Marginal Jew: Rethinking the Historical Jesus*. Volume I: *The Roots of the Problem and the Person* (Anchor Bible Reference Library; New York: Doubleday, 1991), though these arguments are weak, reversible, or assume their conclusions. Fredriksen mentions *Thomas* only twice in *Jesus of Nazareth* (81, 269), describing it in both instances as 'late'. Vermès (*Religion*), refers to *Thomas* just once (82), asserting without argument that *Gos. Thom.* 31 is literarily dependent on the synoptic gospels. Pearson ('Gospel According to the Jesus Seminar') criticizes the Jesus Seminar for using *Thomas*, for the usual variety of reasons, but additionally criticizes them for positing an early edition of *Thomas*. He states, 'No convincing case can be made...for an early "first edition" of the *Gospel of Thomas*.' It is interesting that here Pearson says no such case *can* be made, not that no such case *has* been made: the idea is simply impossible as far as he is concerned. In fact arguments *have* been made for the existence of an early stratum of Thomas (convincing or not) by a variety of scholars, including extended arguments on this issue by myself (William E. Arnal, 'The Rhetoric of Marginality: Apocalypticism, Gnosticism, and Sayings Gospels', *HTR* 88 [1995]: 471–94) and more recently in April D. De Conick, 'The Original Gospel of Thomas', *VC* 56 (2002): 167–99.

46.   E.g., Crossan, Mack, the Jesus Seminar, and many others.

dependence on the synoptic gospels.[47] But it is worth noting two peculiar features of the debate about *Thomas*' applicability to historical Jesus research. The first is that those who offer reasons for rejecting *Thomas* as a source tend to do so on three grounds: (1) it is a late document; (2) it is dependent on one or more of the synoptic gospels; (3) it is Gnostic in its theological orientation.[48] What is interesting about this set of arguments is that *even if* all three of these assertions were accurate, that would still provide no logical reason *whatsoever* for rejecting *Thomas*' applicability to historical Jesus research. As it happens, the exact same types of arguments indisputably[49] apply to the Gospels of Matthew and Luke: (1) they are late compositions, ranging in date somewhere between 85–120 CE; (2) they are dependent on other synoptic sources (Mark and Q); (3) they promote their own distinctive theologies. Yet those scholars who reject *Thomas* on these grounds are happy enough to mine Matthew and Luke for potentially 'authentic' Jesus material, and rightly so, since being late, or dependent, or theologically-biased hardly *precludes* the presence of earlier, authentic material that could not have been gleaned from other sources.[50] In short, the reasons given for rejecting *Thomas*' utility are duplicitous, since these arguments are applied selectively. When such claims can be made about non-canonical writings, these potential sources are set aside as irrelevant. When such claims can be made about canonical sources, by contrast, they are made in the service of methodological rigor, rather than wholesale dismissal. Thus, again, the *reasons* given for the repudiation of *Thomas* as a source for the historical Jesus demonstrate a lack of

---

47. See, however, the extended and convincing argument for *Thomas*' independence from the synoptics offered by Stephen J. Patterson, *The Gospel of Thomas and Jesus* (Sonoma, CA: Polebridge, 1993). So far, I have yet to find a compelling refutation of Patterson's claims; indeed, my own work on *Thomas* has convinced me that Patterson's argument is actually understated. Meier's arguments regarding *Thomas* in *A Marginal Jew I* cannot even be taken seriously. A recent claim has been made, however, that *Thomas* is dependent on the Diatessaron and was originally composed in Syriac: so Nicholas Perrin, *Thomas and Tatian: The Relationship between the Gospel of Thomas and the Diatessaron* (Leiden: E.J. Brill, 2002). While this thesis strikes me as inherently implausible, I have not yet read Perrin's book, and so must reserve judgment until I have familiarized myself with his arguments.

48. See, e.g., Meier's discussion in *A Marginal Jew I*; cf. Pearson, 'Gospel According to the Jesus Seminar', 15; and many others. Note that each one of these points has been contested: the date, literary status, and theology of *Thomas* are still matters of considerable debate.

49. As opposed to *Thomas*, in fact, where all three claims are in dispute.

50. The classic example being the parable of the Good Samaritan, Luke 10.29–37. This parable is generally thought to go back to Jesus in some form (without its Lukan applicative clauses), even though (1) it is singly-attested; (2) in a late (possibly second-century) source; (3) which is dependent on Mark and Q; (4) and which uses the parable to promote the author's own theological-ethical agenda.

consistency, a duplicity, in the treatment of canonical over against non-canonical sources.

The second peculiar feature of this debate is precisely the co-ordination between the use of *Thomas* as a source and the scholarship that allegedly produces a 'non-Jewish' Jesus. This is peculiar precisely because *Thomas* is no less 'Jewish' than the synoptic gospels! In other words, were *Thomas* to offer us a genuinely non-Jewish Jesus, were it to show no concern with the 'religious' features of ancient Judaism, were it to address Gentile concerns or presume a Gentile audience, then its use as a source for reconstructing Jesus would quite naturally and comprehensibly co-ordinate with changes of a 'non-Jewish' Jesus.[51] Likewise, were the Gospel of Mark to promote the 'religious' features of ancient Judaism, were it to stress the Judaism of Jesus, and to take a Jewish audience for granted, then its use as the primary source of information among 'Jewish Jesus' advocates would make perfect sense: the tendencies of the reconstructions would reflect the character of the sources used.[52]

But this does not seem to be the case. Mark does not actually give us a Jesus who positively interacts with the supposed features of the 'common Judaism' of his time. It is Mark who has Jesus abrogate dietary laws wholesale (7.14–19), who variously violates the Sabbath (especially Mark 2.23–28[53]), who feels the need to explain (incorrectly![54]) the purification practices of 'all the Jews' in the third person (7.3–4), and who ultimately

---

51. I want to stress that *very* few scholars use *Thomas* as the primary source for their reconstructions of Jesus. Crossan, the Jesus Seminar, and others typically use *Thomas* as one source, alongside Q, Mark, and even singly-attested material from Matthew and Luke. The complaint is not, in most cases, that *Thomas* has been used exclusively or predominantly, but that it has been used at all. This is especially clear in Pearson, 'Gospel According to the Jesus Seminar', 15–16, where he complains that the Jesus Seminar attempted to use *Thomas*, but then goes on to acknowledge that *Thomas* had no influence at all on the resulting portrait of Jesus.

52. I am focusing on Mark here because it serves as the source for the bulk of narrative material in Matthew and Luke. Thus concentration on reconstructing especially the activity of Jesus from the three synoptic gospels boils down to information ultimately derived from Mark. I have noted elsewhere ('Major Episodes in the Biography of Jesus: Methodological Observations on the Historicity of the Narrative Tradition', *Toronto Journal of Theology* 13 [1997]: 201–26) that Sanders' list of 'indisputable facts' about Jesus is little more than a plot summary of the Gospel of Mark.

53. I chose this example because it is *not* susceptible to the claim that what is at issue is halakhic debate over the fine points of Sabbath observance. It is clear from Jesus' response in Mark that he is denying the applicability of Sabbath regulations (at least to himself), not disputing what they are.

54. So, e.g., Amy-Jill Levine, 'Matthew, Mark, and Luke: Good News or Bad?' in *Jesus, Judaism, and Christian Anti-Judaism: Reading the New Testament after the Holocaust* (ed. Paula Fredriksen and Adele Reinhartz; Louisville, KY and London: Westminster/John Knox, 2002), 77–98, at 81.

lays responsibility (and, arguably, divine vengeance) for Jesus' death at the feet of the Jewish religious leaders and even the whole crowd present in Jerusalem for the Passover festival.[55] Conversely, it is the *Gospel of Thomas* that insists, against Mark's version of Jesus, on the necessity of both fasting and Sabbath observance: 'If you do not fast as regards the world, you will not find the Kingdom. If you do not observe the Sabbath as a Sabbath, you will not see the Father' (*Gos. Thom.* 27). *Thomas*, rather than disparaging Jesus' family as Mark does (Mark 3.21, 31–35), asserts the leadership and centrality of his brother James the righteous (*Gos. Thom.* 12), traditionally presented as a nomistic rigorist (cf. Gal. 2.12). *Thomas* alludes to or quotes Hebrew scriptures,[56] uses the pious Jewish locution 'kingdom of heaven',[57] assumes that the Pharisees and scribes possess the 'keys of knowledge' (*Gos. Thom.* 39), discusses angels and prophets (*Gos. Thom.* 88), and takes it for granted that his readers' history is Jewish history.[58] He offers an interpretation of the parable of the tenants that, unlike Mark's, is not anti-Jewish at all,[59] and an interpretation of the parable of the banquet that, unlike Matthew's or Luke's, has nothing to do with promoting or justifying a Gentile mission.[60]

55.   While Levine, 'Matthew, Mark, and Luke', 82–83, quite correctly notes that Mark is much more overtly hostile to Jewish groups than to Jews in general, the one shades over into the other in the account of Pilate's offer to free Jesus in Mark 15.6–15. Mark does stress that the crowds called for Jesus' execution because 'the chief priests stirred up the crowd' (15.11), but it is still precisely that generalized 'crowd' that cries out 'crucify him' when Pilate asks about what should be done with Jesus (Mark 15.13–14). Matthew's gloss on this passage, 'and all the people answered, "his blood be on us and on our children" ' (Mt. 27.25) merely makes explicit what Mark has already implied.

56.   See *Gos. Thom.* 66, quoting Psa. 118.22–23; and *Gos. Thom.* 17, which may allude to Isa. 64.4 and 65.17.

57.   E.g., *Gos. Thom.* 20. *Thomas* is not consistent in this, however, and evidently does not use the phrase to avoid the words 'god/s' or 'Father', both of which are used in the text. But then, Matthew is not perfectly consistent in this respect, either.

58.   See *Gos. Thom.* 46: 'from Adam until John the Baptist'.

59.   *Gos. Thom.* 65 lacks entirely the allegorical dimensions that make the version in Mk. 12.1–9 so polemical. John S. Kloppenborg, as well, has recently shown that the version in Thomas is not only more original than that in Mark, but that the parable's allusion to Isaiah 5.1–7, in Mark's version, is drawn from the LXX and assumes Egyptian viticultural techniques, while that of *Thomas* is more realistic and reflects Palestinian viticulture. See John Kloppenborg, 'Isaiah 5.1–7, The Parable of the Tenants and Vineyard Leases on Papyrus', in *Text and Artifact in the Religions of Mediterranean Antiquity: Essays in Honour of Peter Richardson* (ed. Stephen G. Wilson and Michel Desjardins; Studies in Christianity and Judaism/Études sur le christianisme et le judaïsme, 9; Waterloo, Ont.: Wilfrid Laurier University Press, 2000) 111–34.

60.   Even Matthew's version (Mt. 22.1–14), for all of its suspicion of the negative consequences of a Gentile mission (see 22.10–14), understands the parable in this fashion, and, moreover, emphasizes the motif that a Gentile mission is akin to punishment – along

My point is not that *Thomas* is a 'Jewish' text and Mark is not. There are many places in Mark, obviously, where scripture is cited, where the importance of Jewish 'religious' practices are emphasized or taken for granted, and the action quite clearly takes place, for the most part, among Jews. So too there are instances in the *Gospel of Thomas* of the sorts of 'non-Jewish' or 'anti-Jewish' features noted in Mark.[61] My point, however, is that neither Mark nor *Thomas* are consistently 'Jewish' or 'non-Jewish'. In short, while there is a very strong correspondence between the rejection of *Thomas* as a source (on inconsistent grounds) and the construction of a traditionalistic 'Jewish Jesus', this correspondence cannot be traced to *Thomas*' actual content, which gives us no more nor less 'Jewish' a Jesus than Mark does.

The correspondence, therefore, must be the result of some other factors than the actual contents of the sources in question. I suggest, then, that the clear rejection of *Thomas* as a source for Jesus by 'Jewish Jesus' advocates, and the rejection of reconstructions of Jesus that do make use of *Thomas*, confirms my claims above about at least part of the agenda behind this scholarship and the manufactured 'debate' over Jesus' Jewishness. That agenda appears at least in part to revolve around the retrenchment of traditionalist religious identity, particularly Christian identity. A Jesus who can *be* a Jew *only* by being an identifiably religiously-focused Jew of a certain traditionalistic sort of course implies a particular vision of religious identity. A Jesus who does not conform to this stereotype implies an opposite vision of religious identity. And so also with the treatment of canonical versus non-canonical documents as sources for Jesus. Although there is no logical relationship between a 'Jewish Jesus' and eschewing the *Gospel of Thomas* as a source, the two positions are clearly correlated; they are correlated, I submit, by their common subtext. For those whose vision or imagination of what Christianity *is*, is as it is defined by its traditional adherents, the notion that non-canonical, 'heretical' sources might be accurate or should even be given consideration is as unattractive, even unthinkable, as is a 'secular'

---

with the destruction of Jerusalem! (22.7) – for Jewish misdeeds, both by associating the call to Gentiles with the violence of the original proposed guests (as opposed to Luke's version [Lk. 14.16–24], where they simply reject the invitation rather than killing those who offer it); and in his positioning of it immediately after his version of the parable of the tenants (Mt. 21.33–46), where the same motifs are developed. Some recent work has suggested that Luke's version of the parable may not reflect concern with a Gentile mission, as has generally been supposed.

61. See, for instance, *Gos. Thom.* 14, which denigrates fasting, prayer and almsgiving, and which appears to dismiss dietary regulations; *Gos. Thom.* 43, which refers to 'the Jews' in the third person and seems to assume a distinction between them and Jesus' disciples; and *Gos. Thom.* 53, which implies that circumcision is useless.

Jesus. And again, the reverse is true. Those scholars who, for whatever personal or intellectual reasons, wish to open the boundaries of Christianity to secular, reformist or non-traditional alterations are consistently inclined to be liberal in their use of sources as well. This tendency is especially marked in the work of Crossan, who not only uses *Thomas* as a source, but also appeals to, *inter alia*, the Egerton Gospel or the 'Cross Gospel' as early and valuable texts. The problem, then, may not be that *Thomas*' contents are inimical to either traditional Christian theological views or traditional historical reconstructions (though this may be a factor too[62]); *Thomas* is to be rejected regardless of its contents or their implications (the interpretation of which remains under dispute) simply because it is not canonical.[63] Since *Thomas* is not part of the traditional construction of the Christian religion, it cannot be part of the historical *re*construction of a traditionalist Christianity. Thus those who depend on 'Jesus the Jew' to support traditionalistic reconstructions also reject *Thomas*, even though the use of *Thomas* need not lead to a 'non-Jewish' Jesus; and those whose agenda of reform, broadening, or some form of 'secularization' generates the accusation of a 'non-Jewish' Jesus tend to make some use of *Thomas* and other non-canonical sources, not because these sources are more 'secular' than the canonical gospels, but precisely because these scholars are not wedded to the traditional Christian canon.

It would seem, then, that for some contemporary scholars, Christianity (or any 'religion') in a secular world will be saved by keeping a tight hold upon its dogmatic roots, its traditional identity, its distinctively *religious* nature, as opposed to and autonomous from the secular world around it. For other scholars, Christianity (or any 'religion') in a secular world can only be saved by accommodation to that secularity, an assertion of the socio-cultural relevance of Christianity as something larger than mere

---

62. So John S. Kloppenborg, *Excavating Q: The History and Setting of the Sayings Gospel* (Minneapolis: Fortress; Edinburgh: T & T Clark, 2000), 2: 'Q – along with the Gospel of Thomas, the epistle of James, and the Gospel of Peter – lets us see that the process that led to the formation of the Gospels was incomparably richer, more complex, and more experimental than earlier models have supposed.'

63. Should anyone doubt this claim, I invite them to consider Meier's 'argument' in *A Marginal Jew I* on the value of non-canonical sources. Not only are Meier's arguments on the secondary character of *Thomas* logically worthless – more to the point, he argues that having dispensed with a small number of non-canonical sources, this should put to rest any notion that non-canonical sources in general and as a whole may be of any utility to the historical Jesus quest! I could ask for no clearer evidence that Meier, at least, is thinking in terms of two classes of objects – canonical and non-canonical texts – rather than in terms of discrete and individual texts. In other words, he is clearly assessing the value of his sources in terms of canonicity, rather than in terms of the actual evidence on a case-by-case basis.

dogma and worship. This agenda influences not only how Jesus is constructed, but also seems to determine what sources are allowable – regardless of the actual *content* of those sources. It is important to note here, in passing, that the significance of this particular subtext cannot be measured wholly in terms of the personal agenda or beliefs of the scholars in question themselves. In some cases, of course, it can be so measured, and quite easily. That scholars such as Pearson or Meier – never mind apologists like N. T. Wright – have something of a religious agenda of their own that revolves around a traditional understanding of the identity of Christianity is quite obvious.[64] Likewise, with scholars such as Crossan, Funk or Patterson, it is fairly clear that there is a personal investment in Christianity, but that the Christianity in question is felt to require reform, including reform of its actual identity. With other scholars, however, the situation is not nearly so clear. On the 'Jewish Jesus' side of the 'debate', scholars such as Fredriksen or Sanders do *not* make it clear (at least not to me) what personal religious commitments they may have, if any, and of what sort those commitments might be. On the other side of the 'debate', it is unclear to me what interest Richard Horsley, for example, has in contemporary Christianity and, while Burton Mack's agenda is fairly clear, it certainly cannot be described as a *theological* agenda.

But in at least one sense, the question of *personal* agenda is irrelevant. As I hope I have shown, there is a *correspondence* between the 'Jewish Jesus' and a (subtextual) defense of traditionalistic understandings of discrete religions. This correspondence is what is important; not the personal beliefs of individual scholars. There need not be a notion here of direct cause and effect. That is, one need not say that the subtext *causes* the particular characteristics of the historical reconstruction. They just go together, and the one stands in for or supports the other. The subtexts may, however, explain the *heat* generated in a 'debate' over Jesus' Judaism in which no one denies that he is Jewish. The anger, recriminations and misrepresentations derive their energy from the subtexts that each type of reconstruction supports. In addition, these subtexts also have a determining effect on the *reception* of this scholarship. So, regardless of, say, Sanders' personal religious beliefs, traditionalistic Christians will tend to approve of his version of the historical Jesus much more than they will of, say, Crossan's; while Christians who are alienated from or distressed about their religious tradition will tend to find Crossan much more helpful

64. Note that 'traditional' here need not mean politically conservative or 'fundamentalist'.

and illuminating than Sanders.[65] There can be little doubt that the historical Jesus, as has always been the case, is being invoked to save our souls.

Saving our Postmodern Souls

The final subtextual matter I wish to address concerns the ways in which reconstructions of the historical Jesus as a particular type of Jew can be correlated to a cultural malaise of our own time, a malaise which is sometimes expressed by the tag 'postmodernism'. Too often, 'postmodernism' is understood to be an epistemological conclusion which boils down to little more than hermeneutical relativism.[66] As anyone should realize, however, philosophical relativism is an old, old view, and we hardly needed 'postmodernism' to introduce us to it. The term 'postmodernism' originally appears to have arisen in connection with *architecture*: it described a building style fiercely at odds with the high-modern styles that generated those appalling high-rise housing projects that mar the surface of large cities today. Postmodernist architecture rejected the values of uniformity, functionality, aesthetic coherence and geometric

---

65. Should anyone doubt this conclusion, I suggest they consult www.amazon.com (or similar sites) and browse through the reader reviews of books by Crossan, the Jesus Seminar, etc., on the one hand; and those of Fredriksen or Sanders, on the other. They will find there much more straightforwardly religious-based fulminations against Funk or Crossan, and much more general approval – from those coming from an obviously Christian, but not fundamentalist, perspective – for Sanders or Fredriksen. For instance, regarding E.P. Sanders' *The Historical Figure of Jesus* (Harmondsworth, Middlesex: Penguin, 1993), we find the following representative reader assessment: 'The important point for me is that this excellent historical study of Jesus will not undermine the faith (beliefs), in the slightest, [of] any practicing Christian.' Conversely, for John Dominic Crossan's *Jesus: A Revolutionary Biography* (San Francisco: HarperSanFrancisco, 1994), we get: 'This book, even to an amateur student of the historicity and reliability of the gospels' account of Jesus, is utterly ridiculous. Crossan works from the perspective that what the Bible says must be wrong, and tries to fit all his evidence to fit that perspective. Relying on a number of historical documents that date much later than the gospels themselves is awfully bias [*sic*] for a supposedly objective scholar.' Clearer still is this reader's rejoinder to Crossan: 'In summation, this book adds up to ... not much. The Jesus presented here would be unrecognizable to believers throughout history, including those who walked with him while he was on this earth. In attempting to make Jesus "relevant" to a politically-correct post-modern world, Crossan strips him of all his uniqueness and presents him as a powerless figure unworthy of worship or following in any religious or spiritual sense. This picture of Jesus is like a jigsaw puzzle with 95% of the pieces missing.'

66. Such a view appears just as often in the promoters of a 'postmodern' perspective as its detractors. See, most strikingly, Stephen D. Moore, *Literary Criticism and the Gospels: The Theoretical Challenge* (New Haven: Yale University Press, 1989). Of course such a view of postmodernism is also implied by N.T. Wright's formulation of 'critical realism' as an alternative.

precision, preferring instead frivolity, mixtures of styles (often jarring), quotation,[67] ornamentality, and geometric anarchy. This architectural style and the values behind it very quickly spread to other areas of culture: literature, art, film, and academic work.[68]

The best explanation for this flood of distinctively postmodern cultural preferences has been an appeal to a postmodern *condition*, which is socially, politically, and/or economically distinctive enough from high-modernity and its expectations that it has generated its own distinctive cultural forms of expression as well.[69] The conditions of postmodernity are ones under which we *all* live, and so in some sense any and every reconstruction of the historical Jesus is 'postmodern'. Crossan may be accused of having produced a 'postmodern' Jesus, but the alternatives to his Jesus, no matter how different they may be, are also being generated out of a postmodern context.[70] And what is this postmodern condition? It is to be found, primarily, in the corrosion of social and political categories, as its cultural expressions would imply in *their* corrosion of taken-for-granted categories. Much more recently, this condition has come to be referred to as 'globalization'.[71] Since the 1970s, and at an accelerated pace since the 1990s, the expectation of social and economic stability from cradle to grave, of working at a single job for one's whole life, in a traditional industry, has been supplanted by an 'information economy', the actual contents or productiveness of which are not immediately apparent, and the stability of which is minimal. We have also seen the erosion of the autonomy and power of the secular state: free trade agreements, currency fluctuations and increasing internationalism, and the autonomy of corporate entities have tended to transfer especially economic power from the state to private corporations. Moreover, the internationalization of trade and economics has eroded social and cultural distinctions that could be taken utterly for granted even 30 years ago. I

67.   That is, the use of a 'signature' element of one particular style to allude to that style in a building whose style is completely different. An example would be the use of high Corinthian columns on the façade of a small private dwelling.

68.   The most thorough and compelling discussion of postmodernism that I have yet encountered is Frederic Jameson, *Postmodernism; Or, The Cultural Logic of Late Capitalism* (Durham, NC: Duke University Press, 1991).

69.   This view is best described and explained by David Harvey, *The Condition of Postmodernity: An Enquiry into the Origins of Cultural Change* (Oxford: Blackwell, 1989).

70.   This is part of the problem with N. T. Wright's criticism of Crossan in 'Taking the Text with Her Pleasure: A Post-Post-Modernist Response to J. Dominic Crossan, *The Historical Jesus: The Life of a Mediterranean Jewish Peasant*', *Theology* 96 (1993): 303–309. He seems to assume that 'postmodernism' is merely a philosophical theory, to which one might offer reasonable alternatives. To my mind, by contrast, Crossan's alleged 'postmodernism' should be assessed as a symptom, not as the assertion of a philosophical model.

71.   Predictably, 'postmodernism' as a positive term and as an academic movement has proved to be something of an ephemeral trend. One is reminded of ... *disco*.

can no longer assume, for instance, that Canada's cultural identity is (at least partly) Christian; I do not need to go to the Middle East to see a mosque: they are all over Canada, as are various mixed-up traces of other cultures from all over the world. If I can experience 'world culture' at home in Saskatchewan, which is a backwater if ever there was one, then the concept of 'a culture' has to be revised a great deal. My point is not that we Canadians and Americans are born racists who are disturbed by the presence of 'other' cultures in our midst. Rather, I am suggesting that this mix, fostered by economic internationalism – globalism – is forcing upon us a redefinition of what culture *is*,[72] and is in fact eroding the cultural distinctions – and identities based on them – that we have taken for granted in the past.

Whether we call it postmodernism or globalization, the relevance of this condition to historical Jesus reconstructions may not be immediately obvious, but strikes me as clear enough. What is at issue is offering some sort of response to the erosion or fragmentation of social and cultural identities, and the simultaneous homogenization of global culture that is implied by globalization or the postmodern condition.[73] What we see, then, in the differing presentations of the Jewish Jesus are different conceptualizations of what culture is, in the face of the need to respond, somehow, to its actual and inevitable reconfiguration in a 'postmodern' world. As I have said elsewhere:

> Typically, this response is one of resistance. It sometimes manifests itself in a reaffirmation of the validity of that which is lost, its proponents behaving with idealist assumptions and imagining that the struggle to retain our souls is being fought at the level of ideas. With such an assumption, the response involves the continual affirmation to the mind, with as much evidence as one can muster, that the concepts on which we base our worldview are still valid. The struggle for our souls, for our selves, for our very identities, therefore takes place at the level of asserting and intellectually defending those very comfortable and threatened conceptions – or means of conceptualizing – which are

72. For instance, we have tended in the past to associate culture with ethnic or national identity, and, as my examples suggest, this is no longer possible. Being a Muslim and a Canadian at the same time is not only possible, but common. Islamic religious (i.e., cultural) identity need not imply Middle Eastern national identity, American security agencies to the contrary.

73. The irony here is only superficial, in fact. That national or traditional cultural identities are being eroded does not necessarily bring with it an end to totalizing conceptions of human behavior. Quite the reverse! The failure of national and cultural identities to retain their salience by retaining their boundaries opens the door to a totalizing global culture based solely on consumerism. If both the Buddha and Mohammed have been set aside, the vacuum may be filled in both instances with McDonalds and Disney World.

losing their resonance, in an effort to rebuild them, revivify them and thus once again live in a (conceptually) stable universe.[74]

This agenda, I suggest, is precisely what is behind some of the insistence on a reified Judaism in antiquity, and on a reified and anachronistic assertion of Jesus' 'religion'. What is being insisted upon here is precisely the *stability* of culture, and precisely the *distinctiveness* of cultural identity. If being a Jew can be easily and sharply defined, and if the application to a person of this classification can allow us easily to reconstruct their identity, then, by implication, my Canadian identity is likewise stable, clear and distinctive. Here cultural distinctiveness and identity is being offered as a response and challenge in the face of conditions in which precisely these features of identity are becoming more and more questionable.

It is notable, in support of this claim, that Fredriksen's and Reinhartz's *Jesus, Judaism, and Anti-Judaism*, a text ostensibly about ancient history and religion, opens with a preface that refers copiously to globalization, and sees in it a direct threat to distinctive religious identity:

> Like a second Flood of biblical proportion, the global democratization of technology, finance, and information threatens to efface all that stands in its way... [H]ow is it, amidst the homogenizing and totalizing power of economic globalization, that *particular* faith communities – like those of Judaism and Christianity – will be able to preserve, let alone deepen, their *specific religious* heritage? If our world's post-Cold War economy has proven itself no respecter of culture, neither will it be a respecter of religion. The implication ... is clear: Jews and Christians are in the same boat. Both will struggle mightily to *preserve their own respective traditions...* Both Christians and Jews face the common challenges of maintaining *particular* and *historically connected* faiths in the face of an impending deluge of economic globalization.[75]

Thus even among scholars who have no personal faith commitment to either Judaism or Christianity, a normative subtext may lurk behind their characterizations of the historical Jesus and of his 'religion'. Why, for instance, would a non-Christian scholar be interested in promoting the traditionalistic definition of religion, Judaism and Christianity that I have

74. William E. Arnal, 'Making and Re-Making the Jesus-Sign: Contemporary Markings on the Body of Christ', in *Whose Historical Jesus?* (ed. William E. Arnal and Michel Desjardins; Studies in Christianity and Judaism/Études sur le christianisme et le judaïsme, 7; Waterloo, Ontario: Wilfrid Laurier University Press, 1997), 308–19, at p. 312.

75. Carey C. Newman, 'Foreword', in *Jesus, Judaism, and Christian Anti-Judaism: Reading the New Testament after the Holocaust* (ed. Paula Fredriksen and Adele Reinhartz; Louisville, KY and London: Westminster John Knox, 2002), ix–xi, at pp. ix–x (emphasis added).

suggested underlies some historical Jesus reconstructions? Because at issue is not simply the identity of Christianity, but the matter of identity itself.

Of course, this reaction to postmodernity is not the only one possible. Again, I have commented on this elsewhere:

> The alternative, if one approaches the [postmodern] malaise from a materialist perspective, is to recognize that conceptions are products of the actual construction of the world of social humanity itself, and that the failure of certain conceptions to persist in a meaningful way is due less to intellectual stagnation than it is to a world whose human relations suggest different and changing patterns to the mind... Since the subject or sense of personal/human groundedness cannot be created *ex nihilo*, it must be constructed within and upon the material culture in which we now subsist, a task which requires not only working *with* the conceptual framework dictated by those circumstances but also changing those actual circumstances in such a way that we are left with a world better suited to modern human needs. Such a perspective lends itself to ignoring and even opposing conceptual archaisms such as 'religion', and reifications thereof, including 'Judaism'. From this stance comes the passion and interest invested by advocates of the Cynic hypothesis and other opponents of the 'Jesus the Jew' reconstruction, which derive from the assumption that these ideal conceptions are not only archaic and meaningless, but counterproductive.[76]

Thus again we see behind the alleged debate over a Jewish Jesus yet another subtext, in which 'Jewish' is being offered as a cipher for the reification of cultural identity, religious or otherwise. Promotions of an identifiably and distinctively Jewish Jesus are resisting postmodern or globalizing homogenization and fragmentation precisely in their insistence on the coherence of 'Jewish' identity. Reconstructions of a less visibly 'Jewish' Jesus are offering their own response to postmodernism and globalization: not exactly an accommodation to its cultural tendencies, but a certain acceptance of the reality of current conditions, and a desire to work within those conditions for a better world, however that may be imagined:

> When previously persuasive discourses no longer persuade and previously prevalent sentiments no longer prevail, society enters a situation of fluidity and crisis. In such moments, competing groups continue to deploy strategic discourses and may also make use of coercive force as they struggle, not just to seize or retain power, but to reshape the borders and hierarchic order of society itself.[77]

---

76. Arnal, 'Making and Re-Making the Jesus-Sign', 312, emphasis original.
77. Bruce Lincoln, *Discourse and the Construction of Society: Comparative Studies of Myth, Ritual, and Classification* (New York and Oxford: Oxford University Press, 1989), 174.

Conclusion

I have spent a great deal of time attempting to describe the undercurrents, the biases, the hidden agenda that I see lurking behind historical Jesus scholarship, including both scholarship with which I sympathize and that with which I emphatically disagree. The fact that such agenda can be claimed for *both* sides in the 'debate' should serve as an indication that I neither exempt myself from such subtextual interests nor regard their existence as an indication of the factual falsity of the scholarly conclusions with which they are associated. The one simply does not follow from the other. I have been accused in my own work on Q[78] of projecting my circumstances onto those of the Q people (whom I describe as, essentially, alienated low-level intellectuals, a characterization that *certainly* reflects my own self-conception) while criticizing others who do likewise. I can hardly deny the accusation, but, at the same time, the actual evidence I cite supports my reconstruction (or fails to, as the case may be) *regardless* of the congeniality of my conclusions. Indeed, I would claim – at least in moments of supreme self-confidence – that it is precisely the congeniality of these views that *allowed* me to see the historical *Sitz* behind Q accurately.

So likewise, I must stress that focusing on the subtexts that may underlie the work of, say, Paula Fredriksen, is not in itself *any* indication that her views are wrong, and is not offered as such. Fredriksen (or Sanders, or Crossan, or Mack) *could* indeed be so massively biased that their reconstruction of Jesus is nothing but projection; yet that reconstruction could still be correct, and we owe it to these scholars to examine and assess the evidence they offer and the arguments they actually make, regardless of their personal agenda or the agenda behind the reception of their work. And it is equally true that scholarship which has no bias at all, should such an animal exist, could nonetheless produce a historical Jesus which is, factually speaking, one hundred percent wrong, or, alternatively, poorly argued. Our aim as scholars, therefore, must not and cannot be the impossible task of approaching our subject matters objectively. We cannot do so, and as human beings, in my opinion, we should not do so. Our task as scholars, rather, is to provide *reasons* for the claims we make, *reasons* for our rejections or approvals of the conclusions of our scholarly colleagues – and these reasons should, at least in theory, be comprehensible, assessable and 'testable'[79] by our scholarly peers. I

---

78. Particularly, William E. Arnal, *Jesus and the Village Scribes: Galilean Conflicts and the Setting of Q* (Minneapolis: Fortress, 2001).

79. By 'testable' I do not mean experimental testability as is expected in the natural sciences. I think this technique is probably impossible for the humanities. I simply mean that our arguments should be of a sort that any reasonable person should be able to assess them: they should not appeal to personal preferences, transcendent insights, or data that cannot be accessed by others.

may vehemently dislike the *implications* of Paula Fredriksen's Jesus and quite like the *implications* of Burton Mack's Jesus.[80] The trick for me as a scholar, however, is to keep my mind open to Fredriksen's arguments, and their potential strengths, as well as Mack's arguments, and their potential weaknesses. And should I conclude that I do, on scholarly grounds, think that Mack is more correct than Fredriksen, my reasons for this conclusion should be limited as much as possible to the cogency of their arguments.

Naïve though it may be, I offer here a plea for a certain scholarly ethic, one which has been characterized by Bruce Lincoln as 'mythology with footnotes'.[81] As scholars, we are still human beings, and we in the humanities especially engage in the generation of human meaning, in the production of worldviews, in the *pensée sauvage* that organizes the universe around us. We are thus mythmakers ourselves even in our analysis of myth. In our reproductions of the historical Jesus, we are doing essentially the same thing that the gospel writers did, whether or not we are Christians or even attracted to the figure of Jesus: we are projecting our own beliefs onto a story (history) and so using narrative (of a sort) to create a myth. The responsibility that sets scholars apart from the more usual (especially religious) practitioners of myth-making is the care that we must take to *document* our claims, such that someday perhaps those claims may survive the inevitable desuetude of the myths they were designed to sustain.

80. Note my stress here on my like or dislike for the *implications* of these figures, and not on my like or dislike of the figures themselves. It has become fashionable in our field to assume that we will project the features we *like* onto the objects of our study: we will make Jesus or Paul or the Q people into replicas of ourselves. This strikes me as a presumptuous and simplistic notion of how bias works in our field. For some of us, there is simply no investment in Jesus, and no need to make him, in particular, 'like us'. Nor do I imagine that the Jesus of E.P. Sanders, for example, actually reflects his own behavior (at least, I hope not!). The point is rather in the way that the conceptualizations behind constructions of Jesus accord, or fail to accord, to our own worldviews, regardless of whether Jesus himself be presented as attractive or unattractive.

81. Bruce Lincoln, *Theorizing Myth: Narrative, Ideology, and Scholarship* (Chicago: University of Chicago Press, 1999), 209; cf. 207–16.

Compassion is to Purity as Fish is to Bicycle and Other Reflections on Constructions of 'Judaism' in Current Work on the Historical Jesus

Paula Fredriksen

Boston University

Jesus of Nazareth was a Jew. This seemingly unremarkable observation has been the starting-point for all serious scholarly work in this last cycle of historical Jesus research, the so-called 'Third Quest'. Earlier scholarship and much more distant treatises of ancient Christology have of course made the same affirmation. What distinguishes the claim in its current form is the effort that modern scholars have made to link their quest for the historical Jesus to an equally vigorous quest for his historical context, late Second Temple Judaism. The scholarly definition of ancient Judaism frames and facilitates the scholar's reconstruction of Jesus.

However, this procedure, common to current questers, has yielded no consensus in results. Instead, the last quarter-century has witnessed a proliferation of contesting historical reconstructions both of Jesus of Nazareth and of his native historical context. We can agree neither on the content of Jesus' message nor on the goals of his mission. Was Jesus an apocalyptic teacher, or not? Was his mission intended to challenge or reform some significant practices and beliefs of his people – indeed, perhaps, to reject some? Did his teaching represent something that was in some way radically new, which the majority of his compatriots (both before his execution and after) then rejected?

Over these ostensibly historical questions a host of others hover. What does it mean to assert that Jesus prophesied that the Kingdom of God was about to occur or arrive, given that he was so manifestly wrong? Is an apocalyptic Jesus, in short, a theologically usable Jesus? Is a reformist or rebellious Jesus an anti-Jewish Jesus? And if reform and radical critique were not his program, then what? Is a (normatively) Jewish Jesus a theologically usable Jesus? And do reconstructions of Jesus as reformer or critic succor Christian anti-Judaism and Western anti-Semitism?

These last are second-order questions. Yet they seem to arise with urgency in our current scholarly context. Too often, they shape or seem to shape the first-order questions by which we direct our research. The goal of this volume is to give several of us, who stand on different sides of debate about Jesus, Judaism, and apocalyptic, a chance to consider critically the relation of these second-order questions to our primary, historical ones. Today, in brief, our question is: What is *at stake* in current reconstructions of Jesus?

I propose to respond by taking a seemingly circuitous route. Let's leave modern New Testament scholarship for the moment, and drop in somewhere else: the ancient Mediterranean.

I

Linguistically, geographically, sociologically, early Christianity developed in two distinct Mediterranean contexts. Jesus himself lived and moved in the overwhelmingly Jewish environment of Galilee and Judea. His spoken language was most probably Aramaic, his biblical tradition (whether written or, more likely, oral) Aramaic or Hebrew, his culture primarily that of villages. The earliest texts through which we know about Jesus and the movement that begins in the wake of his mission are, of course, in Greek. Their provenance is the Eastern Mediterranean. Their social environment is (probably) the mixed Jewish and pagan milieu of diaspora synagogues in the Graeco-Roman city. Their biblical tradition is written, and Greek (the LXX).

Despite their differences, however, much unites the early Jesus movement in both its matrices – 'home' (Galilee, Judea, Jerusalem, the Temple) and abroad (Greek-speaking Jewish communities in the Diaspora) – with ancient Mediterranean culture in general, and with what we think of as 'religious' culture in particular. To present this common cultural context, I offer two egregious generalizations:

> *In antiquity, gods ran in the blood.*
> *In antiquity, all monotheists were polytheists.*

To divine/human hematology first. Ancient gods lived with humans in two different ways. First, gods attached to particular places, whether natural or man-made. Groves, grottos, mountains; cities, temples and, especially, altars: all these might be visited or inhabited by the god to whom they were sacred.[1] Gods tended to be emotionally invested in the precincts of their habitation, and they usually had distinct ideas about the etiquette they wanted observed when humans approached them there. What offerings, at what times, of what sorts, in what manner, by what sorts of

---

1. For a lively evocation of this context, see Robin Lane Fox, *Pagans and Christians* (New York: Alfred A. Knopf, 1986), 11–261.

persons, prepared in what ways: Gods typically communicated this necessary information to their worshipers through various media (theophanies, prophetic inspiration, sacred texts, and dreams). Exodus through Deuteronomy, in the Bible, give us Jewish examples of this sort of communication; epigraphy and classical literature provide copious pagan examples.

Humans, in consequence, took care to safeguard the purity, sanctity, offerings and financial security of holy sites because it mattered to the god. And the god would know because, in a simple way, the god was there: gods 'lived' in their precincts, and especially around their altars. We catch a nice statement of this common ancient idea in the Gospel of Matthew, wherein Jesus observes that 'he who swears by the Temple [in Jerusalem], swears by it and by *him who dwells in it*' – the god of Israel, who abides in his temple (Mt. 23.21; cf. similarly for Paul, Rom. 9.4).

But divinity attached to humanity in a more intimate way. For ancient people, gods really did run in the blood. Put differently: cult, as enacted and as imagined, defined ethnicity. It identified one's people or kinship group, the *genos*. Herodotus, in his *Histories*, exemplifies this way of thinking when he defines 'Greekness' (*to hēllenikon*) in terms of shared blood (*homaimon*), language (*homoglōsson*), sanctuaries and cult (*theōn hidrumata koina kai thusiai*), and customs (*ēthea homotropa*, 8.144.2–3).[2] When distinguishing *Ioudaismos* against *Hellenismos*, the author of 2 Maccabees employs a similar definition: his heroes defend 'the temple, the city, and the laws' (2 Macc. 2.21).[3] Colloquially, deities were known by the people who worshiped them: the god of Israel, the gods of Rome, the god at Delos, and so on (cf. Acts 19.28: 'Great is Artemis of the Ephesians!')

This family connection between gods and their humans was also expressed and imagined in terms of descent. Rulers – kings of Israel, or Alexander the Great, or Julius Caesar, for example – were deemed the 'sons' of their particular god.[4] So too might whole peoples be. Hellenistic and later Roman diplomats wove intricate webs of inter-city diplomacy through appeals to consanguinity inaugurated, in the distant past, by

2. See esp. the essays assembled in *Ancient Perceptions of Greek Ethnicity* (ed. I. Malkin; Washington DC: Center for Hellenic Studies, 2001), many of which consider the quotation from Herodotus 8.

3. Daniel Boyarin, 'Semantic Differences; or, "Judaism"/"Christianity"', in *The Ways that Never Parted* (ed. A.H. Becker and A.Y. Reed; Tübingen: J. C. B. Mohr [Paul Siebeck], 2003), 65–83, esp. 67–71; though cf. the argument of Denise Buell, reference below, n. 6.

4. Alexander was descended from Heracles; Julius Caesar's house, through Aeneas, from Venus. These divine connections proved politically useful. For the Israelite king as God's son, see, e.g., 2 Sam. 7.14, Ps. 2.7, and frequently elsewhere. Later Christian exegesis referred these biblical passages to Jesus.

prolific deities.[5] Jewish scriptures frequently referred to Israelites as the sons of their god. The apostle Paul, repeating this biblical commonplace, distinguished his kinship group (*suggenos*) in terms reminiscent of Herodotus. To his *genos*, Paul said, through their god, belonged sonship (*huiothesia*), the presence of the deity (*doxa*, a reference as well to the altar and the Temple), customs ('covenant' *diathēkai* and 'law' *nomothesia*, that is, Torah), and cult (*latreia*, also a reference to the Temple, where the cult was performed; Rom. 9.4). Later in the second and third centuries, when non-Jewish Christian communities sought to formulate their identity, they too would fall back on this native Mediterranean language of divinity and blood-kinship or ethnicity.[6]

The embeddedness of the divine in antiquity, and consequently the normal multiplicity of gods, should help us to better understand what we call ancient 'religion', and what we call ancient 'monotheism'. The existence or non-existence of the gods of outsiders (much less 'belief' in them) was not at issue: other gods obviously existed, just as their peoples did. True for pagans, true for Jews, true for those former pagans who eventually became Christians of various sorts. Jewish biblical tradition clearly acknowledged the existence of these gods (e.g., Mic. 4.5, and frequently elsewhere). Hellenistic Jewish biblical traditions accommodated Greek gods more respectfully than did their Hebrew prototype, the Canaanite deities: Exod. 22.27, for example, 'Do not revile God', became 'Do not revile *tous theous*, the gods' (Exod. 22.28 LXX).

Jews of apocalyptic bent typically had more of an attitude. The End, they said, would bring with it the destruction of the images of these divine personalities worshiped by the nations. The End would establish globally what Jewish apocalypticists argued with particular fierceness: not that these other gods were not 'real', but rather that *their* god, the God of Israel, had precedence over the gods of the nations, and was the sole rightful object of human piety. Paul serves as a good case in point. Non-Jewish gods, he tells his Gentiles-in-Christ, are celestial light-weights, mere cosmic *stoicheia* (Gal. 4.8–9). They may have some power now; they might even frustrate the 'Christian mission' (an anachronistic term for this period, but let it stand, 2 Cor. 4.4); but Christ when he returned would destroy them (1 Cor. 15.24). 'There are many gods and many lords', Paul tells the Corinthians; but they must stop worshiping them and worship only the god of Israel through his Son (1 Cor. 8.5–6). Baptized into Christ, receiving the Spirit, Paul's ex-pagans would thus gain protection against *two* kinds of divine wrath: that of their insulted native deities (who can do no harm, Paul assures them, now that they are 'in Christ'), and that of

---

5. C.P. Jones, *Kinship Diplomacy in the Ancient World* (Cambridge: Harvard University Press, 1999), esp. ch. 6, on Lycians and Jews.

6. Denise Buell, 'Race and Universalism in Early Christianity', *JECS* 10 (2002): 429–68.

God the Father and of his Son (who have had enough of majority culture, e.g., Rom. 1.18–36; cf. 1 Thessalonians *passim*).

A century after Paul, ex-pagans of sufficient education brought the principles of *paideia* to bear on their construction of the Christian message as they saw it mediated through the LXX. This second wedding of *paideia* and the LXX – the first was performed by Alexandrian Jews in the centuries preceding our period – marks the birth of Christian theology. Christian intellectuals of various stripes, using philosophy and the constructs of Hellenistic science, systematized their culture's religious commonplace, namely, that divinity was on a gradient. The High God was the pinnacle of this gradient; but divinity flowed through the super-celestial and celestial intelligences residing in and structuring *kosmos*,[7] through the superhuman messengers (*angeloi*) who communicated between these different strata, to, finally, the special human beings who functioned as heaven's agents (not least among whom, to either side of 312 CE, the emperor). What distinguished Christian 'monotheism' specifically from Jewish monotheism, and from various forms, high-brow and low, of pagan monotheism,[8] was the introduction of the Son, himself 'another god' (*heteros theos*), identified both with the creator god of the LXX and with the historical personage of Jesus.[9] 'Monotheism' in antiquity defined divinity's pyramid architecture, not its absolute numbers. With the (Christian) Son of God or without, the Mediterranean cosmos was a thickly populated place.

II

I could, of course, go on; but I fear that I have gone on for long enough. I embarked on our quick tour through Mediterranean culture in order to make some general observations about ethnicity, religious etiquette and ancient theology. With these points in mind, I would like to address the theme of this volume: Whence the urgency of questions about apocalypticism, anti-Judaism and theological significance in current work on the historical Jesus?

---

7. The architecture of the universe was ecumenical, as we see both in archaeological remains (such as the zodiac mosaics evident in pagan, Jewish and Christian buildings) and in texts. For a pagan statement of this cosmology: Sallustius, *Peri theōn kai kosmou* (ed. and trans. A.D. Nock; Cambridge: Cambridge University Press, 1926); Jewish: Philo, *De Opificio Mundi* (ed. and trans. F.H. Colson and G.H. Whitaker (LCL; Cambridge, MA: Harvard University Press, 1929–1962); Christian: Origen, *On First Principles* (trans. G. W. Butterworth; New York: Harper & Row, 1966; repr. Gloucester, MA: Peter Smith, 1990).

8. See the essays assembled in *Pagan Monotheism* (ed. P. Athanassiadi and M. Frede; Oxford: Oxford University Press, 1999).

9. Justin Martyr, *Dialogue with Trypho*, ch. 56 on Jesus's identity as 'another god' and as the personality appearing in the theophanies of the LXX.

Concerns about anti-Judaism arise for good reason in our work. For at least the past 16 centuries, Christianity has articulated its ideal views of itself by constructing 'Jews' and 'Judaism' to serve as its negative anti-type. This identity-building enterprise has had horrific social consequences, whether tolerating, sponsoring, encouraging, or actually causing violence against real Jews. On this score, the last century was the worse so far. And the new millennium is not off to a glorious start. In the current climate of Israeli/Palestinian belligerence, anti-Zionism has given respectable cover to anti-Semitism; Israeli policies have been criticized by invoking the blood libel and traditional charges of deicide; and a pop movie on Jesus' passion has extravagantly exploited anti-Jewish prejudices.[10] Who among us would want her or his scholarship to be usable in support of such things?

As authors, we have little or no control over how our work is read or used. And all our reconstructions, as William Arnal's essay makes clear, can be construed as supporting particular agendas, whether that be our intention or not. But as scholars, our choice in preferring one colleague's Jesus over another's can only be made in terms of our assessment of the coherence of his or her argument, its plausibility, its success in addressing problems in the evidence, and so on. I assume that each of us produces our respective reconstructions because we believe that we are doing the best, *historically*, that we can do.

I have presented my case for an apocalyptic Jesus, and I have criticized different construals of a non-apocalyptic Jesus, in several publications, and will not repeat my earlier arguments here.[11] I readily grant that a non-apocalyptic Jesus often presents a figure who is ethically more usable to us than is his apocalyptic counterpart. We are right, I think, to feel strongly about such issues as sexism, racism, colonialism, and economic oppression; and to deplore discrimination on the basis of sexual preference. But I do not think that Jesus need have worried about these issues as I conceive them in order to justify my own position on them. I'm a Massachusetts Democrat; he was not. My two points are, first, that arguments from utility (whether ethical or, as I'll explore below, theological) cannot settle

10. On Christology, the blood libel, and anti-Israel political commentary, see Paula Fredriksen, 'What Does Jesus Have to Do With Christ? What Does Knowledge Have to Do With Faith? What Does History Have to Do With Theology?' in *Christology: Memory, Inquiry, Practice* (ed. A.M. Clifford and A.J. Godzieba; Maryknoll, NY: Orbis, 2002), 3–17, at p. 13, and nn. 26–28. On the marketing of Mel Gibson's cinematic Passion play, and the ways that his advertisement has fed into classic deicide accusations, see www.seethepassion.com and www.supportmelgibson.com. (This last website explicitly correlates Gibson to Jesus, and Abe Foxman, head of the Anti-Defamation League, to Caiaphas.)

11. See primarily *From Jesus to Christ* (New Haven: Yale University Press, 2nd edn, 2000); *Jesus of Nazareth, King of the Jews* (New York: Alfred Knopf, 1999); 'What You See is What You Get', *Theology Today* 52 (1995): 75–97.

arguments about historical plausibility; and, second, that anachronism is the first and last enemy of the historian. I cannot but suspect the historicity of any Jesus whom I would gladly vote into public office. (For the record, I wish desperately that John Dominic Crossan's Jesus would put his hat in the ring.) This is not to say that an apocalyptic Jesus is *eo ipso* more likely to be historical, or any less potentially anachronistic. We have to decide in each case.

This tendency of current constructions of a non-apocalyptic Jesus – imputing to him the sort of politics that makes him an attractive figure to us – functions in another, I think unfortunate, way. In this phase of the Quest, with its characteristic emphasis on Jesus' Jewish context, these same putative ethical concerns are marshaled, *à l'inverse*, to describe the Judaism of Jesus' contemporaries. Thus, Jesus was egalitarian; other Jews affirmed and insisted upon hierarchy. He was kind to women, the ill, the poor; his contemporaries scorned them. Jesus focused on ethics; they focused on ritual. He preached compassion; they practiced purity. And so on.[12]

Are these putative 'descriptions' of Judaism demeaning? Unquestionably. In our culture, at our moment, 'inclusive' and 'egalitarian' rate higher than (understand: 'are morally superior to') 'exclusive' and 'hierarchical'. But are they thereby intrinsically anti-Semitic? To put the question this simply is to confound it, because it distracts by virtue of its sensationalism from the chief problem. These descriptions, *au fond*, are quite simply unbelievable. If we think ourselves back to the ancient Mediterranean that is supposed to be their context, they appear impossible.[13]

If, for instance, what we think of as 'religion' corresponds to ancient constructions of ethnicity, then to construct a Jesus who is 'anti-nationalist' or 'anti-racialist' is simple nonsense.[14] Our post-nineteenth-century concepts of 'nation' and of 'race' sit too loosely upon ancient ones to have such a putative description to be useful. Further, the god whom

12. For my criticisms of the work of John Dominic Crossan, Marcus Borg, and N.T. Wright on this point, see 'What You See', 83–84, 86–91, 94–97; also *From Jesus to Christ*, preface to the new edition, xxvi–xxviii.

13. For a similar conclusion on other points of ancient religious practice, and specifically ancient Jewish practice that scholars will deny affected Jesus, see E.P. Sanders, 'Jesus, Ancient Judaism, and Modern Christianity: The Quest Continues', in *Jesus, Judaism, and Christian Anti-Judaism* (ed. P. Fredriksen and A. Reinhartz; Louisville: Westminster John Knox, 2002), 31–55, esp. 34–36 ('Jesus as the Only Modern Man who Lived in the Ancient World').

14. This formulation is N.T. Wright's particular contribution. See his *Jesus and the Victory of God* (Minneapolis: Fortress; London: SPCK, 1996). Wright thinks of his Jesus as 'apocalyptic', but he so redefines the term that it is scarcely usable as a description for his Jesus, who pursues an elaborate, highly metaphorized program, and who also thinks he is god.

Jesus worshiped, and the god whom Paul urged that his Gentiles commit to exclusively, was quite specifically the god of *Israel*. He might be the god of the universe, but he was also, and precisely, the god of Abraham, Isaac and Jacob; the god who hardened Pharaoh's heart to free his people from Egypt; the author of the laws and the promises; the divine father of Paul's kinsmen. The ethnic specificity of this deity, and of his message as tendered through Jesus and, later, through Jesus' apostles, should neither offend nor upset us. Ancient gods *were* ethnic. So too ancient 'religions' – even Christianity.

A related example of a modern, ethically pleasant misconstrual: Paul's much-misconstrued sound bite in Gal. 3.28. Champions of the non-eschatological Jesus have referred to Paul's statement to describe Jesus' 'social policy' as well.[15] But this sentence did not mean in the first century what we like to think that it means now. Paul thought that Gentiles should remain Gentiles (for his most intemperate statement of his position, see Galatians) and that they not convert to Judaism, that is, not 'become' Jews (itself an incoherent thought in antiquity).[16] He shared this conviction with the majority of his *suggenoi*: the only Jews in antiquity who seem to have mounted actual missions to Gentiles in order to turn them into Jews were Paul's Christian-Jewish colleagues, whom he repudiates.[17]

If we take the finale of Romans as some sort of polished statement of his idea of what he was doing, Paul still operated within the polar universe – Israel and the nations – that described the framework both of his Bible and of his social experience. He worked toward building a better Gentile, a 'Gentile-in-Christ'. But the point of the Gentile's being 'in Christ' was that he or she acted less like a 'normal' Gentile (one of *ta ethnē ta mē eidota ton theon*, 1 Thess. 4.5) and more like an 'apocalyptic' Gentile – a Gentile still, for sure, but one who now knew (the Jewish) God, and who worshiped him exclusively. In this way, these ethnically-mixed *ekklesiai* served as a prolepsis for the Kingdom, when all the nations would turn to

15. Thus, explicitly, John Dominic Crossan, *The Historical Jesus* (San Francisco: HarperSanFrancisco, 1991), xii, 263; on the post-ethnic (that is, post-Jewish or post-Zionist) Jesus more generally, see 'What You See', 81–91, 95–97.

16. Since ancient gods and religions were ethnic, what we term 'conversion' was an odd idea in antiquity. In the period before Christianity, conversions to Judaism were imagined and presented on the analogy of forging political alliances; see Shaye J.D. Cohen, *The Beginnings of Jewishness* (Berkeley: University of California Press, 1999), 125–39, 156–74. Aristocrats who switched alliances could be perceived, and treated, as traitors; Cassius Dio, *Historia Romana* 67.14.1–2 (Domitian).

17. Paula Fredriksen, 'What "Parting of the Ways"? Jews, Gentiles, and the Ancient Mediterranean City', in *The Ways that Never Parted* (ed. A.H. Becker and A.Y. Reed; Tübingen: J.C.B. Mohr [Paul Siebeck], 2003), 48–56; also 'Judaism, the Circumcision of Gentiles, and Apocalyptic Hope: Another Look at Galatians 1 and 2', *JTS* 42 (1991): 532–64.

the Jewish god. Just as 'neither slave nor free' certainly did not mean that Paul repudiated slavery; and just as 'neither male nor female' certainly did not mean that Paul repudiated gender-specific social and ritual activities, so also with 'neither Jew nor Greek'. And if Paul, the 'apostle to the Gentiles', then *qal va-ḥomer* Jesus, who on the evidence scarcely ever bumped into any Gentiles at all, and who left no clear instructions (again, on the evidence) on something we might construe as 'Gentile' policy.

So too with other pleasant ethical/political abstractions, imputed to Jesus, denied to his Jewish contemporaries: the prime *intellectual* problem with the caricatures of Judaism that they presuppose or present is *not* that said caricatures demean Judaism (which they do), but that they fail as historical thinking. Purity rules, for another example, normally inform etiquette regulating divine/human encounters in antiquity. The closer to the hot-zone of this encounter (a temple, an altar), the thicker the webbing of rules. To call purity a 'politics', to contrast it to 'compassion', and to assign concern for the one to 'Jews' (or 'priests') and the other to Jesus is to signal a modern ethical position ('compassion is nice'). But by any measure relevant to ancient Mediterranean cultures in general and to late Second Temple Judaism in particular, such a construal of purity wildly misdescribes its function, and weds it to a totally false antimony: compassion is to purity as fish is to bicycle. Historically, this supposed contrast gets us nowhere, and requires us to overlook all the evidence of normal purity concerns in the Jesus tradition.[18]

An apocalyptic Jesus is awkward for other reasons. As Dale Allison's essay lays out, such a Jesus is problematic both for ethics and for theology. Jesus' ethics end up confined to what he thought would be the brief interim between his proclamation of the Kingdom and its advent. And he ends up being wildly wrong in his time-keeping: Jesus preached the Kingdom, but it was the SNTS that arrived. In what sense could the author of such an emphatically disconfirmed prophecy be 'god'?

Again, here I think that we have to go back to the context within which this claim was first made. Originating early with Paul and with John; sustaining various systematic developments in the Christian *paideia* of Valentinus, Marcion, Justin, Ptolemy; reifying into doctrine in the period of imperially-sponsored councils: claims about Jesus' super-human, divine status took shape within a culture when such thoughts were thinkable. Such a claim, in such a culture, could be advanced without calling into question either the integrity of Jesus' humanity, or the ontological distinctiveness of the High God. And the claims of Christology, however constituted, expressed views of redemption that cohered and coordinated with other ideas about flesh, body, soul, time, cosmos, and so on.

18. Paula Fredriksen, 'Did Jesus Oppose the Purity Laws?' *Bible Review* 11 (1995): 18–25 and 42–47.

If theology – or, specifically for our question now, Christology – has fallen on difficult times, I think that that is due more to the changes in our culture (and specifically in philosophy) since the Renaissance, than to any challenge posed by an historical construction of an apocalyptic Jesus. In our disenchanted universe, God no longer has quite so many neighbors: post-sixteenth century divinity is not on the gradient it once was. To designate a human being 'god' complicates modern monotheism unbearably. It also assaults current conceptualizations of 'human'. 'Flesh' and 'mind' or 'spirit' do not define 'human' for us in the ways that they did in antiquity: modern humans seem constituted rather by genes, memory, contested definitions of 'self'. In short, Platonizing metaphysics – the matrix of classical Christology – has died a natural death. But the old christological formulae remain, embalmed by institutional sanction.[19]

Modern believers have several options. At one extreme, they can opt to become keepers of the museum, dusting the traditional formulae and not thinking too hard about them. Fundamentalists – enslaved, ironically, to precisely the over-valuing of empirical reality that they decry in 'secular' science, and which arises, again, in the Renaissance – can just assert more and more loudly that everything they believe is simply what the Bible says, and that their beliefs are accordingly (in this simple, empirical way) 'true'. But the source of liberal alarm is not dissimilar: If Jesus is 'divine', how could he have been so wrong?[20] Here antiquity's greater flexibility with the meaning of texts served it well. Ancient theologians could either allegorize what Jesus meant by the coming Kingdom; or – more typically for the Latin West – they might interpret the second, bodily 'coming of the Son of Man' as the establishment of the Church, since the Church is Christ's body.[21] Seen in this light, Jesus' prophecy had already been realized, beginning at Pentecost.

We no longer read texts with these various levels of 'truth' or meaning – the allegorical, the aetiological, and so on – in mind. But to wring modern meaning from traditional texts, we still must wrestle with the angel of interpretation. (What I say here of Christianity I also think true for Judaism and Islam as well.) We'll come away limping, no doubt; but that, in biblical perspective, is the consequence of close encounters with the divine. An apocalyptic Jesus will lead to one kind of theological struggle; a non-eschatological Jesus, another. Absent fundamentalism – a principled refusal to think – I see no way out of this. Perhaps the difficulty of the situation is what occasions the sense of urgency in our discussions.

That said, I would like to make the pitch, *as an historian*, that we

---

19.   Fredriksen, 'What Does Jesus Have to Do With Christ?'
20.   See the finale of Dale Allison's essay for further thoughts on this issue.
21.   The *locus classicus* for this argument is Augustine, *City of God*, Book 20; he cribbed the interpretation from the Donatist theologian Tyconius.

beware a sort of creeping fundamentalism in our own work, a sort of fallacy of intention. The problem is this: to legitimate or authorize an ethical belief, too often, scholars impute that belief to Jesus himself. (Hence Jesus the feminist, Jesus the champion of peasant land reform, Jesus the anti-nationalist agitator, and so on.) To legitimate or authorize a theological belief about Jesus, that belief is imputed to Jesus himself. (Thus, Jesus thought that he was god; that he wanted to establish a non-Jewish biblical community; that he knew he had to die for the sins of the world.) In both modes, if Jesus did not himself think a thought – a social or political thought in the first instance; a theological thought in the second – then that thought seems less than legitimate for the tradition.

I would prefer to leave the historical Jesus in his own century, and put the obligation to make sense of Christian traditions about him where it belongs – not on him, but on us. Different Christians of different denominational affiliations will do so differently: that has been the case, on the evidence, since the movement itself began. I would also prefer to judge the adequacy of our reconstructions of Jesus not by criteria of ethical or theological utility, but by the usual standards by which any historian judges a historical description. To do that, we need to reconstruct Jesus' contemporary context. Hence my quick tour at the beginning of my essay.

I would like to close with a brief meditation on styles of historical thinking and ways of doing history because, in a sense, that question of style fuels our foregrounded issues of apocalyptic, anti-Judaism, and theology. We have no consensus about methods. Some of us examine texts *à la loupe*, getting in as close as possible to passages, sentences, phrases, words. John Kloppenborg's work on Q, and the essays by A.-J. Levine and by Robert Miller for this volume, are examples of this kind of approach. Some of us rigorously apply methods derived from so-called social sciences; others do literary analysis, and so on – methodologically, we're a promiscuous bunch. I think that's just fine.

But, to draw on a cinematographic metaphor for a moment, I want to make a pitch for the virtue of the wide-angle lens, for establishing the broad sweep before moving in for the close-up. If we considered the sort of data about the developing traditions on Jesus that we find in Paul – who writes at least one generation before the evangelists – then I think that we could have some surer traction up the slopes of the gospel material. If we worked with a better sense of ancient Mediterranean culture generally, I think that it would be harder to make some of the claims about Jesus and Judaism that we still see in print fairly routinely. And if we look not just to patristic material, but to the range of inscriptional and archaeological evidence that we have access to, we could establish a surer historical context within which to place our particular reconstructions of early Christianity, and also of the historical Jesus.

In the first instance, for example, we find a Pharisee going to pagans and walking them into a social no-man's land by demanding that they stop showing respect to their native deities and make an exclusive commitment to the god of Israel, *without* converting to Judaism. He does so explicitly because the Kingdom of God – heralded already by the resurrection of his Son – is about to arrive. In the second instance, we find that *all* ancient peoples saw ancestral custom and antiquity (understand: 'ethnicity') as the measure of proper 'religion' and as an index of piety; and that when Gentile Christianity of various sorts becomes visible in our evidence, these people make the same claim: that they too are a *genos*, and that that *genos* is also legit, because ancient. In the third instance, we see that Jews and pagans, and eventually Jews, pagans and Christians, mixed and co-celebrated in various religious functions throughout this period, in both pagan venues (gymnasia, theatres, law courts, town councils) and in Jewish ones (the Temple, until 70 CE; in 'synagogues' on either side of the War).

In Paul's case, we have an early statement from a contemporary of the original apostles who was in contact with those others who had known Jesus before Easter. This group itself chose to give up its Galilean roots – if they had any – and to live in Jerusalem. They all experience Christophanies; they believe that the Kingdom is coming; they are concerned to integrate non-practicing pagans – Gentiles, that is, who are willing to make an exclusive commitment to the god of Israel – into their communities. All these data cluster coherently around strong themes in Jewish apocalyptic. If we want to scissor the historical Jesus out of this context, we of course can, and some do. But then all this behavior – the earliest we have evidence for from this movement – becomes that much more difficult to account for.

With ancient ethnicity, it means that we have yet one more reason to exorcise some of the routinely employed language of invidious comparison when describing ancient Judaism. Jews may be one of the few Western groups now for whom ethnicity and religion closely coincide; back then, it was the least odd thing about them. And with the ancient urban evidence, it means that we should stop imputing to ancient Christianity the 'novel' idea that Jewish scriptures could be shared with non-Jews, or that Gentiles were 'no longer impure', or that the religious mixing of Jews and non-Jews was Christianity's revolutionary new concept.[22] It gives us an extra reason to be aware that our assumption that Christianity and Judaism were two distinct, even antagonistic, religions or movements or groups is extravagantly anachronistic: what was clear to Justin Martyr or Tertullian in the

---

22. Fredriksen, 'What Parting?', 40–48.

second century was obviously unclear to Origen's or Chrysostom's shul-hopping congregations in the third century and in the fourth.[23]

As for the ideological uses that any or all of our Jesuses can be put to, I can only observe that, if we ourselves do this, we will still have to make our case by an appeal to evidence; and that we all need to count on each other for collegial criticism for help in seeing, or hearing, what we ourselves say. And while we can control what we write, we cannot control how we are interpreted, as anybody who has ever had his or her book reviewed knows full well. Here again, collegial colloquy can only help. And so, again, for all of us, I thank the Jackman Symposium for enabling this particular round of thinking with, speaking with, and listening to each other.

23. Origen, in Caesarea (c. 230 CE), tells his Gentile Christian congregation not to discuss in church questions they heard raised the day before in synagogue, and not to eat meals in both places (*Hom. Lev.* 5,8; *Select. Exod.* 12,46). Chrysostom, notoriously, before the high holidays in 387 in Antioch, complains that members of his church fast, keep Sabbath, go to synagogue, take oaths in front of torah scrolls, and co-celebrate Passover and Sukkot ('When did they ever celebrate the Pasch with us?' *Against the Judaizing Christians* 4.3; see passim). Church canons go on forbidding this sort of behaviour on through the Visigothic and Byzantine period in the seventh century: see A. Linder, *The Jews in the Legal Sources of the Early Middle Ages* (Detroit: Wayne State University Press, 1997).

APOCALYPTICISM AND ANTI-SEMITISM: INNER-GROUP RESOURCES FOR INTER-GROUP CONFLICTS

John W. Marshall

University of Toronto

Constructions of the historical Jesus as 'apocalyptic prophet' predate the vibrant concern of our discipline to avoid presenting Jesus in a manner that facilitates anti-Semitism.[1] In fact, the possibility exists that the model of apocalyptic prophet has more potential for misuse in service of anti-Semitism than some competing models. I propose that the intensity of in-group conflict in Jewish apocalyptic materials and the habitual appropriation and deployment of these and similar materials by early Christian readers predisposes apocalyptic materials – with their scenes of judgment, visions of sins piled up the heavens, and overviews of the places of punishment – to use in the service of anti-Semitism. While there is nothing anti-Semitic about apocalyptic literatures and modes of thinking *per se*, an apocalyptic Jesus may play into the tropes of later Christian anti-Semitism, quite apart from any judgment of questions of the historical accuracy of such a model for Jesus. The 'real' Jesus might not be the Jesus who is least potent in an anti-Semitic discourse.

My plan then is to reflect briefly on the role of Jesus' Jewishness in relation to the question of anti-Semitism and then undertake an examination of what an apocalyptic prophet might be and how that relates to creating the type of materials that have been deployed with such horrible power in the history of Christian anti-Semitism. Following this I

---

1. Compare Johannes Weiss, *Die Predigt Jesu vom Reiche Gottes* (Göttingen: Vandenhoeck & Ruprecht, 1892); ET *Jesus' Proclamation of the Kingdom of God* (ed. trans. Richard H. Hiers and David Larrimore Holland; Philadelphia: Fortress, 1971) and Albert Schweitzer, *Von Reimarus zu Wrede. Eine Geschichte der Leben-Jesu-Forschung* (Tübingen: J.C.B. Mohr [Paul Siebeck], 1906) with Marcel Simon, *Verus Israel: étude sur les relations entre chrétiens et juifs dans l'Empire romain, AD 135–425* (Paris: Boccard, 1948) and John G. Gager, *The Origins of Anti-Semitism: Attitudes Toward Judaism in Pagan and Christian Antiquity* (Oxford: Oxford University Press, 1983).

want to draw a few examples from the apocalyptic literature of Second Temple Judaism to illustrate the contours of inner-Jewish conflict as seen in apocalyptic literature and a community oriented to apocalyptic expectation. Finally, a short examination of Christian deployments of Jewish materials: I intend to illustrate two key ingredients in the history of Christian anti-Semitism – the role of the apocalyptic genre and worldview in raising the pitch of inner-Jewish conflict to cosmic proportions, and the toxic redeployment of inner-Jewish criticisms by Christians in course of Jewish-Christian conflict and Christian self-definition. If Jesus was an apocalyptic prophet – and on a 'purely' historical basis (*pace* William Arnal) I am convinced such is an apt model for him – his legacy to Christianity bears with it some decidedly dangerous side-effects.

Judaism and Anti-Semitism

A scene near the end of James Joyce's *Ulysses* assembles the contradictory forces of historicism and anti-Semitism illuminatingly. The hero, Leopold Bloom, recounts an altercation in which the issue of Jesus' Jewishness in connection to anti-Semitism comes to the fore. In an account of the scene, Bloom relates that:

> He called me a jew, and in a heated fashion, offensively. So I, without deviating from plain facts in the least, told him his God, I mean Christ, was a jew too, and all his family, like me, though in reality I'm not. That was one for him. A soft answer turns away wrath. He hadn't a word to say for himself as everyone saw. Am I not right?[2]

Joyce illustrates with alacrity the way in which the 'fact' of Jesus Jewishness holds little force in relation to an anti-Semitic animus. The historicity of Jesus' Jewishness has no purchase on the anti-Semite; the aggressor is unchanged by the historical insight. The 'blasphemy' that the anti-Semite perceives in any discourse on Jesus' Jewishness shows that a commitment to history is much less deeply embedded than the anti-Semitic impulse.

---

2. James Joyce, *Ulysses* (Paris: Rodker, 1922): 'Eumaeus'. See also *Ulysses*, 'Cyclops' [Bloom speaking first]:
– Mendelssohn was a jew and Karl Marx and Mercadante and Spinoza. And the Saviour was a jew and his father was a jew. Your God.
– He had no father, says Martin. That'll do now. Drive ahead.
– Whose God? says the citizen.
– Well, his uncle was a jew, says he. Your God was a jew. Christ was a jew like me.
Gob, the citizen made a plunge back into the shop.
– By Jesus, says he, I'll brain that bloody jewman for using the holy name. By Jesus, I'll crucify him so I will. Give us that biscuitbox here.

In the ancient world, the *Epistle of Barnabas* seems nearly the counterpart of the Leopold Bloom's aggressor. The anathema pronounced against those who say the covenant is both theirs and ours[3] is animated by the same unwillingness to see the other at the origin that makes an offence out of the 'plain use of the facts' by Leopold Bloom. *Barnabas'* pseudepigrapher and Bloom's interlocutor guard the origins of their faith against what they perceive as the impurity of Judaism with a vitriol that inoculates them against history. The confusion of origin and essence that Jacques Derrida has elucidated throughout so much of western thought[4] is the basis of the offence for both Joyce's anti-Semite and the writer of *Barnabas*. That Judaism – Christianity's intimate other – could lie at the basis of Christianity is literally a *skandalon*, a stumbling block, that has confounded confessional and academic approaches to Jesus.

An Apocalyptic Prophet

Turning to the apocalyptic prophet, the influential description of the apocalyptic literary genre led by John J. Collins is foundational.[5] Collins's 'morphology of the genre' has several features that have no obvious correlate outside the realm of literary production, but Collins boldly distinguishes from the apocalyptic literary genre an 'apocalyptic worldview' that need not be instantiated in terms of the literary form – mediators, pseudonymity, narrative framing. The characteristics of the apocalyptic literature that make most sense as elements of a worldview are the breadth of context, the reach beyond empirical modes of knowledge, the particular intertextual habitus, the expectation of a boundary-crossing intervention, and the strong moral concern. In combination with the prophetic mode, this worldview would produce a prophet who makes his or her case concerning the present situation in relation to a much larger frame of reference (creation, eschaton, God's ideal realm, ultimate adversaries, the farthest reaches of the cosmos). Such a prophet would claim knowledge of realms beyond everyday human cognition (the future, the heavens, the book of life) though the articulation of such knowledge

---

3. 'Watch yourselves now, do not be like some people by piling up your sins and saying the covenant is both theirs and ours. For it is ours.' *Barn.* 4.6–7 (Bart Ehrman, *The Apostolic Fathers* [LCL; Cambridge, MA and London: Harvard University Press]).

4. 'The question of origin is at first confounded with the question of essence.' Jacques Derrida, *Of Grammatology* (trans. Gayatri Chakravorty Spivak; Baltimore: Johns Hopkins University Press, 1974 [1967]), 74.

5. John J. Collins, 'Introduction: Towards the Morphology of a Genre', *Semeia* 14 (1979), 1–20, at p. 3.

would take place in dialogue with a set of oral and textual materials specific to a cultural trajectory and which would form resources to buttress the claims to knowledge, vision and insight. The point of such prophecy is to make claims about the present situation which are conditioned by this larger context, either by direct intervention, or by the knowledge that the larger context provides. Who is an apocalyptic prophet? The list might contain Paul, Theudas, the 'Egyptian', the Samaritan deliverer, the Teacher of Righteousness, John the Baptist and, of course, Jesus.[6]

Inner-group Conflict

Apocalyptic-prophetic action – because it raises the stakes so high, because it sets the problems it addresses in such a context of surpassing value – is not consistently conciliatory within a social context, to say the least. The righteous are absolutely right. Opponents of the author/prophet are cast as opponents of God, as colleagues of the devil, as the damned. The characteristic bridge-building activity of apocalyptic-prophetic action is beyond the social rather than within the social. With the benefit of the evidence we have in the form of literary apocalypses, admittedly not susceptible to a complete mapping onto the non-literary prophetic model under consideration, the intensification of in-group conflict that characterizes a significant strand of that literature becomes clear.

The Animal Apocalypse[7]

Set within the corpus of Enochic revelatory literature, and originating in the middle of the second century BCE, the Animal Apocalypse retells the history of creation and of the people of Israel by means of an animal allegory that spans the period from creation through the Maccabean revolt and beyond to an eschatological utopia. The text shows strongly how the events of the mid-second century BCE were the sites of deep divisions within Palestinian Judaism. The section that deals with the Second Temple and the Maccabean crisis puts its focus on the willful

---

6. This is of course a compressed list of figures who fit the description above; Josephus, the New Testament, and the Dead Sea Scrolls form the richest primary literature for this group. See David E. Aune, *Prophecy in Early Christianity and the Ancient Mediterranean World* (Grand Rapids, MI: Eerdmans, 1983) and Richard A. Horsley and John S. Hanson, *Bandits, Prophets, and Messiahs: Popular Movements in the Time of Jesus* (Harrisburg, PA: Trinity Press International, 1999).

7. See George W. Nicklesburg, *1 Enoch: A Commentary on the Book of 1 Enoch* (Hermeneia; Minneapolis: Fortress, 2000) and Patrick A. Tiller, *A Commentary on the Animal Apocalypse of 1 Enoch* (Early Judaism and its Literature, 4; Atlanta: Scholars Press, 1993).

disobedience of the bulk of the sheep (the sheep are the Jews). Since the apocalyptic genre pays such constant attention to the active role of God in the cosmos, the causal proximity of that God to the actions of Gentile oppressors is not mitigated by the habits of a historical narrative of usually self-sovereign actors, but can actually occlude the actions of Gentile rulers: the Lord himself oppresses and slaughters his own sheep without the intervention of Gentiles.

> And he sent many other sheep to those sheep to testify to them and to lament over them. And after this I saw how when they left the Lord of the sheep and his tower, they went astray in everything, and their eyes were blinded; and I saw how the Lord of the sheep wrought much slaughter among them in their pastures until those sheep themselves invited that slaughter and betrayed his place. (*1 En.* 89.54–56)

The apocalyptic mode has cut out the Gentile middleman. The diverse responses to exterior hegemony that characterized Second Temple Judaism in the Hellenistic period are allegorized and evaluated without reference to the actions of and pressures from those Gentile rulers. The allegorical mode and the cosmic proportions of this account of the history of Israel culminate in a very violent vision of the resolution of that history:

> And I saw at that time how a similar abyss was opened in the middle of the earth which was full of fire, and they brought those blind sheep, and they were all judged and found guilty and thrown into that abyss of fire, and they burned; and that abyss was on the south of that house. (*1 En.* 90.26)

Jews judged unfaithful by the author are sent to essentially the same fate as the daemonic spiritual rulers of the Gentile nations. This is insider conflict raised to the highest register. Compare the conflicts among Jews described in the Maccabean literature: bitter denunciation, forced circumcision, and murder (2 Macc. 2.20–38). The tensions were just as strongly felt by the chroniclers of the Maccabees, but historically situated narrative is necessarily a smaller canvas. Jason's epitomizer did not paint with the vivid colours that fill an apocalyptic palette. In the Animal Apocalypse, the genre has raised the insider conflict to a higher register. The Animal Apocalypse provides a compelling example of the intensity of insider conflict considered in the apocalyptic mode.

The Dead Sea Scrolls
The Animal Apocalypse was among several apocalypses attributed to Enoch found among the Dead Sea Scrolls and known through other textual traditions. Though the community that produced the Dead Sea Scrolls apparently did not generate any literary apocalypses, they copied them faithfully and extensively, and integrated the themes of revealed

eschatological knowledge into the documents that do seem central to their sectarian identity. Many have also argued that the teacher of righteousness was understood as an eschatological prophet.[8] The case is strong that the community that produced the Dead Sea Scrolls represents an instance of an apocalyptic community with ideals of prophetic (and priestly) leadership.[9]

The *Community Rule* of the Dead Sea Scrolls describes a separation from the outside community that any detailed reading will understand as separation from other Jews who do not assent to the tenants and practices of the covenant community. The particular topics of assent are described in terms of one of the characteristics of an apocalyptic worldview that I have described as 'the reach beyond empirical modes of knowledge'.[10]

> He [the convert to the community] should swear by the covenant to be segregated from all the men of sin who walk along paths of irreverence. For they are not included in this covenant since they have neither sought nor examined his decrees in order to learn the *hidden matters* over which they err by their own fault and because they treated *revealed matters* with disrespect; this is why wrath will rise up for judgement in order to effect revenge by the curses of the covenant, in order to administer fierce punishments for everlasting annihilation without there being any remnant.

The result of the inattention to revealed matters is everlasting annihilation without remnant. This section of the *Community Rule* concentrates the apocalyptic characteristics of the community: the focus on special revelation to the leaders of the community in combination with a complex and value-laden appropriation of an authoritative realm of discourse, namely the writings of the Hebrew Bible, as well as a complex of that might be called an Enochic corpus consisting not only of revelations attributed to Enoch, but also texts such as *Jubilees*, *Aramaic Levi*, the *Temple Scroll* and others.[11]

Another document of the sect focuses the issues on the prophetic figure and the textual universe that provides the context for an apocalyptic prophet's work. The *Pesher Habbakuk* interprets the prophet of the Hebrew Bible in terms of the author's present, usually understood as the

8. Aune, *Prophecy*, 132, and Horsley and Hanson, *Bandits*, 153.

9. John J. Collins, *Apocalypticism in the Dead Sea Scrolls* (London and New York: Routledge, 1997).

10. 1QS 5.10–13; cf. 1QS 1.9 [Trans.: Florentino García Martínez (ed.), *The Dead Sea Scrolls Translated: The Qumran Texts in English* (New York: E.J. Brill; Grand Rapids, MI: Eerdmans, 1996) (emphasis added).]

11. Gabriele Boccaccini, *Beyond the Essene Hypothesis: The Parting of the Ways between Qumran and Enochic Judaism* (Grand Rapids, MI: Eerdmans, 1998) and *The Roots of Rabbinic Judaism: An Intellectual History from Ezekiel to Daniel* (Grand Rapids, MI: Eerdmans, 2002).

mid second century BCE. The Teacher of Righteousness appears in the pesher as the authoritative interpreter of the word of God in the last days. The interpretation he offers claims that his opponents have excluded themselves from the covenant in the last days, presumably by means of a regime of doctrinal obstinacy and gross sin: 'repulsive acts of filthy licentiousness' in the later words of the pesher (1QpHab 8.13). No one can doubt the intensity of bitterness that characterized the separation of the Qumran community from the larger fold of Judaism in the Second Temple period, and the forms this bitterness takes are clearly conditioned by the apocalyptic worldview of the community: the surpassing stakes of moral value that a conception of 'last days' implies, the claim to authoritative continuity with the normative textual heritage, the framing of the topic of contention as the subject of trans-empirical cognition. In the Qumran sectarians' characterization of their opponents as a 'congregation of Beliar' (1QH 10.22), we have undoubtedly found the verbal 'weapons of mass destruction' that an apocalyptic vision is so apt to create.

Jubilees

The book of *Jubilees* – which is known in its entirety in multiple Ethiopic versions as well as original Hebrew fragments from Qumran and the remains of translations into Greek, Latin and Syriac[12] – recounts the history and pre-history of Israel with a distinctive emphasis on the eternal validity of the law that was revealed to Moses and on the centrality of calendrical purity to proper piety. Its position within Second Temple Judaism is a controversial subject, but its strident descriptions of judgment against a portion of Israel clearly suggest a measure of sectarian identity.

In between its transmission of the narrative of Abraham's circumcision and the account of the appearance of the Lord to Abraham at the oaks of Mamre, that is to say in the space between Genesis 17 and 18, *Jubilees* recounts a very extensive speech from the revealing angel to Moses, the recipient of the revelation. The speech warns that the example of Abraham will not be followed and that the consequences within Israel will be disastrous.

> But I warn you that the sons of Israel will not keep this rule, neither will they circumcise their sons in accordance with this law; for, though circumcised themselves, they will neglect the circumcision of their sons and the miscreants, all of them, will leave their sons uncircumcised, just as they were born. And great will be the Lord's wrath against the sons

---

12. See C. Rabin, 'Jubilees: Introduction', in *The Apocryphal Old Testament* (ed. H.F.D. Sparks; Oxford: Oxford University Press, 1984), 1–10 [revising R.H. Charles' translation]. Quotations use the Rabin and Charles translation.

of Israel, because they have forsaken his covenant and turned aside
from his word, and provoked him and shown their contempt for him by
not observing the rule as regards this law; for they have treated their
members like the Gentiles and will be removed and uprooted from the
land. And though there is forgiveness and pardon for all sins, they will
never be pardoned or forgiven for this transgression, not even in
eternity. (*Jub.* 15.33–34)

Clearly the author of *Jubilees* takes issue with decisions about observance
of circumcision made by other Jews. That is to say that an insider conflict
forms at least part of the document's exigence. The ethical intensity of
Jubilees which shows up here and elsewhere has close parallels in the
teachings attributed to Jesus: the sin that cannot be forgiven – in *Jubilees'*
case circumcision at variance with calendrical standards, in Jesus' case
blasphemy against the Holy Spirit (Mk. 3.28–29 and parallels); or the
elevation of intention to action – in *Jubilees'* case a condemnation of
discussing work on the Sabbath day, to discuss it is as significant as to
desecrate the day by doing work; in Jesus' case a condemnation of the
thought of adultery, to look with lust is as sinful as to commit adultery.[13]
The revelatory context of *Jubilees* explains some of the intensity of its
polemic, but it needs to be noted that the commitment to Judaism never
wavers. The issues of calendar and circumcision in *Jubilees* involve
Gentiles and also judgment against Jews, but there is no passing to the
Gentiles of God's favour. In fact it is the Jews who acclimatize to Gentile
cultural values who are the subject of judgment. The intensity is that of
conflict within the family and yet the scale within which 'the family' is
judged is eternal and infinite.

Fourth Ezra
Fourth Ezra, written in the aftermath of the destruction of the Second
Temple, is saturated with the bitterness of despair more than the bitterness
of conflict.[14] Characterizations of the tone and message of the work as a
whole are controversial, but there is no doubt that the visionary is
shattered by the destruction of the Temple and paints a very bleak picture
of Judaism as it wrestles with these events.

The fourth vision of Ezra levels criticism at Israel for mistreating the
prophets and suggests that covenant does not guarantee salvation: 'Many
have been created, but only a few will be saved' (8.3). The law in the next
of Ezra's visions stands as a heavenly principle which will endure in spite

---

13. See *Jub.* 50.8 on the Sabbath. Compare Mt. 5.28 on the equation of the lustful gaze
with adultery and Mt. 5.22 on the elevation of anger in thought and speech to the standards
applied for killing.

14. Michael E. Stone, *Fourth Ezra: A Commentary on the Book of Fourth Ezra*
(Hermeneia; Minneapolis: Fortress, 1990).

of those who do not keep it. It is not the means of maintaining the benefits of covenant, because the people who try to keep it are secondary and perishable relative to the eternal law (9.32–37). The heavenly Zion grieves because her children are overwhelmingly headed for destruction.

> For Zion, the mother of us all, is in deep grief and great affliction...
> And from the beginning all have been born of her, and others will come;
> and behold, almost all go to perdition, and a multitude of them are
> destined for destruction. (10.7, 10)

Though the emotion attributed to the visionary Ezra is grief, the evaluation of many past as well as contemporary (i.e. early second-century) Jews that Ezra's grief implies is ultimately negative. Many have noted a 'turn' in *Fourth Ezra*, shortly after the grief of Zion, that introduces a messianic figure who will destroy the Roman Empire and an angelic mediator who appears and makes some progress in transforming Ezra's attitude. These efforts address some of the problems that the figure Ezra raises. The 'turn', however, does not erase Ezra's judgment nor does it remove the insight into Jewish despair in the aftermath of the destruction of the Second Temple. Even if we call the author an eventual optimist, it is clear he addressed a substantially demoralized audience. *Fourth Ezra*'s description of damnation is the corollary of despair rather than the bitter fruit of enmity, but that does not lessen the reality of supposing a considerable portion of one's fellow Jews have rejected the prophets, disregarded the law, and are thus destined for destruction rather than salvation. Though *Fourth Ezra* does not extensively pursue an indictment of those over which the lady Zion grieves, the raw materials for such an indictment are active in the text.

Summary on Inner-group Conflict
At this point caveats are in order, specifically because of the heritage of Christian anti-Semitism and mischaracterization of Judaism. The apoca-lyptic framing of inner-Jewish critique is not the kernel of Judaism, nor is it the centrepiece of a movement. These texts do not constitute a movement or a theology. What I have observed in these examples are the tropes of insider conflict in an apocalyptic mode. None of the documents I've examined were ever intended to represent Judaism to those outside it. Each is built on massive assumptions and allegiances to the heritage of Judaism. Each struggles from within the religion. In some cases, these are the desperate cries of peripheral groups within Judaism struggling with their marginal status. The afterlife of some of these and similar documents makes clear the shameful consequences of disregarding these caveats. Let me reiterate that each of these documents is an important instance of Jewish apocalypticism of the Second Temple period and that the community I have focused on is, in terms of the available scholarly

data, the pre-eminent example of a community constituted on the basis of an apocalyptic worldview.[15] Given these caveats and this claim, I hope to have illustrated the shape of insider conflict in apocalyptic discourse – especially its tendency to raise difference to the highest levels of significance.

Christian Deployment

What then can happen when the materials of a conversation within a group fall into the hands of those outside the group? *Fourth Ezra* is itself the most subtle example of Christian deployment. The only manner in which it survives is by the hands of Christian copyists. Jews did not preserve it, and I think that the very things that made it attractive to Christian readers – the emphasis on rejecting the prophets, the accusation of not keeping the law, and the relation of these charges to the destruction of Jerusalem – likely made it unattractive for long-term preservation by Jews. Moreover it survives only with a Christian introduction, *Fifth Ezra*, which describes God turning to other nations, condemns Jews as defiled by murder, and suggests that Israel's place in heaven has been permanently revoked.[16] Without changes being made to the text itself, *Fourth Ezra* has been wrapped in the tropes of Christian anti-Semitism. Jonathan Culler's adage that 'meaning is context-bound, but context is boundless'[17] implies that the creation of specific meaning relies on the binding of context; in the case of *Fourth Ezra*, it was literally bound to *Sixth Ezra*[18] and to the Christian *Fifth Ezra* to create a new context that redirects its filial grief over the travails of second-century Judaism to its millennia-spanning history as *2 Esdras* and the latter's role in negative Christian conceptions of Judaism and Jew-blaming interpretations of the fate of the Second Temple.

Beyond the example of *Fourth Ezra*, two other deployments of Jewish

---

15. Collins, 'Morphology'.

16. *5 Ezra* 1.24–26, 35; 2.10.

17. Jonathan Culler, *On Deconstruction* (Ithaca, NY: Cornell University Press, 1982), 128.

18. *6 Ezra* is usually thought of as a Christian text, though this question is open to further examination. T. Bergren has made the most thorough recent examination and concluded that it ought to be identified as Christian, though he depends heavily on understanding Revelation as a Christian document and thus reasoning on the basis of *6 Ezra*'s reliance on Revelation that *6 Ezra* too must be Christian. See Theodore Bergren, *Sixth Ezra* (Oxford: Oxford University Press, 1998), 15–16, 115. *6 Ezra* makes no mention of Jesus, or a Lamb, no indication of churches, claims no distinction from Jews or Judaism, makes no clear allusions to Christian documents, no reference to Christian rituals. See John W. Marshall, *Parables of War: Reading John's Jewish Apocalypse* (ESCJ, 10; Waterloo, Ont.: Wilfrid Laurier University Press, 2001) for the case that Revelation itself is a Jewish text.

materials in the context of Christian anti-Semitism may serve to illuminate the characteristic dynamics of that phenomenon.

The Epistle of Barnabas

The *Epistle of Barnabas* is an early second-century Christian tract that seeks to justify Christianity and respond to exegetical challenges to Christianity made from the Hebrew Bible.[19] The *Epistle of Barnabas* takes up *Fourth Ezra* and the Animal Apocalypse in the course of its strident denunciation of Judaism, deploying the insider criticism of apocalyptic literature in its Christian diatribe against Judaism.[20] One of the characteristic strategies of the *Epistle of Barnabas* is to suggest a dual audience for texts in the Hebrew Bible that contain both critique and instruction. In the letter's exegetical scheme, positive instructions are directed to Christians, and negative critiques are directed to Jews. The deployment of Isa. 58.4–6 is one of multiple examples of this strategy in the letter of Barnabas. In Isaiah 58, the prophetic critique of Israel is genuine, but the instruction and promise that follow are equally directed to Israel. There is, of course, no shift in implied audience between the critique and the instruction.

Look, you fast only to quarrel and to fight and to strike with a wicked fist. Such fasting as you do today will not make your voice heard on high. ...	*To them* he says then again concerning these things, 'Why do you fast for me ...'
Is not this the fast that I choose: to loose the bonds of injustice, to undo the thongs of the yoke, to let the oppressed go free, and to break every yoke? ... (Isa. 58.4, 6)	*But to us*, he says, 'Behold this is the fast which I choose ...' (*Barnabas* 3.1, 3 [emphasis added])

When the multifaceted materials of conflict that fill the prophetic tradition in the Hebrew Bible find their way into Christian anti-Jewish writing, the complex amalgam of loyalty, requirement, demand, forgive-

---

19. See Reidar Hvalvik, *The Struggle for Scripture and Covenant: The Purpose of the Epistle of Barnabas and Jewish-Christian Competition in the Second Century* (Tübingen: J.C.B. Mohr [Paul Siebeck], 1996) and James Carleton Paget, *The Epistle of Barnabas: Outlook and Background* (WUNT, 2/64; Tübingen: J.C.B. Mohr [Paul Siebeck], 1994) for recent scholarship.

20. See *Barn.* 12.1 quoting *4 Ezra* 4.33; 5.5 and *Barn.* 16.5 alluding to *1 Enoch* 89.

ness and self-examination is refined into pure and hard crystals of judgment that have the deceiving appearance of self-incrimination, though the guilty plea is extracted through what must be seen as textual torture.

Testaments of the Twelve Patriarchs

While the *Epistle of Barnabas* appropriates a prophetic text, another composition of Christian provenance from slightly later in the second century bases itself on a Jewish apocalyptic text. The *Testament of Levi* continues in a Christian setting the visionary testament known in fragments from the Dead Sea Scrolls and the Cairo Geniza and referred to as *Aramaic Levi*.[21] The earlier Jewish materials are very fragmentary, but several close intersections with the Greek Christian materials are evident on matters of testamentary setting, heavenly ascent, and so on.

Judgment of the descendents of the patriarch, however, is the sticking point where Christian reworking of the Jewish Levi materials becomes so problematic. The Jewish materials contain promises or threats of judgment over issues of sin and purity, and so on (4Q213 2.6). In the mode of inter-texture that characterizes apocalyptic literature and preaching, they look to the figure of Enoch to enumerate the future sins of the sons of Levi and the ensuing judgment (4Q213 5.3.6–11). They imply future judgment and restoration – revelation on a temporal axis (4Q541 9.1–7), and they promise knowledge of the secrets of the abyss – spatial revelation commonly associated with places of punishment (4Q541 7.1). Judgment and restoration are both movements within the context of covenant.

When the Christian *Testament of Levi* takes up these topics – future sin, judgment, and restoration – the tropes of Christian anti-Semitism invade the discourse and the judgment stays with Judaism while the restoration is assigned to Christianity. Israel is said to have sinned against the law itself and the sign of this is at the site of strident Christian anti-Judaism: the cross and the tearing of the temple veil.

> I am innocent of all your ungodliness and of the sin you will commit at the end of time against the Saviour of the world ... and together with the rest of Israel, you will sin against the law, so that he will not bear with Jerusalem because of your wickedness, but will tear in two the temple veil ... and you will be scattered as captives among the Gentiles and be... trampled under foot ... as it stands written in the book of the righteous Enoch. (*T. Levi* 10.2–6)

---

21. See M. de Jonge, *The Testaments of the Twelve Patriarchs: A Critical Edition of the Greek Text* (PVTG, 1; Leiden: E.J. Brill, 1978) and 'Testaments of the Twelve Patriarchs', in H.F.D. Sparks (ed.), *The Apocryphal Old Testament* (Oxford: Oxford University Press, 1984), 505–600; R.H. Charles (ed.), *The Apocrypha and Pseudepigrapha of the Old Testament*, II (Oxford: Oxford University Press, 1912–1913); 1Q21, 4Q213, 4Q214, 4Q540, 4Q541.

The sin against the world saviour is the Christian intensification of the inner Jewish complaint of not heeding the prophets. In combination with the destruction of the Temple and understanding the diaspora as punishment, the historical phenomena of the destruction of the temple and dispersion become venomous.

> And so the temple, which the Lord will choose, will be laid waste because of your uncleanness, and you will be captives of all the Gentiles. And you will be an abomination to them and bear the eternal shame of having been condemned by the righteous judgment of God. (*T. Levi* 15.1–2)

The obviously Christian elaboration of judgment culminates in the accusation of Christ-killing, with all its horrible power:

> You will brand as a deceiver a man who renews the law in the power of the Most High, unaware of who he is, and you will finally kill him, as you suppose, and through your wickedness bring innocent blood upon your heads. (*T. Levi* 16.3–4)

In a complex fusion, the Gospel of Matthew's intensification of the Pilate narrative is here retrojected onto a testamentary prophecy by the fictive patriarch of the Jewish priesthood. A pseudepigrapher of Levi prophecies *ex eventu* the incident that the writer of the Gospel of Matthew retrojects onto the life of Jesus. This is extraordinary knowledge indeed, but its consequences are dispiritingly mundane: the accusation that Jews are Christ-killers.

Summary: Inter-religious Deployment

The materials that are part of a painful but potentially healthy conflict of opinion, practice and vision within a group are intensified to dangerous levels by the context of universal significance that characterizes apocalyptic literature. They become nearly toxic when they are deployed in an interreligious context, especially after the relative power of one group over the other surpasses that of the other as we see in the history of Jewish-Christian relations.

Conclusion

The Jesus we want, the Jesus we get, and the Jesus that forms the strongest bulwark against anti-Semitism – these three Jesuses are not especially likely to intersect. William Arnal has noted helpfully how ubiquitously Jesus is characterized as Jewish and how little agreement actually proceeds from that. I want to suggest that no model of Jesus will be enough to contain anti-Semitism, that the power of a religious figure to inspire his followers is a dangerous power after the danger to the nascent religion has passed, and that the power of Jesus to be a tool of anti-Semitic thought and action is as much a product of the immense power that Christianity has often wielded as of the particularity of any model of Jesus.

The messy reality of history is never as supportive of ideology as a canned, re-worked and massaged version of history can be made to be. The task of the historian is, according to Jonathan Z. Smith, 'to complicate rather than to clarify'.[22] Many of have watched, with reactions from chagrin to glee, as our work undermines elements of ahistorical religious narratives that make untenable historical claims (some admirable and some not). This activity of our profession is the strongest bulwark against our work becoming fodder for anti-Semitism and, by its nature, such a bulwark is not impenetrable.

The flip side of this complicating movement is the simplifying or generalizing. This is a less 'safe' activity and comes always with a cost or a risk of cost. It is not a cost we can consistently avoid paying, nor a risk that we can continually avoid taking. Smith's praise of the complicating mode of historiographical production has its counterpart in his treatment of distortion as absolutely necessary to the 'creation of value' in historical research. His analogy is the map, which he has so famously distinguished from territory. The map that does not distort some elements of the territory is no map at all and brings no value to the enterprise of mapping, but the distortion that necessarily accompanies mapping – in scale, in making a sphere into a plane, in highlighting political or physical geography – must be thoroughly understood and clearly articulated. Our efforts both to locate Jesus within Judaism and to specify that location in its particularities can be in tension with one another.

In many ways the risks involved in these operations parallel the risks of insider criticism. And we see Jews today and in history taking that risk in their at best passionate and at worst vituperative arguments over what is right and true within Judaism and within the world. The task we must face as historians and scholars of religion is to respect the risks taken by insiders, to take it upon ourselves to understand the ramifications of those risks, and to refrain from reproducing the ahistorical distortions that our sources practice upon one another.

Jesus the 'Jew against Judaism' is a trope of Christian anti-Semitism and we are not served by playing into this dynamic. When the pendulum swings too far from an acknowledgement of the reality of inner-religious contestation, however, we get the Jesus whose position within Judaism is eviscerated of any of the tension of genuine interaction.

Getting Jesus 'right' is a matter of importance in both historical and moral terms, but it will be of little use apart from a successful and public communication of Second Temple Judaism that neither flinches from the

---

22. Jonathan Z. Smith, *Map is Not Territory* (SJLA, 23; Leiden: E.J. Brill), 208.

hard realities of that period nor promotes as central the damning elements of Christian apologetic characterizations of Judaism. To think that getting 'right with Jesus' is the solution is to slide subtly away from our task as historians to value the period and to slip quietly towards a Christian fixation on the saviour figure in our contention that misunderstandings of that figure are the basis of the problem.

THE EARTH MOVED:
JESUS, SEX, AND ESCHATOLOGY

A.-J. Levine

Vanderbilt University

Both the readings for this symposium and the two essays that I've seen (those of William Arnal and Robert Miller) offer numerous options for approaching the conjoined subjects of our topics: apocalypticism, anti-Semitism, and the historical Jesus.[1]

1. We could continue to fuss about approach: Do we start with the framework or individual pericope? To what extent do we utilize John, Paul, Thomas, or anything else outside the synoptics? What sources – literary, material, cross-cultural, scholarly models – do we use?
2. We can fuss about what we mean by apocalypticism and anti-Semitism, let alone what we mean by 'Judaism'.
3. We could debate the extent of anti-Semitism or anti-Judaism still present in contemporary study rather than, as William Arnal does, blithely state that it 'is simply not a problem today'.[2] Or, to query what we see as the responsibility of the academy, we might observe that academic publications are actually read by laity, and much of that laity has no clue as to whether Jesus was Jewish or what would

---

1. [Ed. note: Two readings were circulated prior to the symposium in order to help focus the discussion: Robert J. Miller (ed.), *The Apocalyptic Jesus: A Debate* (Santa Rosa, CA: Polebridge, 2001) and Paula Fredriksen, *Jesus of Nazareth, King of the Jews: A Jewish Life and the Emergence of Christianity* (New York: Alfred Knopf, 1999), 261–70.]

2. William Arnal, 'The Cipher "Judaism" in Contemporary Historical Jesus Scholarship', p. 24. Arnal's note is insufficient. First, my studies of work on Jesus by scholars writing from social locations outside the Western 'mainstream' do not limit the reason for the prevailing anti-Judaism to the ministers' libraries or to the residue of missionary propaganda. To the contrary, I argue that the recrudescence of anti-Judaism in this literature results from Western education: 'In delineating the evils of colonialism (as well as the complicity of the indigenous male population), some feminist critics identify Jesus with their own self-articulated abject situations, and they identify those biblical peoples who do not follow Jesus

have made him so. Thus, rather than see titles that announce Jesus to be Jewish as 'shrill',[3] we might see them as providing education and corrective.

Me, I'd prefer to talk about sex. The point here is not to be prurient, but rather to break out of some of the methodological strangleholds in which our subjects appear to lie (or lay). I also find sex a productive lens through which I can address some of the questions Kloppenborg posed to us.

I begin with Kloppenborg's 'guiding issue', which is, 'Not whether, at the level of evidence and argument, the Jesus of history should be regarded as an apocalypticist [yes, he should] and what sort of Judaism he represented [obviously, his own] but instead what is at stake in these questions'. I then turn to the benefits of 'sex'.

First, to the stakes of this discussion – there are many; for me, two are pressing.

The first concerns, as Robert Miller already notes, family values. The questions are not simply academic. I cannot count the number of people I've met, especially male college students, terrified that if they masturbate, Jesus will condemn them; or the number of women stuck in abusive marriages because Jesus forbids divorce. Sexual ethics within an apocalyptic context will likely differ from those developed in the context of a long-term project.

The second point concerns the anti-Judaism – at least as I would define it – of many of those who write on Jesus' views of sex and gender. Jesus remains seen as the liberator of all, but especially women, from Judaism's promulgation of purity (always characterized as marginalizing, constraining, or otherwise barbaric), patriarchy (rarely defined) and partitions (such as the belief that in Judaism women cannot appear in public and are

---

– that is, "the Jews" (rarely the Romans) – with their oppressors.' Amy-Jill Levine, 'The Disease of Postcolonial New Testament Studies and the Hermeneutics of Healing', *Journal of Feminist Studies in Religion* 20.1 (Spring 2004), 91–99, here p. 92, and see the responses to this roundtable, p. 132. See also my 'Lilies of the Field and Wandering Jews: Biblical Scholarship, Women's Roles, and Social Location', in *Transformative Encounters: Jesus and Women Re-Viewed* (ed. Ingrid Rosa Kitzberger; Leiden: E.J. Brill, 2000), 329–52. Because much of this material is published by Western presses (e.g., Orbis, World Council of Churches), it does appear in mainstream Western contexts. It is, in fact, a staple in many Divinity School classrooms.

3. Arnal, 'Cipher', p. 26, in this volume. Arnal misses the point of these titles. He asks, 'If no one denies that Jesus was Jewish, why this constant reiteration'? (26). The reiteration is there not only because many, especially outside of the Society of Biblical Literature, do deny it, but because even with many who proclaim it, there is no content to the term. The presumption of authors who put 'Jew' or 'Jewish' in the title is that the book itself will describe how Jesus fits within 'Judaism' or practices 'Judaism'. Then again, what is one to make of titles such as Paul Zahn's *The First Christian: Universal Truth in the Teachings of Jesus* (Grand Rapids, MI: Eerdmans, 2003)?

not allowed to speak with or touch men). This misperception of Judaism is not merely an academic issue either, for Christians in classrooms and pews are introduced to an anal, exclusivistic, misogynistic, clannish, focused-on-externals, heartless, and atavistic Judaism.

G-d forbid such an impression be given of any other ethnic group!

The flip side of this is that those of us (myself, Ross Kraemer, Kathleen Corley, and others, most recently John Elliott[4]) who do not see Jesus as egalitarian – here a distinction from most of the 'guys' including Dale Allison and Marcus Borg – are classified either as 'anti-Jewish' (because we do not see first-century Judaism as accommodating an egalitarian system; of course, we don't see any first-century movement as capable of this) or as bad feminists (because we do not locate a usable past). *Ad hominem* arguments extend to feminist discourse, as, most recently, a glance at Fiorenza's *Politics of Interpretation* demonstrates.[5]

The Method: A Few Remarks

A focus on Jesus' view of sexuality provides one escape from the methodological debates of the essay collection assigned to this conference's participants as background reading. In this case,

1. I need not start with an external frame – such as millenarian movement or political revolution or perceived disempowerment or sapiential subversive wisdom honed in peasant experience – and so skew the data. Thus, Steve Patterson will not accuse me – I hope – of failing to schlogg through the historical-critical muck.[6]
2. Nor need we quibble to any great extent over what is or is not historical Jesus, since sexual and familial statements permeate all layers of the tradition – M, L, Q, Mark, Paul, John, Thomas – and since they are consistent. Otherwise put, even if one doesn't agree that all the statements adduced under the topic are original, it would be very odd to deny all of them.
3. We still get to locate Jesus not only between John the Baptist and Paul but also between John the Baptist and Thomas.

4. Kathleen E. Corley, 'Gender and Class in the Teaching of Jesus: A Profile', in *Profiles of Jesus* (ed. Roy W. Hoover; Santa Rosa, CA: Polebridge, 2002), 137–60; John H. Elliott, 'The Jesus Movement was not Egalitarian but Family-Oriented', *Biblical Interpretation* 11.2 (2003): 173–210.

5. Elisabeth Schüssler Fiorenza, *Jesus and the Politics of Interpretation* (New York: Continuum, 2000).

6. Stephen J. Patterson, 'Assessing the Arguments', in Miller (ed.), *The Apocalyptic Jesus*, 124.

4.   We avoid the problems of determining Jesus' 'Jewishness' since the reconstruction locates Jesus within discussions current in Second Temple circles (and, indeed, less so in Roman Gentile ones).

My Hypothesis

My thesis is that Jesus' views on sexuality are best understood in an apocalyptic-eschatological context. I suggest that Jesus – anticipating the final tribulation, general resurrection, the incoming of the exiles, a last judgment, even his own end-time role – did not expect there to be a next generation. He thought of himself as inaugurating the new age, when people would be like the angels, when marriage and childbirth would be no longer needed. To advocate a celibate lifestyle for everyone is no simple social program; it signals the end of the age. Thus it is the apocalyptic setting that substantially drives his so-called 'moral' program.

The focus on sexuality yields not only an apocalyptic Jesus, but also a Jewish one. The particulars are both based in Jewish scriptures and consistent with other Jewish movements (or at least texts) of the period. The new life is grounded in that old ideal of *Urzeit/Endzeit*, with the *Urzeit* being the Garden of Eden as understood within the parameters of Jewish exegesis.

And these parameters take us, somewhat indirectly, to Kloppenborg's observation on the vigor by which the non-apocalyptic Jesus has been met. Here, I want to state my objections to the way the model of the apocalyptic Jesus is sometimes played out. Leaving authorial intention aside as well as the debates about what is or is not authentic, too often the model when spelled out conveys an image of Judaism that makes a mockery of its practices and reduces its beliefs to a series of universalistic ideals. What is specifically Jewish is regarded as bad; only what Judaism shares with the church is worth preserving.

First, for the non-apocalyptic Jesus, there is no place for law; Jesus is seen as abrogating or relaxing law. Ignored or treated as 'later' is all evidence that in some cases he intensified Torah; ignored are the extensive debates and pronouncements on orthopraxy within Jewish sources.

Second, there is no place for purity, but the promulgators of this view typically overlook the role of purity throughout the empire, the continuation of purity practices by the early church, the leveling of social boundaries purity creates (the high priest can be impure; the slave and Gentile can be pure), the ease of living in an environment where purity is practiced, and the personal meaningfulness of purity practices as a form of sanctifying the body and recognizing contact with the Holy.

Third, in this non-apocalyptic setting we hear about the Temple domination system, when no evidence is produced to show that such a system was seen by anyone as such. Numerous Jews did find the leadership corrupt, but this was not the case with the institution itself (we might compare our own political views: the idea of government is good; the particular people holding office may not be). As for the Temple's elitism, this is the place where both Pharisee and tax collector, Jew and Gentile, male and female, can and do worship. Nor do those who speak about this domination system reflect on temples throughout the empire. Finally, the scholarship remains tendentiously selective in its comparison basis: nowhere, for example, do we find Acts 15's forbidding of eating food offered to idols treated as a protest against the Athenian or Ephesian temple domination system.

Fourth, the non-eschatological Jesus is typically seen as breaking down ethnic barriers. Eliminated is the focus on the people of Israel as a distinct group (Jews knew they were not Gentiles or Samaritans). Jesus, however, did not inaugurate the Gentile mission; he did not think it was necessary, for what happens eschatologically to the Gentiles is accomplished by divine fiat. The historical Jesus did not break down ethnic barriers, for an eschatological Jesus did not need to do so.

Fifth, this apocalyptic-eschatological model, we are told, promulgates, in Robert Miller's terms, 'a God of coercive violence',[7] as opposed to Jesus' nice, humble, slightly inept if not befuddled *abba*. Yet both Testaments as well as ongoing Church and Synagogue traditions attest a G-d who punishes the wicked, and, as Dale Allison notes, Jesus had a view of hell.[8] Of course this view is antithetical to our liberal-academic ethos that decries capital punishment, war, and gun ownership.

Sixth, Miller also claims that this thesis of the non-eschatological/non-apocalyptic Jesus has a 'price tag', namely, 'It means that Jesus rejected the G-d of the Exodus, the Yahweh whom the Israelites praised as a warrior. This puts Jesus at a critical distance from his tradition.'[9] The point is overstated. 'His tradition' is certainly not limited to militarism. 'His tradition' also speaks of suffering servants and harmony with nature. Miller's claim is tantamount to saying that because Martin Luther King, Jr. resisted violence, he was 'at a critical distance from his tradition' given that both Exodus and Revelation were part of his Bible as well.

What then is the payoff of a non-eschatological Jesus? The G-d of mercy is also a G-d of justice. The non-eschatological model offers no justice, and mercy without justice gives us either a divine doormat or a divine irrelevancy. Those who don't find a problem with justice in the world – such as the non-eschatological Sadducees – didn't need a resurrection. What of the rest?

7. Miller, 'Theological Stakes in the Apocalyptic Jesus Debate' (below, p. 117).
8. Dale C. Allison, *Jesus of Nazareth: Millenarian Prophet* (Minneapolis: Fortress, 1998), 131–36.
9. Miller, 'Theological Stakes in the Apocalyptic Jesus Debate' (below, p. 116).

Finally, the non-eschatological model is typically set up, whether intentionally or not, as the antithesis to an apocalyptic model (Marcus Borg's article in *The Apocalyptic Jesus: A Debate* breaks this pattern somewhat by talking about priorities). This is a false premise and indeed one inconsistent with Judaism. A speaker of wisdom may well be eschatologically oriented. The book of Daniel offers both wisdom and apocalyptic, as does Zechariah, the *Apocalypse of Abraham, 1 Enoch, 2 Baruch*, and so on. It would be odd to find in a Jewish context a text or a group in which wisdom and apocalyptic do not appear side by side. Dale Allison puts this succinctly: 'Apocalyptic thinkers need not be monomaniacs.'[10]

So, let's turn to the question at hand.

The Sexual Ethic

Jesus promulgated a lifestyle modeled not only on the *Jubilees* (the more common theory) but also on the Garden of Eden.[11] Comparable are both CD 2.14–6.1 and 11QTemple 57.17–19 on citing Genesis as the bulwark against not only remarriage but also polygamy.

Via an *Urzeit/Endzeit* view of history, he anticipated a kingdom in which his followers would be like the angels, neither married nor given in marriage. He therefore encouraged them to become 'eunuchs for the kingdom of heaven' and to be like children, that is, like those who do not procreate. While he forbade divorce (using Genesis to trump Deuteronomy, and consistent with Mal. 2.10–16),[12] his primary concern was with remarriage, which he abhorred. Nor did he expect his married followers to engage in conjugal activities. There is no longer any need 'to be fruitful and multiply and fill the earth'; that's been done.

In this sense, Jesus stands against one major Jewish position, which is that being fruitful and multiplying is a good thing to do. This is Josephus, with an appeal to Genesis 1 (cited by Brant Pitre[13]): 'Shun eunuchs and flee all dealings with those who have deprived themselves of their virility and of those fruits of generation, which God has given to men for the increase of our race; expel them even as infanticides who withal have

---

10. Dale C. Allison, 'Jesus was an Apocalyptic Prophet', in *The Apocalyptic Jesus: A Debate* (ed. Robert J. Miller; Santa Rosa, CA: Polebridge Press, 2001), 89.

11. See Joseph A. Fitzmyer, 'The Matthean Divorce Texts and Some New Palestinian Evidence', *TS* 37 (1976): 197–226; James R. Mueller, 'The Temple Scroll and the Gospel Divorce Texts', *RevQ* 38 (1980): 247–56.

12. The authenticity of the divorce logion is rarely debated, but see Mary Rose D'Angelo, 'Re-Membering Jesus: Women, Prophecy, and Resistance in the Memory of the Early Churches', *Horizon* 19 (1992): 199–218, esp. 214–16, for an alternate view.

13. Brant Pitre, 'Marginal Elites: Matt 19.12 and the Social and Political Dimensions of Becoming Eunuchs for the Sake of the Kingdom' (unpublished paper presented at the Annual Meeting of the Society of Biblical Literature, Boston, MA, November 1999), 8.

destroyed the means of procreation. For plainly, it is by reason of the effeminacy of their soul that they have changed the sex of their body also' (*Ant.*, 4.290–291).

Jesus' view is consistent with that of other Jews, including John the Baptist and the Essenes as described by Josephus (*War* 8.2), Philo, and Pliny the Elder.[14]

Further, this view is consistent with Paul as well as Thomas (neither of whom is thrilled with lust, sex or procreation). The major text that promotes discontinuity from this celibate ethic, the propagation-happy 1 Timothy 2, proves the rule by using the same Genesis model of Adam and Eve to argue its case even as it attests to the popularity of Christian celibacy.

The Eunuch

Matthew 19.10–12, voted 'pink' by the Jesus Seminar, reads: 'There are eunuchs who have been so from birth, and there are eunuchs who have been made eunuchs by others, and there are eunuchs who have made themselves eunuchs for the sake of the kingdom of heaven. Let the one able to accept, accept.'

Three common definitions are offered for this saying: first, that the eunuch is someone who cannot have sexual intercourse; the second is that the eunuch is a slave; the third is that the eunuch represents someone excluded from the community (back to purity again; here Deuteronomy 23). All three are incorrect. Eunuchs could and did have sexual relations; eunuchs could be either slave or free; eunuchs could participate in eating heave offerings, in *halitzah* ceremonies, and so on, at least according to *m. Yebamot*. In turn, there is no evidence of their exclusion save for idealized Temple systems. The one consistent marker for the eunuch was that he could not produce children.

The eunuch is not a symbol for a slave (as Kathleen Corley argues[15]), and no one in the early church took the statement in that way. To equate eunuch and slave not only runs counter to Acts 8, it also dismisses the Jewish tradition. The *seris* Potiphar is no slave; Nehemiah did quite well for himself; the eunuchs blessed by Isaiah – 'the eunuchs who keep my Sabbaths, who choose the things that please me and hold fast to my covenant' will have 'a monument and a name better than sons and

14. It is also consistent with that of Jeremiah, who, as John Meier puts it (*A Marginal Jew: Rethinking the Historical Jesus* Volume III. *Companions and Competitors* [Anchor Bible Reference Library; New York: Doubleday, 2001], 507), 'had seen himself called to celibacy as a sign "embodying" the crisis and judgment looming over Israel (Jer 16.1–4)'. And, Meier continues, so 'Jesus, the eschatological prophet, may have seen his celibacy as a sign that the present order of things was soon to cease'.

15. Corley, 'Gender and Class', 149–50.

daughters...an everlasting name, which shall not be cut off' (I think that's a pun; Isa. 56.4–5), are not slaves, and legends concerning Daniel speak of his being a eunuch, but not a slave.[16]

Notably, Isaiah's pronouncement is made in an eschatological context, and Daniel is pre-eminently associated with apocalyptic eschatology. The eunuch thus can symbolize more than just the end of a particular person's lineage. The eunuch rather is the male who does not procreate.

Pitre points out that Matthew (or Jesus, for that matter) could have used the language of virginity (*parthenos*) or the unmarried state (*agamos*), but chose *eunouchos* instead.[17]

A final note: neither the eunuch nor any of the other statements on sexual ethics should be seen as feminist, let alone egalitarian, unless one considers the complete devaluation of procreation liberating for women. On the one hand, the eunuch is a male symbol (*pace* Germaine Greer); thus, the androcentricity of Jesus' program is confirmed, rather than challenged, by its disinterest in procreation. On the other, as Aristotle put it (*Generation of Animals* V, vii), 'all animals when they are castrated change over into the female state'. Thus, at best, we have here not an appreciation of the feminine, but a cooptation of it, and such gender-bending is characteristic of millenarian movements.

Alternatively, we have an infantilizing image, but for this we need to go to a fourth-century text, Claudian's *In Eutropium*. If we do, we're back to childlessness.

At the very least, we may conclude that Jesus and his immediate followers were celibate and so counter to the dominant ethos in both Judaism and Hellenism. Augustine got it right: Jesus 'gives the palm to those who have made themselves eunuchs for the kingdom of heaven, meaning the youths of both sexes who have extirpated from their hearts the desire of marriage and who in the church act as eunuchs of the King's palace'.[18]

Indeed, the idea of the eunuch for the kingdom complements the idea of Jesus as bridegroom, and his followers as 'sons of the bridal chamber'. The term *eunouchos* may well derive from *eunē* ('bed' or 'marriage bed') and *echō* ('hold, guard'). They guard it, and themselves.

The Bridegroom

Jesus' role is that of brideless bridegroom. Why? Certainly one facet is the representation's insistence on celebration, for feasting is the hallmark of

16. *B. Sanh.* 93b; *Pirke R. Eliezer* 52; Jerome, *Commentary on Isaiah*; Origin, *Commentary on Matthew* xv.5.
17. Pitre, 'Marginal Elites', 7–9.
18. Gary Taylor, *Castration: An Abbreviated History of Western Manhood* (London and New York: Routledge, 2000), 67–68.

the wedding. The image is also one of anticipation, of a glorious consummation and then the start of a new life. The bridegroom, like Jesus, and so like the world itself in his view, is in a liminal moment: about to make the transition from anticipation to fulfillment.

In the parable of the ten virgins (Mt. 25.1–13), the focus is on the bridegroom. In the parable of the wedding feast (Mt. 22.2), among those not attending is the just-married man. In these wedding parables no one is married: not the bridegroom, for there is no bride; not the father, for no mother of the groom is mentioned; not the guests, for they are virgins.

Further, this bridegroom is accompanied by what might be considered apocalyptic/eschatological violence: the bridegroom shuts the door in the face of foolish although faithful virgins; the bridegroom's father expels a guest for having the wrong garment; his attendants will fast in his absence. The image of the bridegroom runs through the various levels of the synoptic tradition, and eschatological language and/or apocalyptic imagery accompanies them all.[19]

Divorce

The most common explanation found in both professional and popular works for the divorce statements, is that Jesus is engaged in social engineering designed to prevent Jewish women from being tossed out onto the street because 'the rabbis' said that a man could divorce for any reason such as his wife's burning his dinner or because he found someone prettier.[20] This is sloppy.

Had those proclaiming such a Jewish misogynism noted the role of the *ketubah*; observed that this one very liberal view of divorce is just that, one view among many; recognized that rabbinic statements on divorce were at the time of composition prescriptive not descriptive; glanced at what some of the church fathers were saying about women, marriage and divorce; looked at Jesus' own statements concerning the separation of man and woman; or checked Roman legislation (Augustus had his own program of social engineering, given that patrician divorce rates were nearing the 50 per cent mark), the picture of Jesus becomes quite different.

Jesus insisted that one should not get divorced, for there was no reason to do so. Eschatology resolves the problem of loveless marriages in one

---

19. John 3.29, the pronouncement of John the Baptist, does not follow this pattern, although Revelation's 'marriage supper of the lamb' (Rev. 19.9) shows the image exists within Johannine circles.

20. See discussion in Amy-Jill Levine, 'Jesus, Divorce, and Sexuality: A Jewish Critique', in *The Historical Jesus through Catholic and Jewish Eyes* (ed. L.J. Greenspoon, D. Hamm and B.F. Le Beau; Harrisburg, PA: Trinity Press International, 2000), 113–29.

way; until then, Jesus' new family resolves the problem another way by encouraging the separation of husband from wife (and, as his female followers suggest, wives from husbands). The married state does not require cohabitation.

Moreover, if the man following Jesus leaves everything, the *ketubah* is irrelevant. If the point is to promote celibacy, forbidding divorce again makes sense, for divorce would free the wife to remarry.

Single Followers

Jesus was a single man followed by other single people: single men and women separated from or unattached to other men. As for conjugality, there is no married couple (with the exception of Mary and Joseph and Jairus and his wife [Mk. 5.40]) with whom Jesus speaks. (Mary Magdalene, Mary and Martha of Bethany, the Syro-Phoenician woman, the Samaritan woman, all appear without marriage or husband. Joanna seems to have left [divorced? deserted? been deserted by] her husband, Herod's stewart Chuza.)

Similarly, the men following Jesus do so without spousal accompaniment (e.g., Mt. 19.27–29). Jesus heals Peter's mother-in-law, but the text is silent regarding his wife. Paul notes that some apostles are accompanied by a 'sister wife' (1 Corinthians 9); while the term could indicate a Christian wife, more likely it means a wife treated as if she were a sister, one with whom the husband had no sexual congress.

Jesus also encourages his followers to leave their homes and families, as in Luke 14.26, 'Whoever comes to me and does not hate father and mother, wife and children, brothers and sisters, yes, and even life itself, cannot be my disciple' (cf. Mt. 10.37, which tones down the statement by speaking of relative [in both senses of the term] love; see also *Gos. Thom.* 55, 101). See also Lk. 18.29, 'Truly I tell you, there is no one who has left house *or wife* or brothers or parents or children, for the sake of the Kingdom of G-d, who will not get back very much more in this age, and in the age to come eternal life.' While many commentators assume Luke added 'wife' to this Markan saying, separation of spouses in the context of radical piety – and Jesus is certainly involved in radical piety – is hardly unusual.[21]

We could domesticate these statements to mean 'Don't put anything ahead of your love for G-d or don't get too attached to wealth.' But this is

21. This notice is similar to his citation of Mic. 7.5–6 on disruption between parents and children (cf. Mt. 10.34–39; Luke 12.51–53; 14.25–27, and cf. *Gos. Thom.* 55, 101). See also Kathleen Corley, 'Gender and Class', 151. For fuller discussion, see David C. Sim, 'What About the Wives and Children of the Disciples? The Cost of Discipleship from Another Perspective', *Heythrop Journal* 35 (1994): 373–90.

not what Jesus' earliest followers understood. As Peter puts it, 'We have left everything.' Nor do I see any reason to domesticate, any more than I would reduce forgiving debts or loving enemies to such banalities.

Jesus' point was to create a new family, a 'fictive kinship group'. His program had special appeal to those outside the traditional *oikos*. In his new family, relationship was determined not by biology or *ketubah*, but by voluntary mutual support. In turn, Jesus dismisses the biological family: 'who are my mother and brothers and sisters? those who hear the will of the Father, and do it' (Mt. 12.48–50 // *Gos. Thom.* 99 and see Mk. 3.33–35 // Lk. 8.21).

However, there is no earthly 'father' in this group: mothers follow sons into the movement, no father does so; Zebedee, the father of James and John, remains with his boats. For Jesus, the Father in heaven is sufficient.

As long as the subject of fathers is being addressed, a side note to the almost requisite appeal to the codes of honor and shame in non-eschatological Jesus works but less so in those that see Jesus as apocalyptic or emphasize his Jewishness. Again, Miller's paper for this meeting provides a splendid example. Citing Scott on the Prodigal Son,[22] he speaks of how the 'father shamelessly fawns over his younger son, in utter disregard for male honor, behavior most unfitting the apocalyptic king of the cosmos'.[23] First, not all parables need to be eschatological in order for Jesus to be so. Second, and more pressing, the honor/shame construct is exactly that, a construct, and it is based substantially on limited field work. Carol Schersten LaHurd, who did field work with Arab Christian women, notes that while Kenneth Bailey (upon whom Scott and Miller are so dependent) 'and others have described the father's running in v. 20 as contrary to the dignity of a Middle Eastern patriarch', the Christian Arab women all disagreed. They found it 'a natural reaction'; rather than seeing the father as acting anomalously in that he did not concern himself with whether his son had 'learned his lesson', they instead noted that such a concern is 'a very Western thought' which LaHurd glosses as 'Greek/European, not Middle Eastern/Arab'.[24] An interpretive strategy that relies on a pan-Mediterranean model, especially one that is accompanied by the insistence that *Ioudaios* be translated as 'Judean'

22. Bernard Brandon Scott, *Hear Then the Parable* (Minneapolis: Fortress, 1989), 117.

23. Miller, 'Theological Stakes'.

24. Carol Schersten LaHurd, 'Re-viewing Luke 15 with Arab Christian Women', in Amy-Jill Levine (ed.), *A Feminist Companion to Luke* (Feminist Companion to the New Testament and Early Christian Writings, 3; London and New York: Continuum, 2002), 246–68, here 259.

rather than 'Jew' in all or almost all cases, may inherently marginalize the 'Jewishness' of Jesus.[25]

Granted, the single status does not preclude sexual activity. However, in the case of Jesus and his followers, it does.

Lust

Matthew 5.27–28 not only forbids adultery but asserts: 'Everyone who looks at a woman with lust has already committed adultery with her in his heart.' Jesus also forbids self-gratification. Mark 9.42–48 exhorts: 'If your hand causes you to stumble, cut it off; it is better for you to enter life maimed than to have two hands and go to hell', and Matthew juxtaposes this saying to the pronouncement on lusting (Mt. 5.29). Some rabbis advocated cutting off the hand for masturbation (cf. in a different context, Deut. 25.11–12). As the Mishnah puts it (*m. Nid.* 2.1): 'Every hand which frequently makes examinations, in the case of women is praiseworthy, and in the case of men is to be cut off.'[26] Qumran recognized the metaphoric potential of 'hand' (11QTemple 46.13 calls the latrine as *meqom yad*, the 'place of the hand') and in Semitic languages, 'hand' as well as 'foot' can be a euphemism for 'penis'.[27] I am trusting here that the injunctions are metaphorical, but what one person finds to

---

25. On terminology, see most recently John H. Elliott, 'Jesus was Neither a Jew nor a Christian: Pitfalls of Inappropriate Nomenclature', unpublished paper given at the 67th International Meeting of the Catholic Biblical Association, Saint Mary's University, Halifax, Nova Scotia, August 7–10, 2004. Robert J. Miller's edited *The Complete Gospels: Annotated Scholars Version* (San Francisco: HarperSanFrancisco, rev. and exp. edn, 1994), translates 'Judean' in every case save for Mt. 28.15, where Bernard Brandon Scott, the translator, offers, 'this story [about the disciples' stealing the body of Jesus] has been passed around among the Jews until this very day' (114). For the Scholars Version, 'Judeans' and 'Judean religion' describe figures of the Second Temple period, while 'Jews and Judaism' refers to the 'religion of the rabbis, Talmud, and synagogue.' I wish to express my deep gratitude to Prof. Miller for his gracious responses to my concerns about this matter: his conversation proves that in this very heated, controversial issue, civility and friendship need not be sacrificed.

26. For texts and discussion see W.D. Davies and D.C. Allison, Jr., *A Critical and Exegetical Commentary on the Gospel According to Saint Matthew*, I (New International Critical Commentary Series; Edinburgh: T.&T. Clark, 1988), 524. See also Will Deming, 'Mark 9.42 – 10.12, Matthew 5.27–32, and *B. Nid.* 13b: A First Century Discussion of Male Sexuality', *NTS* 36 (1990): 130–41. Deming argues that Matthew 5, Mark 9 and *b. Nidda* 13b reveal 'a discussion on male sexuality that took place in Jewish and Christian circles sometime in the middle of the first century CE. Comparing these three texts, Deming then makes the case that the gospel's concern for 'scandalizing' the 'little ones' reflects a concern, shared by the rabbinic material, for pederasty or 'some other form of child molestation'.

27. See Hans Dieter Betz, *The Sermon on the Mount* (Hermeneia; Minneapolis: Fortress, 1995), 238 n. 335, denying the idiom lies behind the verse in question.

be hyperbole, another will take literally. The disciplinary effect – thank you, Foucault – is comparable.

Procreation

Jesus, not thrilled with lust, is even less thrilled with procreation.

In his vision, the consummation of the age was not a sexual one; he anticipated a transformation of the body beyond the sexual and a time when we all become 'like the angels[28] in heaven, who neither marry nor are given in marriage' (Mt. 22.30; Lk. 20.35–36). We might compare Josephus, *War* 3.374, on the 'chaste bodies' of the world-to-come. While early Judaism's configuration of angels could include male genitalia, the only ones who so employed their endowments were fallen. Good angels, the angels we are to become, do not do such things.

Apocalyptic literature confirms this impression: the great marriage of Revelation is between a slain lamb and a bejeweled city populated by 144,000 male virgins 'who have not known a woman'.

The only passage in the Jesus tradition that could suggest a positive view of procreation is the intercalation of hemorrhaging woman and dead girl, for in each case procreation, once precluded, becomes a possibility. However, the woman is not shown in a marital relationship; the girl is returned to her parents. More, the woman steals Jesus' power; he does not volunteer to heal.

Children

Celibacy, and especially the lack of children, was a marker of group identity, and this marker may well explain why the disciples sought to prevent parents from bringing their children to Jesus, even as it explains Jesus' multiply attested statement that his followers become like a child (Mk. 10.15; Mt. 19.14; Lk. 18.17).

The child is typically associated with dependence and low social status. While the dependence case holds (adults in the first century are also dependent, so while the case holds, it's hardly a marker of children),

---

28. Ben Witherington (*The Jesus Quest: The Third Search for the Jew of Nazareth* [Downers Grove, IL: InterVarsity, 1995], 169), sees the comparison as indicating not 'asexuality or lack of married condition' but 'immortality'. His appeal to Philo is inconsequential; his emphasis is not supported by other textual materials, and his view erases the specifics of the comparison itself. Also unconvincing are those arguments that see Jesus as looking forward to the end of 'patriarchal' marriage in which women are objectified as tokens of exchange; this may be the result of the statement, but less clear is its function as motivation.

children were not of low social status unless their parents also were. So what then does being like a child mean?

The little child is marked by sexual inexperience and lack of fertility.[29] As Crossan puts it in reference to *Thomas*, 'a kingdom of children is a kingdom of the celibate'[30]; the point originates, I suggest, not in *Thomas*'s asceticism, but in Jesus'. Otherwise put (here in Crossan's terms): Jesus wanted his followers to become little children, not to conceive them.

Consistently, the gospels do not privilege childbearing. According to Lk. 11.27–28, 'A woman from the crowd raised her voice and said to [Jesus], "Blessed is the womb that bore you, and the breasts that you sucked!" He responds, "Blessed rather are those who listen to the word of G-d and keep it".' The major point, also in *Gos. Thom.* 79 (where Lk. 23.29 is added),[31] is, probably, that one's ethic rather than one's fertility is valued. But it also comports with a negative view of procreation.

In an apocalyptic context, Jesus correspondingly blesses wombs that never gave birth and breasts that never nursed (Lk. 23.29). Unlike his prophetic predecessors, the one miracle he doesn't do is cure infertility. There was no need to do so, and every reason to avoid doing so.

Conclusion

Jesus sought to establish a new Eden, to inaugurate a time when people did not divorce, for, as he states, 'from the beginning it was not so', a time

---

29.   On the common reading that children represent those without status, see James L. Bailey, 'Experiencing the Kingdom as a Little Child: A Rereading of Mark 10.13–16', *Word and World* 15 (1995): 58–67; Ernest Best, 'Mark 10: 13–16: The Child as Model Recipient', in J.R. McKay and James F. Miller (eds.), *Biblical Studies in Honor of William Barclay* (Philadelphia: Westminster, 1976), 119–34; J. Duncan M. Derrett, 'Why Jesus Blessed the Children (Mark 10.13–16 Par.)', *NovT* 15 (1983): 1–18; Stephen Fowl, 'Receiving the Kingdom as a Child: Children and Riches in Luke 18.15ff', *NTS* 39 (1993): 153–58; A.O. Nkwoka, 'Mark 10.13–16: Jesus' Attitude to Children and its Modern Challenges', *African Theological Journal* 14 (1985): 100–110; Daniel Patte (ed.), *Kingdom and Children: Aphorism, Chreia, Structure. Semeia* 29 (1983); Hans-Ruedi Weber, *Jesus and the Children: Biblical Resources for Study and Preaching* (Geneva: World Council of Churches, 1979) [my thanks to Kathleen Corley for this list of sources]. Corley notes that *pais* and *paidion* need not mean only children; the terms can also refer to 'slaves'; thus Jesus' point may concern identification with the under-class ('Gender and Class', 125). Nevertheless, not all 'slaves' would be considered beneath the class status of peasants. Nor, as Corley also notes, were (free) children marginalized (citing Mark Golden, 'Chasing Change in Roman Childhood', *Ancient History Bulletin* 4 [1990]: 90–94, esp. 92, against Thomas Wiedemann, *Adults and Children in the Roman Empire* [New Haven: Yale University Press, 1989]).

30.   John Dominic Crossan, *The Historical Jesus: The Life of a Mediterranean Jewish Peasant* (San Francisco: Harper & Row, 1991), 267.

31.   Crossan, *Historical Jesus*, 299–300.

when all were literally of one flesh and not so because of intercourse, a time when procreation was neither necessary nor desirable.

The various pronouncements concerning sexuality are best explained within an apocalyptic-eschatological context. The other models don't work:

1. To tell the poor they are blessed is one thing; to tell them they cannot procreate or masturbate is something else.
2. To take the statements on sexuality as metaphor or joke is contrary to what all of Jesus' earliest followers thought: whether libertine or ascetic, they knew something sexual was up (again, in both senses).

The injunctions against lust, intercourse, procreation and masturbation are more than simply challenges to 'people to re-examine all their priorities, even the most intimate and sacred, in light of the demands of God's present kingdom'. The point here is not 're-examination'; it is 'no sex'.

This is the eschatological program followed by Paul, whose view of marriage was that it was preferable to burn with passion; by the author of the book of Revelation, who stated that the number saved would be 144,000 male virgins 'who had not known a woman'; and on through those metaphorically titled church 'fathers' and 'mothers'. And of all this, I think Jesus would have approved. Then again, he never expected to find fathers of the church.

At the end (where else?) we find not only an eschatological Jesus, but a Jewish one as well. Using imagery consistent with his tradition, such as the *Urzeit/Endzeit* schema with an appeal to Eden; adopting the model of the Jubilee; setting up a fictive kinship group as other Jews (as well as gentiles) had done; radicalizing the Torah by extending the prohibition of adultery to a prohibition of lust; reinterpreting some halakhic concerns in eschatological light such as the forbidding of divorce; appealing to angelology, all mark Jesus as a Jew speaking to other Jews in a Jewish idiom. None of this precludes Jesus from a sapiential perspective. Perhaps his insistence that there be justice, modeled now in the new family of faith and universalized by the in-breaking of the kingdom of G-d, may be seen as the harmony of both eschatological and sapiential modes of thought. The justice that the kingdom brings may not be the justice some of us would wish to see – the place of outer darkness, where there is wailing and gnashing of teeth may be less preferable to a system of restorative justice – but these are the terms Jesus leaves us.

THE PROBLEM OF APOCALYPTIC: FROM POLEMIC TO APOLOGETICS

Dale C. Allison, Jr.

Did Jesus believe that the final judgment and its attendant events, such as the resurrection of the dead, were imminent and, if so, to what extent did his proclamation and ministry mirror such a conviction? This question, especially associated which the work of Johannes Weiss and Albert Schweitzer, is the subject of this paper.[1] My goal, however, is not to take an excursion among the arguments and ask what the truth might be. I intend rather to review some of the *theological* convictions that have encouraged or discouraged fondness for a fervently eschatological Jesus. One rarely reads a book on Jesus without feeling that there is, for the author, immense interest in the outcome; and E.F. Scott's optimistic assertion that 'we have learned to approach the question [of Jesus and apocalyptic] dispassionately'[2] is as ridiculously false now as when Scott penned it, 80 years ago. Weiss and Schweitzer did not produce equanimity but provoked an uproar that has never quieted. Almost everyone who has written about Jesus since 1900 has become embroiled in the fracas; those traveling the straight and narrow road of bona fide impartiality on this issue must be few. So what precisely has been at stake *theologically* with regard to the great eschatological question?

Pro

I begin with those who have sketched for us a Jesus who lived and spoke in the grip of the impending consummation. Perhaps we do well to remember that such a Jesus appeared originally among people outside the

---

1. Johannes Weiss, *Jesus' Proclamation of the Kingdom of God* (Philadelphia: Fortress, 1971) (trans. of *Die Predigt Jesu vom Reiche Gottes* [Göttingen: Vandenhoeck & Ruprecht, 1892]); Albert Schweitzer, *The Quest of the Historical Jesus* (Minneapolis: Fortress, 2001) (trans. of *Geschichte der Leben-Jesu-Forschung* [Tübingen: J.C.B. Mohr (Paul Siebeck), 1906, 1913, 1950]).

2. E.F. Scott, 'The Place of Apocalyptical Conceptions in the Mind of Jesus', *JBL* 41 (1922): 137–42, at p. 137.

church, people wishing to attack those inside the church. If one wants to discredit a religion, discredit its founder. Show, for example, that the founder was wrong about something, preferably something important.

Of all the things that the NT is clearly mistaken about, the most obvious is its conviction, plainly expressed in a good number of places, that the consummation is near to hand. In the seventeenth century, the expositor Matthew Poole wrote that 'the apostles ordinarily in their epistles speak of the world as nigh to an end in their age, though it hath since continued more than sixteen hundred years; which would incline one to think, that they thought it would have been at an end before this time'.[3] The risen Jesus himself says a full three times in Revelation 22: 'I come quickly' (vv. 7, 12, 20). The speaker has failed to keep this promise. It does not surprise that 2 Peter 3 knows of 'scoffers' who ask, 'Where is the promise of his coming? For ever since the fathers fell asleep, all things have continued as they were from the beginning of creation' (v. 4). While we can only wonder about the identity of these so-called 'scoffers', we certainly do understand their critique. We don't need Deuteronomy to realize that 'if a prophet speaks in the name of the Lord but the thing does not take place or prove true, it is a word that the Lord has not spoken' (Deut. 18.22).

Whether the 'scoffers' in 2 Peter 3 had in mind words attributed to Jesus is unknown. It is, however, perfectly clear that there was, in the early church, awareness that some prophecies attributed to him were problematic. John 21 reflects consternation that the Beloved Disciple has died even though Jesus has not yet returned: 'The rumor spread among the brothers that the disciple would not die. Yet Jesus did not say to him that he would not die, but, "If it is my will that he remain until I come, what is that to you?"' Obviously in the background is some saying such as Mk. 9.1 – 'There are some standing here who will not taste death until they see that the kingdom of God has come with power'. This or something like it was, reasonably enough, understood by somebody to mean that not all of Jesus' disciples would die before the consummation.

We do not know whether John 21 is designed to dispel doubt within the church or to confute criticism from without or both; but that some non-Christians at a later date imputed eschatological error to Jesus is not in doubt. In his attack on Christianity, the Neoplatonist Porphyry (233–301) not only ridiculed Paul for misreading the eschatological clock; he also made Jesus guilty of the same misperception. According to Matthew 24, the gospel will be preached throughout all the creation, and then the end

---

3. Matthew Poole, *Synopsis criticorum aliorumque S. Scripturae interpretum* (4 vols. in 5; London: Cornelius Bee, 1667–76); ET: *A Commentary on the Holy Bible* (London: Henry G. Bohn, 1846), 3.572 (on 1 Cor. 10.11). Poole exempts Jesus himself from this error; see pp. 45 (on Mt. 10.23) and 166 (on Mk. 9.1).

will come. Porphyry observed that the gospel had indeed been preached throughout all the creation, and that the end had nonetheless not come. QED: Jesus was wrong.[4]

The attempt to gut Christianity by finding false forecasts in the gospels appears centuries later with the Deists of the seventeenth and eighteenth centuries. H.S. Reimarus is the most famous of them, but he has been, because of Schweitzer's history, given far too much credit: much of Reimarus' reconstruction of Jesus just expands the work of his English predecessors. So let me refer here to one of them, Matthew Tindal. Tindal came to destroy not just the law and the prophets but also the NT; and one of his weapons was the argument that Jesus and his apostles were mistaken insofar as they expected the Second Coming not centuries down the road but in the near future.[5] Tindal was a proponent of the religion of reason, which for him meant censuring the religion of revelation. So he criticized the Bible. It was his desire to do away with traditional, dogmatic Christianity that led him to latch onto unfulfilled prophecies. Tindal asked, regarding the tardy *parousia*, if Jesus and his apostles 'were mistaken in a Matter of this Consequence; how can we be absolutely certain, that any one of them may not be mistaken in any other Matter? If they were not inspir'd in what they said...concerning the...coming of Christ; how could they be inspir'd in [other] Arguments...? And if they taught (that) their Times were the last, no Direction they gave, cou'd be intended to reach further than their own Times'.[6]

If one can, like Porphyry and Tindal, sponsor a strongly eschatological Jesus for polemical reasons, it is equally possible to defend such a Jesus for apologetic ends. Consider the case of Joachim Jeremias, one of the more important questers in the era after Schweitzer. We may fairly offer three generalizations about him. First, Jeremias was conservative with regard to the reliability of the synoptics. He indeed held that 'in the synoptic tradition it is the inauthenticity, and not the authenticity, of the sayings of Jesus that must be demonstrated'.[7]

The second relevant fact about Jeremias is that his own species of

---

4. For the Greek text see Macarius Magnes, *Apoc.* 4.3 ed. Blondel, p. 161. R. Joseph Hoffmann, *Porphyry's Against the Christians: The Literary Remains* (Amherst, NY: Prometheus Books, 1994), p. 71, offers this translation: 'It is as servile a piece of work as ever came from a drudge in a factory: "The Gospel of the kingdom shall be preached in all the world, and then the end will come". Consider that every corner of the world has heard of the gospel; that everyone – everywhere – has the finished product – but that the end has not come and will never come. This saying should be whispered, not said aloud.'

5. Matthew Tindal, *Christianity as Old as the Creation: Or, the Gospel a Republication of the Religion of Nature* (London: n.p., 2nd edn, 1732), 233–36.

6. Tindal, *Christianity*, 236.

7. Joachim Jeremias, *New Testament Theology: The Proclamation of Jesus* (New York: Charles Scribner's Sons, 1971), 37.

Christian theology required a conservative historiography. Here are his words on the place of the historical Jesus in theology: 'We must continually return to the historical Jesus and his message. The... incarnation implies that the story of Jesus is not only a possible subject for historical research, study, and criticism, but demands...these. We need to know who the Jesus of history was...'[8]

My third point about Jeremias is that his Jesus is a direct descendant of Albert Schweitzer's Jesus. According to Jeremias, Jesus announced the messianic woes, the resurrection of the dead, the last judgment, the punishment of the devil and his angels, and the renewal of the world.[9]

Now how is Jeremias' apocalyptic Jesus related to a faith that the synoptic tradition needs to be, as his theology demands and as his historical studies seek to show, relatively reliable? If one wants to regard the canonical gospels as generally accurate icons of Jesus, if in fact one's theology depends upon them being so, then a Jesus engaged with eschatology is a foregone conclusion. One may put it this way: If Mark's Jesus utters the so-called little apocalypse in chapter 13, with its detailed eschatological scenario; and if Luke's Jesus strings together sayings about the days of Noah and the days of Lot and how they typify the coming catastrophe (17.20–37); and if Matthew's Jesus promises that the disciples will not finish going through the towns of Israel before the Son of man comes and otherwise preoccupies himself with such things as eschatological rewards and punishments – then surely, if the synoptics are the good guides that Jeremias desires them to be, Jesus must have had much to say about eschatological judgment and recompense, thought to be imminent. To deny this would be, on a conservative evaluation of the synoptics, to enlarge intolerably the distance between Jesus and his witnesses. In short, because the synoptics have more than a few sayings with what one may fairly call an apocalyptic orientation, those with a personal theology entailing great faith in the synoptics will find such an orientation in Jesus himself.

I come next to a third theological concern that has sometimes encouraged making peace with an apocalyptic Jesus. It is this: such a Jesus can be a good weapon with which to bludgeon opponents for their defective theology. In illustration of this, let me go back a hundred years, to F.C. Burkitt, Professor at Trinity College, whose failure to be cited much anymore is no reflection of his one-time importance, which was considerable. Burkitt dismissed the so-called liberalism of his day. He reckoned it 'a religion not of science but of sentiment. It wanted to find itself in a free world governed by a kind personal God, who would

---

8. Joachim Jeremias, 'The Search for the Historical Jesus', in *Jesus and the Message of the New Testament* (ed. K.C. Hanson; Minneapolis: Fortress, 2002), 1–17, at p. 8.
9. Jeremias, *New Testament Theology*, 241–49.

distribute a happy personal immortality to everyone.'[10] Such religion was a useless 'compromise between traditional Christianity and present-day philosophy, formed by taking some things out of Christianity and some things out of our modern world'.[11] Burkitt's problem with liberalism was not its modern methods but rather his belief that, whatever Christianity should be, it should be something other than one more manifestation of the *Zeitgeist*. What good is the church if its central teachings are available in the contemporary culture at large? Burkitt could not abide the deistically inspired, common liberal portrait of a Jesus who, as an example of unsurpassed goodness and pure morality, as a purveyor of the perfect scheme of ethical truth, simply confirmed what good people might otherwise believe without benefit of the gospel.

What did Burkitt offer in place of the liberal synthesis and its (to his mind) tepid Jesus? He enthusiastically championed the enthusiastic prophet of Weiss and Schweitzer. Despite that figure's mistakes about eschatological particulars, Burkitt argued that we can never do without hope in the divine utopia. It is the foundation of the gospel, the most important thing in the world, and as 'long as we believe in our hearts that our property, our arts, our institutions, our buildings, our trust-deeds, are the most permanent things in this world, so long we are not in sympathy with the Gospel message'.[12] Given this view of things, one understands Burkitt's sympathy for Schweitzer's sort of otherworldly Jesus, who has no hope in or theory of human progress. An apocalyptic Jesus is irreducibly religious; he dwells in and speaks from and to an imaginative world that can never be assailed by economics, politics or culture.

One also understands why some with more orthodox opinions also early on lauded Schweitzer, whose Jesus had such an exalted self-conception, so much so that he imagined himself able to turn the wheel of history. Herbert Relton thought that 'the Eschatological movement under the leadership of...Weiss and Schweitzer threatens to make it impossible hereafter for Liberal criticism to come to rest in a purely humanitarian view of the Person of Christ. The Eschatologists are seeking to do full justice to the self-witness of Christ and the transcendental character of His claims'.[13] In other words, Schweitzer's eschatological Jesus not only leaves the liberals bereft of their liberal Jesus but also simultaneously shows us that Jesus imagined himself to be somebody. I suppose this is partly why

10. F.C. Burkitt, *'The Failure of Liberal Christianity' and 'Some Thoughts on the Athanasian Creed'* (Cambridge: Bowes and Bowes, 1910), 12.

11. Burkitt, *Failure*, 20.

12. F.C. Burkitt, 'The Eschatological Idea in the Gospel', in *Essays on Some Biblical Questions of the Day by Members of the University of Cambridge* (London: Macmillan and Co., 1909), 193–213, at pp. 210–11.

13. Herbert M. Relton, *A Study in Christology: The Problem of the Relation of the Two Natures in the Person of Christ* (London: SPCK, 1917), 236–37.

most conservatives prefer Ed Sanders' Jesus, who takes himself to be the king of Israel, over the Jesus of the Jesus Seminar, who doesn't take himself to be the king of Israel.

Let me add a footnote to Burkitt. It will serve as a reminder that theological motives always lie beside other motives. To say that Burkitt found Schweitzer's work a means by which to criticize liberal theology is not to say that no other impulse animated him. We do well to remember that Schweitzer's Jesus showed up at a time when there was a growing knowledge of and interest in Jewish apocalyptic literature; and Burkitt, who wrote a book entitled *Jewish and Christian Apocalypses*,[14] shared such interest. With this in mind, consider the following words of C.W. Emmet, penned in 1911:

> It may turn out that the charge of modernizing, and of false modernizing, will lie at the door of those who ascribe to... [Jesus] their own absorbing interest in the recently studied apocalyptic literature, rather than of those who hold that He came to reveal the Fatherhood of God, and the joy of communion with Him. The study of the Jewish Apocalypses is the... [latest cry] and the New Testament student is just now steeped in eschatology. There is a danger in our taking our own enthusiasm and transferring it bodily to Jesus. We assume that He was nourished on apocalyptic literature as His Bible, and breathed daily an atmosphere impregnated by the ideas of the Book of Enoch. Is it not possible that a future generation will reproach the eschatologist himself with creating a Christ after his own likeness?[15]

Someone might write a similar paragraph today about our current enthusiasm for the *Gospel of Thomas*.

I should like to add one more reason why an apocalyptic Jesus has had theological appeal for some. Once one gets around the scandal of a missed date, and indeed lives with it for a while, one can get used to it. Meanwhile, it may occur that it is the end of a story that determines the meaning of what has gone before, and if that is so, then maybe associating Jesus with eschatology is a natural way of stressing his finality and meaning. Perhaps the most explicit transformation of apocalyptic into a claim for ultimacy occurs in the theology of Wolfhart Pannenberg, who once wrote: 'Only at the end of all events can God be revealed in his divinity, that is, as the one who...has power over everything. Only

14. F.C. Burkitt, *Jewish and Christian Apocalypses* (London: H. Milford, 1914). On pp. 14–15 we find this: 'What is wanted...in studying the Apocalypses is, above all, sympathy with the ideas that underlie them, and especially with the belief in the New Age. And those who believe that in Christianity a near Era really did dawn for us ought, I think, to have that sympathy.'

15. C.W. Emmet, *The Eschatological Question in the Gospels: And Other Studies in Recent New Testament Criticism* (Edinburgh: T. & T. Clark, 1911), 34.

because in Jesus' resurrection the end of all things, which for us has not yet happened, has already occurred can it be said of Jesus that the ultimate already is present in him, and so also that God himself, his glory, has made its appearance in Jesus in a way that cannot be surpassed.'[16] As Pannenberg amply proves, this sort of theology welcomes an apocalyptic Jesus with open arms.

Con

Let me now turn to the other side of things. If some have had theological reasons for hoping that Weiss and Schweitzer were going down the right road, others have had theological reasons for hoping that they went badly astray. Obviously there can be strong prejudices here. A miscalculating Jesus causes us Christians to stumble. He is downright damnable to many. Hastings Rashdall wrote, in 1914, 'I do not see how the Christ of Schweitzer... can be "the Way, the Truth and the Life" to anybody.'[17] C.W. Emmet similarly thought it improbable that 'a Jesus dominated by an error and living for an illusion can ever retain the reverence of the world'; the 'Jesus of eschatology it is difficult either to admire or to love; worship Him we certainly cannot'.[18] W.R. Inge summed up Schweitzer's work in one word, 'blasphemous'.[19] Closer to our own time, the evangelical George Eldon Ladd shook the dust of Schweitzer from his feet with these words: 'To imagine that one sees on the horizon the rosy blush of the breaking dawn and in its faint light sets out upon a journey only to wander in the darkness of midnight is utter deception... If Schweitzer was correct in his analysis of Jesus' message, he was right in the conclusion that the historical Jesus was the victim of a *gross* error...'[20]

I remember my own teacher, the late W.D. Davies, expressing a similar concern. He was anxious that I not end up with a Jesus who had an overabundance of eschatological expectations and who kept a calendar. He did not much like the figure who walks through my book, *Jesus of Nazareth: Millenarian Prophet*, a book which makes me Schweitzer's ally. It was Davies' least favorite of my publications. Although never so blunt, he must have felt the same way as Markus Bockmuehl, who in a review of

---

16.   Wolfhart Pannenberg, *Jesus – God and Man* (Philadelphia: Westminster, 1968), 69.

17.   Hastings Rashdall, 'The Creeds', *The Modern Churchman* 4 (1914): 204–14, at p. 211.

18.   Emmet, *Eschatological Question*, 72, 77.

19.   W.R. Inge, review of W. Sanday, *Christologies Ancient and Modern*, *JTS* 11 (1910): 584–86, at p. 586. He went on to comment: 'It has now appeared in English, not, as might have been expected, under the auspices of the Rationalist Press Association, but with commendations from Divinity Professors of both our great Universities.'

20.   George Eldon Ladd, *The Presence of the Future: The Eschatology of Biblical Realism* (Grand Rapids, MI: Eerdmans, 1974), 125–26.

my work wrote that Allison's 'Jesus remains in the end a poor idealistic blighter whose misguided religious zeal got the better of him'.[21]

It is not just people one might label conservative who continue to find a Schweitzerian Jesus problematic. John Dominic Crossan, although he has been more than cordial about our disagreements, is also unhappy with my sort of Jesus. His reasons are candidly theological as well as historical. He has, for example, asserted that I could never claim that God vindicated Jesus: 'Having said that Jesus and all other millenarian prophets were wrong (so far), you could hardly claim that God raised Jesus from the dead to prove he alone was transcendentally wrong.'[22] Crossan is asserting that if Jesus really was off target about the consummation, it will be tough to do much with him theologically.[23]

If miscalculation of the date of the end has often been an obstacle to accepting a strongly eschatological Jesus, there is also the fact that a Schweitzerian Jesus is typically linked with any number of ideas that many find theologically uncongenial or embarrassing. One might worry that, in some respects, such a Jesus shares company with modern fundamentalists, such as the readers of the 'Left Behind' series, whose fancies are captive to a never-to-be-realized apocalyptic scenario. Or one might fret that such a Jesus focused on judgment and really believed in hell, ideas that are not very much in vogue in our pluralistic, relativistic world. Or one might be anxious that a Jesus with too much eschatology had an exalted self-conception, that he indeed imagined himself to be an apocalyptic figure, maybe even, as the synoptics have it, the central figure in the apocalyptic drama. John Knox thought that such a possibility involved 'serious psychological difficulties. Could so sane a person [as Jesus] have entertained such thoughts about himself?'[24] David Friedrich Strauss posed the riddle of self-exaltation this way: If Jesus sincerely foretold his own second coming on the clouds of heaven, then 'he is for us nothing but a fanatic; if, without any conviction on his part he said it of himself, he was a braggart and an imposter'.[25] Hermann Werner put the apocalyptic Jesus in the company of those locked up in 'institutions of the insane'.[26]

21. Markus Bockmuehl, review of Dale C. Allison, *Jesus of Nazareth, JTS* 51 (2000): 637–41, at p. 640.

22. John Dominic Crossan, in *The Apocalyptic Jesus: A Debate* (ed. Robert J. Miller; Santa Rosa, CA: Polebridge, 2001), 55.

23. Cf. Robert J. Miller, 'Is the Apocalyptic Jesus History?', in *The Once and Future Faith* (ed. Karen Armstrong *et al.*; Santa Rosa, CA: Polebridge, 2001), 101–16.

24. John Knox, *The Death of Christ: The Cross in New Testament History and Faith* (New York and Nashville: Abingdon, 1958), 58.

25. David Friedrich Strauss, *A New Life of Jesus* (London: Williams and Norgate, 1865), 322.

26. Hermann Werner, *Die psychische Gesundheit Jesu* (Berlin: Edwin Runge, 1909), 44.

Yet another theological gripe against an apocalyptic Jesus is the perception of his implicit violence. Certainly there is a lot of carnage in the old Christian and Jewish apocalypses, in which the good typically comes only after all hell breaks loose. In Revelation the blood comes up to the bridles of the horses. Crossan has been passionate in his concern that an apocalyptic Jesus may implicitly condone violence. How do you make the world right without violently attacking wrongs? How do you exalt the debased without violently debasing the exalted?

I shall mention one more factor that has made an apocalyptic Jesus an unwelcome guest in many books and articles. Schweitzer offended a host of Christians when he claimed that Jesus had an 'interim ethic', that his moral teaching was inextricably bound up with his belief in a near end. It might be natural to disregard families and money if they are soon to dissipate in the eschaton. But if Jesus promulgated an ethic for the interim, if he did not leave behind a set of general precepts or principles designed for every time and place, what good is his counsel? Not much in the minds of many. Can any moralist, firmly persuaded of history's imminent dissolution, frame an ethical code adequate for those of us who continue to live in history? Presumption of a negative response explains the vehement resistance to Schweitzer's claims about an interim ethic. According to one early critic, Francis Greenwood Peabody, if Schweitzer were right, 'the ethics of the Gospels would give us a teaching, not designed for this world, but preparatory for another…appropriate for those who looked for some great catastrophe, but not to be taken seriously by those who have waked from the apocalyptic dream. The best way of conduct on the approach of an earthquake is not the best rule of conducting a stable world'.[27]

Against Unduly Simplifying

Having outlined some of the theological reasons why some have wanted to embrace an apocalyptic Jesus while others, instead, have longed to push him away, I now wish to issue several caveats. All four of them warn us against making simplistic estimates of people's motives.

My first caveat is that human beings are complex, and sometimes they are conflicted within themselves. Recall Jeremias. Despite the theological grounding of his eschatological Jesus, that Jesus troubled him, as he candidly admitted. Jeremias believed Jesus to be the incarnate Son of

---

27. Francis Greenwood Peabody, 'New Testament Eschatology and New Testament Ethics', in *Transactions of the Third International Congress for the History of Religions* (ed. Percy Stafford Allen and John de Monins Johnson; Oxford: Clarendon, 1908), II, 305–12, at p. 308.

God. This christological dogma entailed a dilemma. How could God incarnate be mistaken in his eschatological expectations? In struggling with this quandary, Jeremias made several apologetical moves. I need not scrutinize them here.[28] Pertinent only is the observation that Jeremias would surely, all else being equal, have been happier with a Jesus who committed no error. So Jeremias had to choose between the lesser of two evils, between a mistaken Jesus and a mistaken synoptic tradition, between assigning unrealized hopes to his Lord or plucking out verses and throwing them away. Why he preferred the former course of action to the latter, in contrast to others who have preferred the latter to the former, I cannot say. We can imagine someone with conservative theological leanings going either way on this issue, just as we can envisage someone else with a more liberal bent opting for either alternative. My point, however, is that Jeremias was not wholly comfortable with his own reconstruction. If his eschatological Jesus harmonized nicely with some aspects of his theology, it also created cognitive dissonance. We cannot, then, simply claim that he produced a Jesus in his own theological image, after his likeness. And it is the same with others. Speaking for myself, I am no millenarian prophet; and a Jesus without eschatological error would certainly make my life easier. I might, for instance, be able to tell my in-laws what I really do for a living; and my pious divinity students would complain less to the Dean about their heretical teacher.

My second caveat is that, if motives are sometimes disharmonious, other times they are just not apparent. Although he has written two important books on Jesus, I am uncertain, for example, what makes Ed Sanders tick.[29] He has been discreetly silent about his personal theology, if he has any at all. So I do not know whether, apart from professional honor, he has much at stake in what he has written about the historical Jesus. Sometimes we keep our theological cards close to the vest. And sometimes there may not be any theological cards at all.

I even find it hard to pin down the motives of the great Schweitzer himself, despite all the biographical information we have about him. We can of course speculate. He once wrote: 'I live my life in God, in the mysterious divine personality which I do not know as such in the world,

28. See Joachim Jeremias, 'Die Naherwartung des Endes in den Worten Jesu', in *Kerygma und Mythos, VI-6: Aspekte der Unfehlbarkeit: kritische Untersuchungen und Interpretationen* (TF, 56; ed. Franz Theunis; Hamburg: Herbert Reich, 1975), 139–45.

29. E.P. Sanders, *Jesus and Judaism* (Philadelphia: Fortress; London: SCM, 1985); *The Historical Figure of Jesus* (Harmondsworth, Middlesex: Penguin, 1993). On p. 2 of the former he writes: 'I am interested in the debate about the significance of the historical Jesus for theology in the way one is interested in something that he once found fascinating. The present work is written without that question in mind, however....'

but only experience as mysterious Will within myself.'[30] Someone who does not find God at large in the world might well be attracted to an other-worldly Jesus.

I nonetheless remain unclear as to what extent a theological agenda suggested to Schweitzer his sort of Jesus. One suspects that his otherworldly ideology was partly a product of his otherworldly Jesus. Schweitzer claimed that Jesus' 'significance for us is that He fights against the spirit of the modern world, forcing it to abandon the low level on which it moves even in its best thoughts and to rise to the height when we judge things according to the superior will of God, which is active in us, and think no more in terms of human utilitarianism but solely in terms of having to do God's will – becoming forces of God's ethical personality'.[31] My bet is that this evaluation of things was not firmly in place before Schweitzer's historical Jesus showed up but instead came later; it was the interpretation of an apparent discovery, not the motivating impulse behind that discovery. But whether this is so or not, motives can remain obscure.

I come now to my third caveat, which I should like to underline: motives need not be ideological. Some people can take this or that position on an issue not because they care about the issue but because they enjoy playing Devil's advocate. Furthermore, people often do things – maybe most things they do – simply out of habit. This matters so much for our purposes because we may justly suspect that many or even most NT scholars hold the view of Jesus that they do because it was instilled in them at a young age by their education; and once they came to see things a certain way, they found it difficult to change their minds. Intellectual inertia can be obstinate. Are there any important historians of Jesus whose views in their fifties or sixties were radically different from their views in their twenties or thirties?

Imagine with me a young graduate student in a department of religion. She becomes convinced that Schweitzer was close to the truth – or, as the case may be, not close to the truth – because a revered professor, whose arguments she has not yet the means to rebut, persuades her of this. Once her paradigm about Jesus is in place, a cognitive bias will also be in place. We all see what we expect to see and want to see – like highly prejudicial football fans, who always spot more infractions committed by the team they are jeering against than by the team they are cheering for. A

30. Albert Schweitzer, *Civilization and Ethics*. Vol. II. *The Philosophy of Civilization* (London: Adam & Charles Black, 1923), xviii. These words of self-description are close to what he says of Jesus himself in *Christianity and the Religions of the World* (New York: George H. Doran, 1923), 32: for Jesus, God 'is a dynamic Power for good, a mysterious Will, distinct from the world and superior to the world'.

31. Schweitzer, *Christianity and the Religions of the World*, 35.

professor of paleontology once praised a student with these words: 'She has no preconceptions, so her observational skills are excellent'. If we hold a belief, we will notice confirming evidence, especially if we are aware that not everyone agrees with us. Disconfirming evidence, to the contrary, makes us uncomfortable, and so we are more likely to miss, neglect or critically evaluate it. After a period of time, then, one might anticipate that our graduate student will have collected her own evidence for her professor's belief and become all the more persuaded of its correctness. As soon, moreover, as she communicates her views in public fashion, say by tutoring undergraduates or publishing a paper, she may be set for life. The prospect of embarrassment from publicly admitting error can make it hard to admit error to oneself, to undertake the difficult cognitive task of rearranging data into a new pattern after one has long been looking at an old pattern. If, in the near future, someone truly demonstrates that my sort of Jesus cannot be the historical Jesus, others would no doubt be quicker than me to see the truth. I would have to reconfigure my entire reconstruction of early Christianity, a task requiring courage and prolonged intellectual effort. Maybe I wouldn't be up to it.

I have a fourth and final caveat, and it is the most important. People, like cats, can be genuinely curious, and surely the desire to find the truth of some things of interest really does partly animate some of us. I think that, if we could call up Albert Schweitzer's ghost as Saul called up Samuel, and if we were to quiz this shade about his reconstruction of Jesus, he would assuredly assert that he thought he had, in all honesty, found the truth: his Jesus was above all a solution to many important historical riddles.

Since E.P. Sanders and John Dominic Crossan are not dead, we could also call them up – on the phone; and if we were to ask them the same question, I am confident that they too would express their conviction that they have come close to the historical truth. Now as Sanders and Crossan have fundamental disagreements, at least one of them must be fundamentally wrong. But being wrong does not mean one has not been looking for the truth, which after all may be difficult to find. The corridors of history are dark.

If one wants to call the appetite for truth just another ideology, so be it. But no one should pretend that people cannot be interested in what really happened, or that they cannot learn new things, or that they cannot change their minds about deeply held theological convictions. Jesus of Nazareth was or was not influenced by Cynic philosophy; he did or did not think the consummation at hand; he did or did not think of himself as Israel's eschatological king. It is the business of the conscientious historian addressing these questions to answer them, when that is possible, honestly, whatever the theological payoff, if any, may be. Doing history means being open to the uncongenial as well as the congenial, the painful as well as the edifying, the useless as well as the useful.

In this connection I think of Johannes Weiss, who was able to keep the historical and theological questions distinct in his own mind. In the preface to the second edition of his book on the proclamation of Jesus (1900), where he claims that his work was accompanied by 'distressing personal conflict', he declares that Albrecht Ritschl's understanding of the kingdom of God cannot be identified with Jesus' understanding of the kingdom. Yet Weiss goes on to endorse Ritschl: his interpretation is 'the most suitable to awaken and sustain for our generation the sound and nourishing religious life that we need'.[32] Here Weiss indicates that his view is not Jesus' view. I admire this confession of distance from Jesus. The honesty remains refreshing to this day, when many still assume that if you contend that Jesus believed something, then you must believe it too. Everything we know about Weiss indicates that he discovered his Jesus while he was conscientiously working as an historian. Some may think that he misconstrued the evidence; but I cannot see that what he took to be a discovery appeared from anything other than a desire to recover the past.

I should like to end this excursus of caveats by dissociating myself from any investigation of theology or ideology that deteriorates into *ad hominem* attack. We can conjecture interminably about what motivated this scholar or that writer. We can ponder the *Zeitgeist* in which Schweitzer lived and moved and had his being, or wonder about the connection between Crossan's peasant Jesus in the midst of an oppressive Roman colonialism and Crossan's own Irish past. In the end, however, Crossan and Schweitzer and the rest have, in their works on Jesus, ostensibly written not about themselves but about him, and they move toward their conclusions by means of arguments, which stand or fall independently of the theology or ideology that may have helped nurture them. We show our historians disrespect if we do not respond in kind, that is, if we imagine our chief task to be the investigation of authors rather than their arguments.

---

32. Johannes Weiss, *Die Predigt Jesu vom Reiche Gottes* (Göttingen: Vandenhoeck & Ruprecht, 2nd rev. edn, 1900), v.

THEOLOGICAL STAKES IN THE APOCALYPTIC JESUS DEBATE[1]

Robert J. Miller

The debate over whether the historical Jesus was an apocalyptic prophet is central to contemporary Jesus research. The answer one gives to this question, and how one goes about answering it, shapes the way one understands much of the gospel evidence. I believe that this particular question is the single most important one about the historical Jesus, for it goes directly to the character of his message and mission. Let me disclose that I am a participant in this debate, not a neutral observer of it. I maintain that Jesus was a non-apocalyptic sage.

My task here is to reflect on what is at stake in this debate. While my purpose is not directly to argue for a non-apocalyptic Jesus, I am sure that my rhetoric leans in that direction. Still, my intention here is to analyze the debate and to press a few key issues in the hope of sparking productive discussion.

Theological Investments in the Apocalyptic Jesus

Albert Schweitzer's milestone work, *The Quest of the Historical Jesus*,[2] put twentieth-century scholarship on notice about allowing theological preferences to set the agenda for constructions of the historical Jesus. Heeding Schweitzer's lesson has sensitized us to the various ways our social, religious and political location can influence our reading of the historical evidence. Among biblical scholars this helped to clinch the argument that pure objectivity in the study of history is a mythic ideal. The greatest benefit of Schweitzer's analysis has been the inculcation of a healthy circumspection about and steady refinement of historical method.

---

1. This paper is a slightly revised version of 'Is the Apocalyptic Jesus History?', in The Jesus Seminar, *The Once and Future Faith* (Santa Rosa, CA: Polebridge, 2001), 101–16. Used with permission.

2. Albert Schweitzer, *Von Reimarus zu Wrede. Eine Geschichte der Leben Jesu Forschung* (Tübingen: J.C.B. Mohr [Paul Siebeck], 1906); ET: *The Quest of the Historical Jesus: A Critical Study of Its Progress from Reimarus to Wrede*, preface by F.C. Burkitt (New York: Macmillan & Co., 1910).

Its most baneful effect is that it has armed scholars with a rhetorical weapon of mass destruction. To accuse an opponent of coming up with a Jesus after his or her own image is singularly satisfying. Not only does it let you discredit your opponent's position without having to engage any of his or her arguments; it is also impossible to refute.

From this vantage point let me offer an observation on how this plays out in the debate over whether Jesus was an apocalyptic prophet.

Schweitzer read Jesus against the background of a thoroughly apocalyptic first-century Judaism. In Schweitzer's mind, Jesus' apocalypticism 'on the one hand, underscored the *commonalities* between Jesus and his environment, and the profound *distance* between Jesus and early twentieth-century Christian theology, on the other'.[3] However, by the mid twentieth-century, this picture was changing dramatically.[4] The European optimism of the late nineteenth and very early twentieth century gave way to foreboding and then to profound disillusionment in the wake of two World Wars, the Holocaust, the Cold War, and the nuclear threat. In this cultural environment the apocalyptic Jesus no longer seemed such a stranger.

More than anyone else, it was Bultmann who made the apocalyptic Jesus safe for liberal Protestantism. In his treatment of the gospels and their traditions, the adjective 'eschatological' served to *distinguish* Jesus from his environment. 'For Bultmann ... the term "eschatological" stands for the novelty of Christianity, its incomparable superiority, the uniqueness of its victorious religion.'[5] A paradigm case of this appropriation of eschatology is *The Charismatic Leader and His Followers* by Martin Hengel,[6] which 'uses the category of "eschatological charismatic" in order to render Jesus incommensurable and unique within Judaism and the Hellenistic world'.[7] Theologians such as Moltmann and Pannenberg found convergence between their reading of Jesus' eschatology and the heart of Christian theology. In this intellectual matrix, eschatology became a cipher for uniqueness and ultimacy.[8] This reversed the polarity that Schweitzer had emphasized: the eschatological Jesus was now set over

3.   John S. Kloppenborg, *Excavating Q* (Minneapolis: Fortress; Edinburgh: T. & T. Clark, 2000), 438, emphasis original.

4.   Stephen J. Patterson, *The God of Jesus* (Harrisburg, PA: Trinity Press International, 1998), 164–69.

5.   Dieter Georgi, 'Rudolf Bultmann's *Theology of the New Testament* Revisited', in *Bultmann, Retrospect and Prospect* (ed. Edward Hobbs; Philadelphia: Fortress, 1985), 82; quoted in Kloppenborg, *Excavating Q*, 438, n. 52.

6.   Martin Hengel, *The Charismatic Leader and His Followers* (Edinburgh: T. & T. Clark; New York: Crossroad, 1981).

7.   Kloppenborg, *Excavating Q*, 438.

8.   Kloppenborg, *Excavating Q*, 439.

against his ancient contemporaries, but was congenial to modern Christianity.

From the perspective of this analysis we can notice some high irony in the proclivity of defenders of the apocalyptic Jesus to cudgel their opponents (all of whom, by the way, seem to be present or past members of the Jesus Seminar) with the Schweitzer stick. These critics readily accuse people like me of refashioning Jesus to conform to our élite academic sensibilities. The irony here is that some of those critics brandish the apocalypticism of Jesus as if it were their certificate of immunization against the nearly irresistible tendency to modernize him. They are either unaware or unconcerned with how easily the eschatological Jesus can accommodate contemporary christological interests.

A second irony takes us into more ominous territory. Advocates of a non-apocalyptic Jesus are sometimes charged with reconstructing a 'non-Jewish' Jesus, as if first-century Judaism were a substance and apocalypticism an essential element of it. This charge is a cheap caricature: for while it may be powerful rhetorically, it is intellectually vacuous. I bring up this 'non-Jewish' charge because of the usually implicit, and sometimes explicit, accusation of anti-Semitism that seems to lurk below its surface. What interests me here is the anxious self-consciousness with which this charge seems to be made.[9] Since the Holocaust, Christian intellectuals have been sensitized to the insidious ways in which anti-Semitism can infect their work. It is as if some believe that an insistence on Jesus' apocalypticism so completely certifies his Jewishness that it repels any lingering whiff of the stench of anti-Semitism. The irony here is that the 'eschatological' Jesus has been co-opted as code for the 'unique' Jesus, a uniqueness invariably understood as superiority. The eschatological Jesus is thus implicated in supersessionism, which is fraught with anti-Jewish overtones. By contrast, a non-apocalyptic Jesus cannot easily be folded into claims for or assumptions about the unique superiority of Christianity.

The Apocalyptic Jesus Was Wrong, But So What?

If the historical Jesus predicted the imminent End,[10] then, obviously, he was wrong. For liberal Protestants in the trail of Bultmann, that doesn't matter theologically. And Catholic scholars seem not to care, probably because Catholic theology doesn't need an infallible Jesus. The problem is acute, however, for evangelical scholars because they need to defend both a strong sense of the historicity of the gospels and the supernatural status

9. Karen King, 'Back to the Future', in The Jesus Seminar, *The Once and Future Jesus* (Santa Rosa, CA: Polebridge, 2000), 77–107, at pp. 89–90.
10. Most explicitly in Mk. 1.15, 9.1, 13.30 and Mt. 10.23, but elsewhere as well.

of Jesus. This puts them in the unenviable position of upholding Jesus' theological inerrancy *and* his apocalyptic predictions. Since this position is clearly untenable, it should not surprise us that most evangelical scholars take the prudent course of ducking the question.[11]

Evangelical demurrals aside, my interest here lies in the theological ramifications of this particular error of the apocalyptic Jesus. Since that Jesus made concrete predictions, his message and mission were, at least to some extent, falsified by subsequent events. What does this error mean about the truth of the rest of his teaching? His conviction that the End was imminent is not just one item among others. It is foundational. How much of his message and mission stands or falls with its apocalyptic foundation?

To frame the question this way entails that if Jesus was an apocalyptic prophet, the Christian theological project has to be a salvage job. If theology is to have any meaningful connection to the apocalyptic Jesus, the theological task must start by assessing the wreckage of his message and mission and deciding how much is usable, how much can be repaired, and how much is lost for good.[12]

Let me offer two examples to show how judgments about the viability of Jesus' message can be affected by the decision about whether he was an apocalyptic prophet.

11.   For example, Charles Holman, in a brief excursus on the 'Historical Jesus', attributes Mk. 9.1, 13.30 and Mt. 10.23 to Jesus. He notes that their non-fulfillment was an embarrassment to early Christians, but somehow avoids raising the question of Jesus' error. See Charles Holman, *Till Jesus Comes: Origins of Christian Apocalyptic Expectation* (Peabody, MA: Hendrickson, 1996), 134–137.

The few evangelical scholars who do face the question try to paper over the problem, but the paper is thin. Scot McKnight (*A New Vision for Israel: The Teachings of Jesus in National Context* [Grand Rapids: Eerdmans, 1999], 138) asks 'Was Jesus Mistaken?' and answers 'no': 'Jesus prophesied that God would wrap things up within one generation. However, instead of saying that Jesus was mistaken, that he was either a false prophet or a misguided fanatic, we ought to admit that his knowledge of the future was limited.' Apparently, false predictions do not constitute error: 'he was not wrong'; 'Jesus was not mistaken'.

Ben Witherington takes a different approach. He poses the problem of how Jesus could have both predicted the End as he did in the Coming Son of Man sayings and declared that he did not know 'the day or the hour' of its arrival (Mark 13.32). Since Witherington does not have the option of judging any saying of Jesus in the canonical gospels to be inauthentic, he concludes that 'Jesus did not proclaim that the end was *necessarily* imminent. At most he could only have spoken of its possible imminence' (*The Jesus Quest: The Third Search for the Jew of Nazareth* [Downers Grove, IL: InterVarsity, 1995], 96).

12.   Even if Jesus' perspective was not apocalyptic, Christian theology still involves a critical sifting of his legacy, not because it collided with historical reality, but simply because his world was so different from ours. The issue of the truth of Jesus' teaching shakes down very differently for a non-apocalyptic Jesus. Since the message of this Jesus is not falsifiable historically, the specifically theological dimension of the issue comes into sharper focus. The question is not whether Jesus was right or wrong about the future. It is whether he was right or wrong about God.

Social Deviance

A good bit of Jesus' 'ethics' recommend behaviors and attitudes aberrant to the business-as-usual of his society. Interpreters of New Testament eschatology commonly understand teachings like this to constitute an 'interim ethic', a way of living necessitated by the eschatological crisis and intended only for the short time until the End. A case in point is Paul's advice on sex and marriage in 1 Corinthians 7. If Jesus taught an apocalyptic message, how much of his teaching should be considered an interim ethic?

For example, consider Jesus' extraordinary demands to renounce family ties (Q 14.26), to walk away from home and family (Mk. 10.29–30), and not to bury one's dead parents (Q 9.59–60). Coming from an apocalyptic Jesus, these sayings seem to be meant literally, in the belief that the social structures of the world-as-we-know-it would soon be irrelevant in the new world that God was about to create. Since Jesus was wrong about the future, was he, in hindsight, wrong to subvert these family bonds? On the other hand, coming from a non-apocalyptic Jesus these radical directives seem less literal and more aphoristic. They challenge people to re-examine all their priorities, even the most intimate and sacred, in light of the demands of God's present kingdom.

Beatitudes

When an apocalyptic Jesus congratulates the poor, the hungry, and the sorrowing, he does so out of his conviction that their circumstances would soon be reversed when God imposed his rule on the earth. Since this kingdom did not come as expected, the apocalyptic Jesus was mistaken to congratulate these unfortunates. Worse yet, he may have been unwittingly cruel in giving them false hope.

On the other hand, if Jesus was not an apocalypticist, the beatitudes mean that the poor, the hungry and the sorrowing enjoy God's favor in their present lives, in light of who they are now, not in light of what might happen to them later. Whether it is true or false that such people are divinely favored cannot be settled by empirical events. In a non-apocalyptic framework our decision about the truth of the beatitudes does not involve an assessment of the living conditions of the poor, the hungry and the sorrowing. It is a theological decision in which we ask ourselves how we imagine God.

More examples could be discussed, but surely the most important question is whether Jesus was right about God. The God of apocalypticism is a Deity who intervenes from outside our world to set things right, to do for us what we cannot do for ourselves. He is a Deity able and willing to use coercive power to effect his will, even if, mysteriously, he always seems to hold that power in reserve for future use. When this God finally exercises that power, however, it will be overwhelming, and he will triumph against otherwise invincible earthly and demonic forces.

The apocalyptic Jesus was proven wrong about God's plan for human history. Was the apocalyptic Jesus also wrong about God? And if so, is there any real point to a theological salvage operation?

Apocalypticism and Divine Violence

There is no evidence that Jesus endorsed a military solution to the ungodly injustice of Roman rule, and abundant indirect evidence that he rejected military resistance to it. We may be inclined to think that Jesus took that position because he was a realist, because he realized that Rome would pay any price to hold onto its rule and so it was impossible to defeat Rome and suicidal to try. We tend to view the Zealots as fanatics and want to think that Jesus would have too, had they been around in his lifetime.

Zealotry was not irrational fanaticism. It was rooted in a particular theology, a view of God; specifically, an apocalyptic view. The Zealots knew they could never defeat Rome on their own, but they believed they weren't on their own. God was on their side. When the time came, God would fight alongside them, and no earthly power could defeat God. Josephus tells us that the Zealots held out to the end expecting legions of angels to intervene. The *War Scroll* from Qumran gave detailed battlefield instructions to the sons of light for the Final Conflict. They too believed that God would send supernatural military assistance. They were mistaken. No angels appeared and both the Zealots in Jerusalem and the Essenes at Qumran were slaughtered by the Romans. Because their hopes proved to be delusions, we are tempted to think that the Zealots and the Essenes were irrational. Yet their hopes were entirely reasonable, given their apocalyptic image of God.

I want to explore the hypothesis that *Jesus' rejection of violence was not tactical, but theological.* He ruled out the option of armed resistance, not because of a hard-headed assessment of the military situation, but because he rejected apocalypticism and the image of God it entails. He rejected the belief that God will solve the problem of human evil by killing the evil humans. Jesus rejected the image of a God who accomplishes justice through violence. Let's not underestimate the price tag for this thesis. It means that Jesus rejected the God of the Exodus, the Yahweh whom the Israelites praised as a warrior. This puts Jesus at a critical distance from his tradition.

The cost of this thesis is high, but so are its benefits. It enables us to account for the central irony in Jesus' notion of the kingdom of God: God has a kingdom, but does not act like a king. Despite the centrality of

God's kingdom in Jesus' teaching, God is never represented by a king in the authentic parables and aphorisms.[13] Instead he is a benevolent parent, addressed as father, but acting at times like a mother, not insisting on patriarchal prerogatives nor even showing concern for male honour (see the Prodigal Son). God's kingdom is imagined, not as the majestic cedar of Lebanon that dominates the landscape, but as the scruffy mustard bush that makes the best of wherever it happens to gain a foothold.

The God of Jesus makes no promise to protect his subjects from their enemies. Instead he directs his subjects to love their enemies and bless their tormentors. He sends sun and rain equally on those who obey him and those who defy him. Such a God is an un-king, a pathetic weakling to those who measure the power of gods by their ability to enforce their will, punish their enemies and protect their subjects. To an apocalyptic mind, the God of the authentic parables and aphorisms is not a king at all, for a kingdom that cannot be imposed on the unwilling is a contradiction in terms.

Proposing a Jesus who rejects the God of violence opens the door to the charge that such a Jesus is non-Jewish. As I said before, this is a disingenuous caricature. And yet, if we ignore the cheap polemic, we can see a legitimate concern, though it has nothing to do with anti-Semitism. It has to do with the issue of divine violence. I take it to be beyond dispute that the Yahweh of the Torah and the Prophets is a God of coercive violence. To be sure, that is not the only way Yahweh is imagined in the scriptures, but there is no point arguing that that is not the dominant image of the Deity in those traditions. Throughout the Law and the Prophets Yahweh works his will through armies and his purpose is manifested in the army of the victor, be it Israelite or Gentile.[14]

So we have to face the question of the Jewishness of a Jesus who believes in a non-violent God, a God who is an anti-king. Characterizing this Jesus as non-Jewish is obviously absurd. But there is a real issue behind it: what kind of Jew was Jesus? From which aspects of his Israelite heritage did he draw his inspiration, and from which did he dissent?

---

13. I am in broad agreement with my colleagues in the Jesus Seminar on which of the parables and aphorisms in the gospels can be traced to the historical Jesus. For a list of the sayings judged authentic by the Seminar, see Robert Funk, Roy Hoover and the Jesus Seminar, *The Five Gospels* (New York: Macmillan, 1993), 549–553.

14. In Genesis, Yahweh annihilates 'all flesh' because (ironically) 'the earth is filled with violence' (Gen. 6.13). In Exodus, Yahweh liberates the oppressed by killing the oppressors' babies and destroying their army. In Joshua, Yahweh mandates campaigns of ethnic cleansing. In Joshua through Kings, Yahweh protects and rewards Israel by going to war against its enemies. In the Prophets, Yahweh punishes sinful Israel by going to war against his own people.

Which aspects of the Jewish tradition were non-negotiable in the first century?[15]

The prophet Amos radically relativizes Israel's election and prophesied the end of Israel as a people (Amos 9.7–8a). Jeremiah calls the Davidic Covenant and its temple theology a lie (Jer. 7.1–15), even though that covenant and theology had been vigorously promoted by Isaiah. The book of Ruth asserts the sanctity of mixed marriages, probably in rebuttal to Ezra's condemnation of them. Third Isaiah condemns animal sacrifice *per se* (Isa. 66.3). Job rails against the deuteronomic principle and Qoheleth calmly considers it to be self-evidently false. And so on. The Jewish tradition is peppered with Jews who reject apparently core elements of their theological heritage.

Consider one more reflection on the rhetoric of the 'non-Jewish Jesus' accusation. This accusation carries the unmistakable innuendo of anti-Judaism and is a thinly veiled attempt to seize the moral high ground. But let's ask who honours Judaism more. Is it one who insists that its God is a Deity of coercive violence, whose will is expressed in every military victory, and that only a non-Jew could think otherwise? Or is it one who sees in Jesus' words and deeds a Jewish experiment in imagining a non-violent God? I wonder.

Parables and the (Non-)Apocalyptic Jesus

The decision about whether Jesus was an apocalyptic prophet influences our understanding of his teaching. A number of Jesus' words and deeds can be taken in either an apocalyptic or a non-apocalyptic sense, as in the case of the Beatitudes discussed above. Both readings are legitimate and the differences in meaning come not from the material itself but from the larger context one uses to interpret it. Since the parables are both the most distinctive way in which Jesus expressed himself and unusually open-ended in their meaning, it behooves us to consider how parables fare in the two opposing interpretive frameworks.

I want to focus on two kingdom parables as test cases, The Mustard and The Leaven. In each case we can track the contrasting interpretations of these miniature stories that follow from an understanding of the kingdom as either apocalyptic or non-apocalyptic.

If the kingdom of God is apocalyptic, these parables are read as growth

15. Many scholars, conservative and liberal, believe that Jesus was loose with purity standards, was deliberately lax about sabbath observance, and openly associated with the unclean. No one calls this Jesus non-Jewish. Evangelical scholars argue for a historical Jesus who believed himself to be the unique Son of God, or Wisdom personified, or even Yahweh in person. How Jewish is this Jesus? N.T. Wright maintains that Jesus believed that his Roman crucifixion would be a definitive expiation for Israel's sin. How Jewish is this Jesus?

stories. This is how the Christian tradition has understood them; indeed, the synoptic gospels seem to take them that way. As growth stories, however, The Mustard and The Leaven are rather banal. A tiny seed grows into the largest of garden plants (Mk. 4.30–32) or a tree (Q 13.18–19). A pinch of leaven causes the rising of a large mass of dough. The referents of 'mustard' and 'leaven' are the literal things denoted by those nouns. They have no connotative value and do not function as symbols. Mustard and leaven are used as comparisons for the kingdom only because they start small and end big. Other examples could have served just as well. After all, every plant starts from a seed. The mustard is actually an unpromising example for a lesson about growth. If the object is to contrast inconspicuous origins with impressive results, why single out the lowly mustard bush? Why not a tree: the rugged olive, or the stately palm? Better yet, why not the strong and lofty cedar of Lebanon, a tree that Ezekiel and Daniel use to symbolize world empires? In the Q version of the parable, the mustard grows into a tree, a botanical impossibility. As an illustration of the triumphant final state of the kingdom, the parable undercuts itself because it implies the *futility* of such a hope. Since the Q parable ends up with a tree, why not use a real one? As an illustration of a glorious apocalyptic kingdom, the mustard is an inept choice.

As parables of an apocalyptic kingdom, The Mustard and The Leaven celebrate the contrast of humble beginning and grand finale as a manifestation of divine power. In this respect, the kingdom of God embodies the same values as the kingdom of Rome, which grew from a small town into a worldwide empire. As growth stories these parables reaffirm that God is on the side of the victor, exactly the lesson Rome wanted to teach its subjects.

On the other hand, as parables of a non-apocalyptic kingdom, The Mustard and The Leaven are wickedly clever satires of imperial values and religious respectability. The mustard takes aim at the cedar of Lebanon. The allusion is established by 'the birds of the air nesting in its branches', a nearly verbatim echo of passages in which the cedar is a metaphor for the empires of Egypt, Assyria, Babylon, and the restored Israel (Ezek. 17.23; 31.6; Dan. 4.12). The lowliness and un-awe-inspiring character of the mustard bush, qualities that reduce the effectiveness of the story as an illustration of eschatological growth, are exactly the point in a parable of the non-apocalyptic kingdom: God's domain does not look majestic, stable, secure, enduring, domineering. The mustard thus subverts the standard markers of imperial power. For the imperial cedar, 'all the birds of the air' who 'nest in its branches' (Ezek. 31.6) represent the conquered peoples living under the 'protection' of empires like Assyria. But in a mustard bush in a garden (Lk. 13.19) or a field

(Mt. 13.31), roosting birds are a nuisance, as are the kind of people Jesus elsewhere declares to be citizens of the kingdom of God.

Furthermore, a non-apocalyptic reading of the parable gives full rein to the symbolic value of mustard. This hardy and aggressive bush is well known for its tendency to spread beyond its allotted place and upset the order of a well-managed garden. The Mishnah (*m. Kilayim* 3.2) forbids the cultivation of mustard in a garden, lest it lead to a violation of the law of like kinds (Lev. 19.19). The mustard-kingdom is thus prone to transgress boundaries of religious purity and social respectability. It blooms where it was not planted, bringing along its unwelcome inhabitants.

Leaven symbolizes the profane, the unholy (Exodus 12). Leavening symbolizes the process of corruption. Paul twice quotes a proverb, 'A little leaven leavens the whole batch of dough' (1 Cor. 5.6; Gal. 5.8), both times to warn his congregation that it risks moral infection by tolerating the presence of certain corrupting individuals. The parable of the leaven therefore likens the growth of the kingdom of God to the spread of moral corruption. It associates the sphere of divine influence with the unholy.

If the parable is about an apocalyptic kingdom, leaven can function only as an agent of growth. It cannot have any symbolic resonance because that would undermine the apocalyptic scenario. God's purpose in the apocalyptic intervention is to impose the hegemony of the holy on the present world imagined as hopelessly unholy and corrupt. The apocalyptic reading of this parable thus must sever the image of leaven from its symbolic value in the Jewish world of meaning. (Which Jesus looks non-Jewish now?)

If mustard and leaven are allowed to be symbols that resonate with the Hebrew scriptures, both of these parables subvert apocalyptic assumptions. They can rightly be considered *anti*-apocalyptic.

If this is true for The Mustard and The Leaven, we should investigate other parables for similar qualities. Two more parables come to mind in this regard, and there may well be others like them. (1) If the father of The Prodigal Son is meant to represent God, he is a sorry excuse for an apocalyptic Deity. He gives no special reward for his elder son's perseverant obedience, which is a primary virtue in apocalyptic moral exhortation. The father shamelessly fawns over his younger son, in utter disregard for his male honor,[16] behavior most unbefitting the apocalyptic king of the cosmos to whom all who defy his authority will be forced to submit. (2) The Good Samaritan promotes an attitude toward the enemy that is antithetical to the apocalyptic dualism of the sons of light and the sons of darkness. My point is not only that these two parables insinuate notions incompatible with apocalypticism. My point is stronger: if the

---

16.   Bernard Brandon Scott, *Hear Then the Parable* (Minneapolis: Fortress, 1989), 117.

image of God and the attitude toward the enemy in these parables are allowed to burrow into the symbolic world of the listener, they can seriously subvert the apocalyptic imagination.

I have no grounds for thinking that scholars with an apocalyptic Jesus read these four parables the way I do. Here I am only guessing, but perhaps scholars who have immersed themselves in the symbolism of ancient Judaism can intuit the anti-apocalyptic tendencies in these parables, just as I imagine Jesus' listeners doing. Perhaps these parables are so well crafted that they can have this effect on the imagination of perceptive listeners without their being fully aware of it. Admittedly, this is wishful thinking. I indulge in it here only because it cannot be a coincidence that scholarly reconstructions of the apocalyptic Jesus give such short shrift to the parables. As I flipped through the four apocalyptic Jesus books on the ready-reference shelf above my desk, here's what I saw. The parables are virtually absent in E.P. Sanders' *The Historical Figure of Jesus*.[17] Paula Fredriksen seems to make no use of them at all in her *Jesus of Nazareth*.[18] John Meier's *Marginal Jew* programmatically marginalizes the parables.[19] Dale Allison's *Jesus of Nazareth* seems to relegate parables to the footnotes, where they serve only to document themes Jesus taught more clearly elsewhere. It is up to these scholars to explain why we should largely ignore Jesus' most distinctive and most original contribution to humanity's treasury of religious teaching. For whatever reason, the parables have been unhelpful in making the case for the apocalyptic Jesus.

17. *The Historical Figure of Jesus* (Harmondsworth, Middlesex: Penguin, 1993).
18. *Jesus of Nazareth, King of the Jews* (New York: Alfred Knopf, 2000).
19. 'Some readers may be surprised to see that very few parables are used in the main part of my argument' [that Jesus was an apocalyptic prophet]. *A Marginal Jew*, Volume II: *Mentor, Message, and Miracles* (New York: Doubleday, 1994), 290.

RESPONSES

Dale C. Allison, Jr.

I shall confine myself to three points, each one having to do with a different presenter.

1. If I understand him aright, I find nothing to disagree with in John Kloppenborg's helpful presentation. Those who have argued for a so-called apocalyptic Jesus have not always done so simply against their wills, as sometimes implied. Apocalyptic can be and has been tamed in several different ways, and indeed turned into a positive theological program. And there have been additional boons for some (in Schweitzer's case the promotion of an unconventional, apocalyptic Jesus brought notoriety). An apologetic use of apocalyptic appeared early on with Burkitt and Bultmann, and it remains with us today in Pannenberg and Wright. So one cannot simply claim the historical high ground by observing that one has an apocalyptic Jesus and others do not. There are personal interests and theological agendas all around. Pretending otherwise is cheap argument.

I should like to stress, however, that the ubiquity of theological and personal interests does not entail that we are necessarily wholly captive to them (and I note that John does not say otherwise). Speaking for myself, I did not reconstruct an apocalyptic Jesus because I wanted him for my own theology. On the contrary, I found such a Jesus and continue to find him in many ways troubling and uncongenial, and my life would be easier without him. The details need not be narrated here. All I need say is that somehow I acquired a conscience, which told me that I should be more committed to the truth than to my own orthodoxy. I have always suspected that any Jesus of which I was too fond could not be the real Jesus, and I have worried about the human proclivity to rationalization, which can be a weakness of the strongest minds. So I take some pride in having come to personally painful conclusions.

The point of all this is not to defend my own Jesus – a task autobiography cannot attempt – but simply to urge that while we are always moved, consciously and unconsciously, by our own ideological agendas, human beings also have the magical ability to be self-aware and self-critical and so to transcend, to some extent, those agendas. If there is no such thing as pure objectivity, we all know scholars who seem less objective and more ideologically driven than others. It is precisely this fact that should comfort those of us who seek, despite all the obstacles, endogenous and exogenous, to be conscientious historians.

2. William Arnal's engaging contribution is, as I see it, a contemporary extension of George Tyrrell's famous Schweitzerian remark that Adolf Harnack looked down the well of history and saw his own reflection, not the historical Jesus. Arnal is able to show, in ways most of us have not fully appreciated, how modern scholars from all parts of the theological – and non-theological – spectrum are finding their own agendas to have been the agenda of Jesus.

I am moved only to add a very minor footnote. Arnal is concerned at one point that what he calls 'a new, progressive, and genuinely North American (or Anglophone) brand of New Testament scholarship' may be losing part of its rightful inheritance. 'We are', he says, 'wont to reject [the older German scholarship] as we invent our own.'[1] My tangential observation is that we are not so much consciously rejecting older works as never learning about them in the first place. The problem, which is a serious one, is that we are, understandably, so preoccupied with the present that we have much too little time for the past. So much is now being published that no one can keep up; and given our common conviction, imbibed from the culture and daily reinforced by our technological, computer-filled lives, that what is new is almost always better than what is old, our tendency in the guild is to read new books instead of old ones (especially if the latter are written in a foreign language and so take more of our time to read). Surely it is, we imagine, safer to neglect the past rather than the present.

It is largely because many New Testament scholars are overwhelmed by the need not to neglect the latest contributions that they are ill-acquainted with earlier, foundational works, not to mention earlier works that were of lesser importance but remain instructive. We have here a circumstance arising less from ideology than from pragmatism, less from considered reflection than from priorities dictated by limited time. Which is just to say that, when we are trying to map where the discipline is, ideology is only one part of the picture. Mundane factors, such as the ever-growing number of books the publishing industry places on our desks, also can push us in one direction rather than another.

3. Although the subject of the symposium was ideology rather than the historical Jesus, perhaps it is not out of place to make a comment about Amy-Jill Levine's provocative reconstruction of Jesus. One might think, given that I myself have elsewhere argued for a strongly apocalyptic Jesus and further contended that some of his behaviour moved in an ascetic

---

1. Ed. note: This comment was part of Arnal's oral presentation, but is not in the printed text above.

direction, that we see eye to eye. But it is not clear to me that we do. Levine at one point speaks of Jesus advocating 'a celibate lifestyle for everyone'. The words that give me pause are the last two, 'for everyone'.

In the gospels as we have them, Jesus addresses an inner circle as well as a wider public, and he sometimes asks of the former things he does not ask of the latter. This is the case, for example, in the various missionary discourses in the Synoptics. The detailed instructions in these closely related texts are not indiscriminately directed at a broad Galilean audience, peasant or otherwise. They rather presuppose, and the evangelists themselves highlight, a distinction between missionaries, whom Jesus is instructing, and their potential audiences, whom he is not instructing. The orders to go without purse and knapsack and sandals and staff and to exorcize are for one group and not for the other. Neither Jesus nor his disciples requires all the missionized to become missionaries. They do not tell everyone to travel from village to village or to proclaim the kingdom or to do without necessities. On the contrary, the messengers accept the hospitality of people who can afford to serve them, the hospitality of individuals who are living at home and have not abandoned their customary lives.

The missionary discourses, which surely reflect some demands that Jesus made, are for me evidence that he sometimes instructed his closest followers in ways that he did not instruct others, and I take this circumstance to be applicable to several parts of the tradition. Even the Reformers, despite being opposed to the medieval distinction between the religious and the non-religious, a distinction which found a dual ethic in the sayings of Jesus, conceded that demands such as Mt. 8.22 = Luke 9.60 (Q: 'Let the dead bury their own dead') and Mark 10.21 ('Sell what you own, and give the money to the poor') were never intended to be general public imperatives. They were instead concrete requirements confined to some who were literally to follow Jesus, individuals who were to participate fully in his missionary ministry. In like manner, I very much doubt that Jesus called everyone away from home and hearth and marriage, or that he issued a general appeal for people to become eunuchs. I do not think that he was that radical.

William Arnal

Why would one wish devote a symposium, or a collection of papers, or indeed any academic work at all to 'subtexts in scholarship'? In the popular imagination, at the very least, and probably among most academics as well, a subtext, an agenda, is something that one should weed out of scholarly work: it is a bias, an error, a failing. One would then think that any discussion of such subtexts among scholars would be either *confessional* or *polemical*: an acknowledgment of the failings of one's own work, or a denunciation of the blunders of one's scholarly interlocutors. Why collect scholars scattered throughout North America, some of them quite prominent, to engage in this sort of potential bloodletting?

At least one reason for doing so is the increasing prominence being given, in our field, to these subtexts. In many cases, this attention is indeed intended polemically: one increasingly encounters accusations of bias mixed together with more substantive arguments against a given scholar's position. In other cases, though, attention to subtexts is being presented more even-handedly, to answer such questions as why certain positions are attractive, or why certain issues generate controversy. Several of the participants in this symposium have published material that aims to do precisely this.[2] The experience of having to compose a paper on this topic, and – even more – of listening to and reading the other participants' papers, has helped me to clarify somewhat my own views on the import and implications of any discussion of 'scholarly subtexts'.

Perhaps the first and most obvious point suggested by all of my colleagues' essays – and indeed by the healthy size of the audience that came to listen to them – is that our work *matters*. To be sure, we are often inclined to exaggerate the impact of our scholarship, and to imagine that our rather obscure historical, textual, exegetical studies will have a direct and salubrious influence on contemporary theology. As I note in my essay, such a belief strikes me as wishful thinking of the most naïve variety. But equally common is the suspicion that the work undertaken in the 'ivory tower' does not engage with the 'real world' much at all; that university professors, especially in historical disciplines, occupy themselves with concerns so murky and arcane as to have no point of connection at all with the daily life of people today. This suspicion is not only imposed on us from without; it is, at times, a source of our own personal misgivings.

Yet the topics that were raised as 'subtexts' in our essays and discussions were by no means trivial or esoteric at all. We did not confine ourselves to ancient ideologies or to the meaning of obscure texts. Instead, our analysis put on the table such heady and relevant issues as anti-

---

2. See, e.g., John Kloppenborg, *Excavating Q: The History and Setting of the Sayings Gospel* (Minneapolis: Fortress; Edinburgh: T. & T. Clark, 2000), especially 271–444; 'A Dog among the Pigeons: The "Cynic Hypothesis" as a Theological Problem', in *From Quest to Q: Festschrift James M. Robinson* (ed. Jon Ma. Asgeirsson, Kristin de Troyer and Marvin W. Meyer; Leuven: Leuven University Press, 2000), 73–117; William Arnal, 'Making and Re-Making the Jesus-Sign: Contemporary Markings on the Body of Christ', in *Whose Historical Jesus?* (ed. William E. Arnal and Michel Desjardins; Waterloo, Ont.: Wilfrid Laurier University Press, 1997), 308–319; *Jesus and the Village Scribes: Galilean Conflicts and the Setting of Q* (Minneapolis: Fortress, 2001), especially 18–21, 59–65; Robert J. Miller (ed.), *The Apocalyptic Jesus: A Debate* (Santa Rosa, CA: Polebridge, 2001).

Semitism and the Holocaust (Arnal, Marshall), attitudes toward the value
of this world (Allison, Kloppenborg, Miller), attitudes toward sexuality
(Levine), and the nature of religion itself (Fredriksen). If a discussion of
subtexts in a fairly obscure field of historical scholarship can balloon so
suddenly and fruitfully into such a range of vital concerns, there is
evidently more going on in the 'ivory tower' than may meet the eye. We
seem to slide very easily from our precise areas of expertise into matters of
broad humanistic concern. Our work is *engaged*, whether we like it or not,
even when its ostensible object seems far removed from modern life; and
our work derives its importance, its relevance, its interest, from that
engagement.

This observation, in turn, suggests another point, one that deserves
special emphasis here because of the way that all of the essays, in their
different fashions, illustrated this point. The issue is the fashion in which
subtexts or agenda influence arguments, and the reception of those
arguments. John Kloppenborg observed that the presence of agenda can
incline us to accept arguments that we would otherwise dismiss as weak or
illogical. I suggested in my paper one such example: the fashion in which
an interest in conventional (and reified) definitions of a religious tradition
(in this case, both Christianity and Judaism) can be linked to the dismissal
of the historical utility of extra-canonical sources (especially the *Gospel of
Thomas*), and, in consequence, the invocation of *demonstrably* duplicitous
arguments in support of that dismissal.

But the situation is even more complex, and doubles back upon itself.
One of the weak and illogical arguments recently deployed with much
vigor in historical Jesus scholarship and accepted with surprising
equanimity, is precisely the argument that the intersection between an
agenda (personal or cultural) and a set of conclusions is itself evidence
relevant to those conclusions (whether for or against). This type of
argument can be framed positively or negatively. The positive form is the
assertion that a particular historical conclusion is a *better* conclusion
because its implications are attractive. To some degree, this position is
invoked (in passing) in Robert Miller's essay on the theological implications of a non-apocalyptic Jesus: 'But let's ask who honors Judaism more.
Is it the one who insists that its God is a Deity of coercive violence, whose
will is expressed in every military victory, and that only a non-Jew could
think otherwise? Or is it one who sees in Jesus' words and deeds a Jewish
experiment in imagining a non-violent God?'[3] Here, the positive social
and theological implications of a non-apocalyptic religious imagination
appear to be cited as arguments for the plausibility of imputing such a
view to Jesus, as if historical plausibility and desirability were in any way

---

3. Robert Miller, 'Theological Stakes in the Apocalyptic Jesus Debate', 118, in this
volume.

related. John Marshall's essay appears to share this assumption, albeit to a limited degree and only implicitly.[4] In showing that an apocalyptic version of the historical Jesus is as susceptible to anti-Semitic or anti-Jewish deployment as any other version of Jesus (a view with which I am in complete agreement), Marshall *appears* to be arguing that, therefore, this reconstruction of Jesus is not intrinsically superior to any others. Marshall quite explicitly draws the conclusion that 'the Jesus we want, the Jesus we get, and the Jesus that forms the strongest bulwark against anti-Semitism – these three Jesuses are not especially likely to intersect'.[5] So at some level his point must be to repudiate the argument that the best historical reconstruction will necessarily be the one that serves our interests. But by approaching the issue in terms of the equal potential for anti-Judaism of an apocalyptic Jesus with a non-apocalyptic Jesus, Marshall essentially cedes the ground to the very argument he intends to reject. Why not instead, for instance, argue that the potential of a historical reconstruction for anti-Judaism has no bearing whatever on its *historical* merits?

The negative side of this argument is more frequently encountered. This appears as the claim that the presence of implications to a historical argument or reconstruction that are positive from the perspective of the historian in question are evidence against that reconstruction. In short, this is an argument that associates congeniality with bias, and correspondingly, the apparent absence of congeniality with the absence of bias and hence the greater rigor and likely accuracy of the reconstruction. One encounters this type of argument with extraordinary frequency in the context of the debate whether the historical Jesus was an apocalyptist or not. Indeed, this argument is assumed in the efforts of John Kloppenborg and Robert Miller in their contributions to this volume to show that the apocalyptic Jesus is *just as congenial* to some modern interpreters, albeit for different reasons, as the non-apocalyptic Jesus is to others. It is also assumed in the use by Dale Allison of the notion of coming to a historical conclusion 'against one's will', involuntarily, uncomfortably, as a sign of scholarly integrity; and in his concession to Kloppenborg that 'those who have argued for a so-called apocalyptic Jesus have not always done so simply against their wills, as sometimes implied', and so as a result, 'apocalyptic can be and has been tamed' (above, p. 122).

It seems to me, however, that we should assume that the presence of potential agenda on *both* sides of any given controversial issue indicates, precisely, that all scholarly conclusions are motivated in some sense or another – we would not study things that held no interest for us. This in

---

4. John W. Marshall, 'Apocalypticism and Anti-Semitism: Inner-Group Resources for Inter-Group Conflicts', in this volume.

5. Marshall, 'Apocalypticism and Anti-Semitism', 80.

turn would imply that, while discussion of the presence of subtexts and agenda is important for clarifying the discourse, weeding out spurious arguments, and elucidating just what it is that we are disagreeing about, we cannot continue to use the evocation of bias as a substantive argument for or against any hypothesis. In short, the absence of bias does not indicate that an argument is 'true' in any way; only that we have failed to see clearly the subtextual agenda promoted in a given reconstruction. And the presence of overt or obvious bias simply means that the author has been less careful to disguise such bias – the bias itself may lead to the *correct* conclusions, may be the route that allows a scholar to see what was 'really there'.

We also need to be careful that we do not assume a *community of agenda* on the part of scholars operating in our field. Indeed, this is one of the reasons that, outside of a well-defined faith (or other) community, such agenda cannot be used as positive or negative arguments against a given hypothesis. If we all wanted the same things and held the same views as normative, we could indeed argue that, since reconstruction *x* violates our common norms and desires, it should therefore be set aside (or, conversely, that it is hopelessly compromised by its congeniality). Failing such agreement, though, this argument cannot be compelling. Interpretations of bias or agenda must recognize the diversity of assumptions that characterize individuals and sub-groupings within our field. An excellent example of the failure to do so, and its problems, is the assumption that an attractive Jesus is the same thing as a congenial Jesus, an assumption betrayed, I think, in Allison's comments about the problems with 'taming' apocalypticism, or again with *all* of the symposium's participants' assumptions that anti-Judaism is something we do *not* want to attribute to Jesus. Such views assume and imply that every scholar reconstructing a historical Jesus already views Jesus as an attractive, positive figure, and so will tend to impute to him those ideas held and those qualities admired by the scholar in question. Even leaving aside the question of whether we all hold the same ideas and qualities to be admirable, what if a scholar does *not* think much of Jesus? What if a scholar despises Christianity, and views the figure of Jesus as a crystallization of everything that is wrong with it? Will not such a scholar then find, precisely, *congenial*, the attribution to Jesus of the most *unattractive* qualities possible? Will not such a scholar tend to impute to Jesus, say, the seeds of later Christian anti-Judaism, or the most alien and 'untamed' aspects of ancient apocalypticism? If so, then *both* the claim that Jesus was, say, anti-Jewish, and was not anti-Jewish, will be equally congenial, albeit to different people. Likewise the claim that Jesus was apocalyptic. And if one can identify *both* sides of a dispute as, potentially, equally congenial, how can congeniality serve as an index of the falsity of any reconstruction? It is only the illusion that we can agree on what is attractive and desirable in a portrait of the historical Jesus that misleads us into thinking that attractiveness and desirability can be associated firmly with particular viewpoints.

And this leads me to a final consideration: the extent to which the personal motivations of any given scholar are available to us, and whether it even matters. Dale Allison points out that, while some scholars do appear to wear their ideologies on their sleeves, others reveal no information that allows us to speculate about their personal beliefs. He draws attention to E.P. Sanders, in particular:

> Although he has written two important books on Jesus, I am uncertain, for example, what makes Ed Sanders tick. He has been discreetly silent about his personal theology, if he has any at all. So I do not know whether, apart from professional honor, he has much at stake in what he has written about the historical Jesus. Sometimes we keep our theological cards close to the vest. And sometimes there may not be any theological cards at all.[6]

Moreover, if scholars *are* using reconstructions of the historical Jesus to advance subterranean agenda about which they are not wholly forthcoming, why should we expect that their explicit theological statements will really reveal everything there is to know about their personal beliefs? The latter could just as easily be ciphers for something else as the former. As with our imaginary anti-Christian described above, we simply cannot be sure *enough* of the actual beliefs of any individual to engage in the psychologically speculative task of inferring their scholarly conclusions directly from their personal attitudes.

Thus I would stress that the task of uncovering subtexts is much less about authorial intention – including identifying the potential individual congeniality of this or that conclusion – than it is about looking at the way that 'individual' reconstructions fit into larger contemporary discourses. What we are really doing in looking at 'agenda' and 'subtexts' is trying to consider *the cultural work performed by* scholarly reconstructions. As Paula Fredriksen importantly observes, 'As authors, we have little or no control over how our work is read or used. And all our reconstructions... can be construed as supporting particular agendas, whether that be our intention or not.'[7] The ellipsis in this quotation hides a reference to my own paper for this symposium, and I can only assume that Fredriksen is reflecting here on the lack of fit between my own speculations about her work, and her actual personal beliefs and agenda. This is exactly on point. What matters about discourse is how it is deployed and how it can be

---

6. Dale C. Allison, 'The Problem of Apocalyptic: From Polemic to Apologetics', 107, in this volume.

7. Paula Fredriksen, 'Compassion is to Purity as Fish is to Bicycle', 60, in this volume.

deployed within a larger cultural framework; not what individual quirks may have motivated it. This being the case, analysis of subtexts will prove much more important for analyzing the *reception* of particular arguments than it will for identifying whether the origins of those arguments were sufficiently pristine to be taken seriously.

BIBLIOGRAPHY

Allison, Dale C., *Jesus of Nazareth: Millenarian Prophet* (Minneapolis: Fortress, 1998).

—'Jesus was an Apocalyptic Prophet', in Robert J. Miller (ed.), *The Apocalyptic Jesus: A Debate* (Santa Rosa, CA: Polebridge, 2001), 17–29, 83–105, 109–14.

Arnal, William E., 'The Rhetoric of Marginality: Apocalypticism, Gnosticism, and Sayings Gospels', *HTR* 88.4 (1995): 471–94.

—'Major Episodes in the Biography of Jesus: Methodological Observations on the Historicity of the Narrative Tradition', *Toronto Journal of Theology* 13.2 (1997): 201–26.

—'Making and Re-Making the Jesus-Sign: Contemporary Markings on the Body of Christ', in William E. Arnal and Michel Desjardins (eds.), *Whose Historical Jesus?* (ESCJ, 7; Waterloo, Ont.: Wilfrid Laurier University Press, 1997), 308–19.

—*Jesus and the Village Scribes: Galilean Conflicts and the Setting of Q* (Minneapolis: Fortress, 2001).

Athanassiadi, P., and M. Frede (eds.), *Pagan Monotheism* (Oxford: Oxford University Press, 1999).

Aune, David E., *Prophecy in Early Christianity and the Ancient Mediterranean World* (Grand Rapids, MI: Eerdmans, 1983).

Bailey, James L., 'Experiencing the Kingdom as a Little Child: A Rereading of Mark 10:13–16', *Word and World* 15 (1995): 58–67.

Baird, William, *History of New Testament Research.* II: *From Jonathan Edwards to Rudolf Bultmann* (Minneapolis: Fortress, 2003).

Bergren, Theodore, *Sixth Ezra* (Oxford: Oxford University Press, 1998).

Best, Ernest, 'Mark 10: 13–16: The Child as Model Recipient', in J.R. McKay and James F. Miller (eds.), *Biblical Studies in Honor of William Barclay* (Philadelphia: Westminster, 1976), 119–34.

Betz, Hans Dieter, *The Sermon on the Mount: A Commentary on the Sermon on the Mount* (Hermeneia; Minneapolis: Fortress Press, 1995).

Boccaccini, Gabriele, *Beyond the Essene Hypothesis: The Parting of the Ways between Qumran and Enochic Judaism* (Grand Rapids, MI: Eerdmans, 1998).

—*The Roots of Rabbinic Judaism: An Intellectual History from Ezekiel to Daniel* (Grand Rapids, MI: Eerdmans, 2002).

Bockmuehl, Markus, 'Review of Dale C. Allison, *Jesus of Nazareth*', *JTS* 51 (2000): 637–41.

Boyarin, Daniel, 'Semantic Differences; or, "Judaism"/ "Christianity"', in A.H. Becker and A.Y. Reed (eds.), *The Ways that Never Parted* (Tübingen: J.C.B. Mohr [Paul Siebeck], 2003), 65–83.

Buell, Denise, 'Race and Universalism in Early Christianity', *JECS* 10 (2002): 429–68.

Bultmann, Rudolf K., *Jesus* (Berlin: Deutsche Bibliothek, 1926).

—*Jesus and the Word* (New York: Charles Scribner's Sons; London: Nicholson, 1934).

Burkitt, F. Crawford, 'The Eschatological Idea in the Gospel', in *Essays on Some Biblical*

Questions of the Day by Members of the University of Cambridge (London: Macmillan & Co., 1909).

—'The Failure of Liberal Christianity' and 'Some Thoughts on the Athanasian Creed' (Cambridge: Bowes & Bowes, 1910).

—*Jewish and Christian Apocalypses* (London: H. Milford, 1914).

Caird, George B., *The Language and Imagery of the Bible* (London: Duckworth, 1980).

Charles, R.H. (ed.), *The Apocrypha and Pseudepigrapha of the Old Testament* (2 vols.; Oxford: Oxford University Press, 1912–13).

Chilton, Bruce D., *A Galilean Rabbi and His Bible: Jesus' Use of the Interpreted Scripture of His Time* (Wilmington, DL: Michael Glazier, 1984).

Cohen, Shaye J.D., *The Beginnings of Jewishness* (Berkeley: University of California Press, 1999).

Colani, Timothée, *Jésus-Christ et les croyances messianiques de son temps* (Strasbourg: Treuttel et Wurtz, 2nd edn, 1864).

Collins, John J., 'Introduction: Towards the Morphology of a Genre', *Semeia* 14 (1979): 1–20.

—*Apocalypticism in the Dead Sea Scrolls* (London and New York: Routledge, 1997).

Corley, Kathleen E., 'Gender and Class in the Teaching of Jesus: A Profile', in Roy W. Hoover (ed.), *Profiles of Jesus* (Santa Rosa, CA: Polebridge, 2002), 137–60.

Crossan, John Dominic, *The Historical Jesus: The Life of a Mediterranean Jewish Peasant* (New York: HarperCollins, 1991).

—*Jesus: A Revolutionary Biography* (San Francisco: HarperSanFrancisco, 1994).

—*Who Killed Jesus? Exposing the Roots of Anti-Semitism in the Gospel Story of the Death of Jesus* (San Francisco: HarperSanFrancisco, 1995).

—*The Birth of Christianity: Discovering What Happened in the Years Immediately After the Execution of Jesus* (San Francisco: HarperSanFrancisco, 1998).

Culler, Jonathan, *On Deconstruction* (Ithaca, NY: Cornell University Press, 1982).

D'Angelo, Mary Rose, 'Re-Membering Jesus: Women, Prophecy, and Resistance in the Memory of the Early Churches', *Horizon* 19 (1992): 199–218.

Daly, Mary, in cohoots with Jane Caputi, *Websters' First New Intergalactic Wickedary of the English Language* (Boston: Beacon Press, 1987).

Davies, W.D., and Dale C. Allison, Jr., *A Critical and Exegetical Commentary on Matthew* (ICC; 3 vols.; Edinburgh: T. & T. Clark, 1988–97).

Dawes, Gregory W., *The Historical Jesus Question: The Challenge of History to Religious Authority* (Louisville, KY: Westminster/John Knox, 2001).

De Conick, April D., 'The Original Gospel of Thomas', *VC* 56.2 (2002): 167–99.

de Jonge, M., *The Testaments of the Twelve Patriarchs: A Critical Edition of the Greek Text* (PVTG, 1; Leiden: E.J. Brill, 1978).

Deming, Will, 'Mark 9.42—10.12, Matthew 5.27–32, and B. Nid. 13b: A First Century Discussion of Male Sexuality', *NTS* 36 (1990): 130–41.

Derrett, J. Duncan M., 'Why Jesus Blessed the Children (Mark 10:13–16 Par.)', *NovT* 15 (1983): 1–18.

Derrida, Jacques, *Of Grammatology* (trans. Gayatri Chakravorty Spivak; Baltimore: Johns Hopkins University Press, 1974 [1967]).

Eddy, Paul Rhodes, 'Jesus as Diogenes? Reflections on the Cynic Jesus', *JBL* 115 (1996): 449–69.

Elliott, John H., 'The Jesus Movement was not Egalitarian but Family-Oriented', *Biblical Interpretation* 11 (2003): 173–210.

—'Jesus was Neither a Jew nor a Christian: Pitfalls of Inappropriate Nomenclature'. Unpublished paper given at the 67th International Meeting of the Catholic Biblical Association, Saint Mary's University, Halifax, Nova Scotia, August 7–10, 2004.

Emmet, C.W., *The Eschatological Question in the Gospels: And Other Studies in Recent New Testament Criticism* (Edinburgh: T. & T. Clark, 1911).

Fitzmyer, Joseph A., 'Matthean Divorce Texts and Some New Palestinian Evidence', *TS* 37 (1976): 197–226.

Fowl, Stephen, 'Receiving the Kingdom as a Child: Children and Riches in Luke 18:15ff.', *NTS* 39 (1993): 153–58.

Fox, Robin Lane, *Pagans and Christians* (New York: Alfred A. Knopf, 1986).

Fredriksen, Paula, 'Judaism, the Circumcision of Gentiles, and Apocalyptic Hope: Another Look at Galatians 1 and 2', *JTS* 42 (1991): 532–64.

—'Did Jesus Oppose the Purity Laws?' *Bible Review* 11 (1995): 18–25 and 42–47.

—'What You See is What You Get', *Theology Today* 52 (1995): 75–97.

—*Jesus of Nazareth, King of the Jews: A Jewish Life and the Emergence of Christianity* (New York: Alfred Knopf, 1999).

—*From Jesus to Christ* (New Haven: Yale University Press, 2nd edn, 2000).

—'What Does Jesus Have to Do With Christ? What Does Knowledge Have to Do With Faith? What Does History Have to Do With Theology?', in A.M. Clifford and A.J. Godzieba (eds.), *Christology: Memory, Inquiry, Practice* (Maryknoll, NY: Orbis, 2002), 3–17.

—'What "Parting of the Ways"? Jews, Gentiles, and the Ancient Mediterranean City', in A.H. Becker and A.Y. Reed (eds.), *The Ways that Never Parted* (Tübingen: J.C.B. Mohr [Paul Siebeck], 2003), 48–56.

Fredriksen, Paula, and Adele Reinhartz (eds.), *Jesus, Judaism, and Christian Anti-Judaism: Reading the New Testament after the Holocaust* (Louisville, KY and London: Westminster/John Knox, 2002).

Freyne, Seán, 'Galilean Questions to Crossan's Mediterranean Jesus', in William E. Arnal and Michel Desjardins (eds.), *Whose Historical Jesus?* (ESCJ, 7; Waterloo, Ont.: Canadian Corporation for Studies in Religion/Corporation canadienne des sciences religieuses by Wilfrid Laurier University Press, 1997), 61–91.

Funk, Robert W., *Honest to Jesus: Jesus for a New Millennium* (San Francisco: HarperSanFrancisco, 1996).

Funk, Robert W., and the Jesus Seminar, *The Acts of Jesus: What did Jesus Really Do?* (San Francisco: HarperSanFrancisco, 1998).

Funk, Robert W., Ray Hoover and the Jesus Seminar, *The Five Gospels: What Did Jesus Really Say?* (New York: Macmillan, 1993).

Gager, John G., *The Origins of Anti-Semitism: Attitudes Toward Judaism in Pagan and Christian Antiquity* (Oxford: Oxford University Press, 1983).

Galvin, John P., ' "I Believe...in Jesus Christ, His Only Son, Our Lord": The Earthly Jesus and the Christ of Faith', *Int* 50 (1996): 373–82.

García Martínez, Florentino (ed.), *The Dead Sea Scrolls Translated: The Qumran Texts in English* (New York: E.J. Brill; Grand Rapids, MI: Eerdmans, 2nd edn, 1996).

Georgi, Dieter. 'Rudolf Bultmann's *Theology of the New Testament* Revisited', in Edward C.

Hobbs (ed.), *Bultmann, Retrospect, and Prospect: The Centenary Symposium at Wellesley* (Harvard Theological Studies, 35; Philadelphia: Fortress, 1985), 75–87.

Gnilka, Joachim, *Jesus von Nazaret: Botschaft und Geschichte* (HTKNT, Supplementband, 3; Freiburg: Herder, 1990).

Golden, Mark, 'Chasing Change in Roman Childhood', *Ancient History Bulletin* 4 (1990): 90–94.

Harvey, David, *The Condition of Postmodernity: An Enquiry into the Origins of Cultural Change* (Oxford: Blackwell, 1989).

Hays, Richard, 'The Corrected Jesus', *First Things* (May 1994): 43–48.

Head, Peter M., 'The Nazi Quest for an Aryan Jesus', *JSHJ* 2.1 (2004): 55–89.

Hengel, Martin, *Nachfolge und Charisma: Eine exegetisch-religionsgeschichtliche Studie zu Mt. 8, 21f. und Jesu Ruf in die Nachfolge* (BZNW, 34; Berlin: Walter de Gruyter, 1968).

—*The Charismatic Leader and His Followers* (Edinburgh: T. & T. Clark; New York: Crossroad, 1981).

Hengel, Martin, and Roland Deines, 'E.P. Sanders' "Common Judaism", Jesus, and the Pharisees', *JTS* 46 (1995): 1–70.

Hoffmann, R. Joseph (ed. and trans.), *Porphyry's Against the Christians: The Literary Remains* (Amherst, NY: Prometheus Books, 1994).

Holman, Charles, *Till Jesus Comes: Origins of Christian Apocalyptic Expectation* (Peabody, MA: Hendrickson, 1996).

Holtzmann, Heinrich Julius, *Die synoptischen Evangelien: Ihr Ursprung und geschichtlicher Charakter* (Leipzig: Wilhelm Engelmann, 1863).

Holtzmann, Oskar, *The Life of Jesus* (London: A. & C. Black, 1904).

Horsley, Richard A., and John S. Hanson, *Bandits, Prophets, and Messiahs: Popular Movements in the Time of Jesus* (Minneapolis: Winston, 1985; repr. Harrisburg, PA: Trinity Press International, 1999).

Hvalvik, Reidar, *The Struggle for Scripture and Covenant: The Purpose of the Epistle of Barnabas and Jewish-Christian Competition in the Second Century* (Tübingen: J.C.B. Mohr [Paul Siebeck], 1996).

Inge, W.R., 'Review of W. Sanday, *Christologies Ancient and Modern*', *JTS* 11 (1910): 584–86.

Jameson, Frederic, *Postmodernism; Or, The Cultural Logic of Late Capitalism* (Durham, NC: Duke University Press, 1991).

Jeremias, Joachim, *New Testament Theology: The Proclamation of Jesus* (London: SCM Press; New York: Charles Scribner's Sons, 1971).

—'Die Naherwartung des Endes in den Worten Jesu', in Franz Theunis (ed.), *Kerygma und Mythos, VI-6: Aspekte der Unfehlbarkeit: kritische Untersuchungen und Interpretationen* (Theologische Forschung, 56; Hamburg: Herbert Reich, 1975), 139–45.

—'The Search for the Historical Jesus', in K.C. Hanson (ed.), *Jesus and the Message of the New Testament* (Fortress Classics in Biblical Studies; Minneapolis: Fortress, 2002), 1–17.

Johnson, Luke Timothy, 'The Humanity of Jesus: What's at Stake in the Quest for the Historical Jesus?' in John Dominic Crossan, Luke Timothy Johnson and Werner H. Kelber, *The Jesus Controversy: Perspectives in Context* (Harrisburg, PA: Trinity Press International, 1999), 48–74.

Jones, C.P., *Kinship Diplomacy in the Ancient World* (Cambridge, MA: Harvard University Press, 1999).

Joyce, James, *Ulysses* (Paris: Rodker, 1922).

Kähler, Martin, *The So-Called Historical Jesus and the Historic Biblical Christ* (ed., trans. and intro. Carl E. Braaten; Philadelphia: Fortress, 1964).

Kant, Immanuel, *Religion Within the Limits of Reason Alone* (trans. Theodore M. Greene and Hoyt H. Hudson; New York: Harper, 1960).

Käsemann, Ernst, 'Das Problem des historischen Jesus', *ZTK* 51 (1954): 125–53.

—'The Problem of the Historical Jesus', in *idem*, *Essays on New Testament Themes* (SBT, 41; London: SCM, 1964), 15–47.

—'The Beginnings of Christian Theology', in *idem*, *New Testament Questions of Today* (London: SCM, 1969), 82–107.

Khan, Shahnaz, *Aversion and Desire: Negotiating Muslim Female Identity in the Diaspora* (Toronto: Women's Press, 2002).

King, Karen, 'Back to the Future', in The Jesus Seminar, *The Once and Future Jesus* (Santa Rosa, CA: Polebridge, 2000), 77–107.

Kloppenborg, John S., 'A Dog Among the Pigeons: The "Cynic Hypothesis" as a Theological Problem', in Jon Asgeirsson, Kristin de Troyer and Marvin W. Meyer (eds.), *From Quest to Quelle: Festschrift James M. Robinson* (BETL, 146; Leuven: Uitgeverij Peeters, 1999), 77–117.

—*Excavating Q: The History and Setting of the Sayings Gospel* (Minneapolis: Fortress; Edinburgh: T. & T. Clark, 2000).

—'Isaiah 5:1–7, The Parable of the Tenants and Vineyard Leases on Papyrus', in Stephen G. Wilson and Michel Desjardins (eds.), *Text and Artifact in the Religions of Mediterranean Antiquity: Essays in Honour of Peter Richardson* (ESCJ, 9; Waterloo, Ont.: Wilfrid Laurier University Press, 2000), 111–34.

Knox, John, *The Death of Christ: The Cross in New Testament History and Faith* (New York and Nashville: Abingdon, 1958).

Ladd, George Eldon, *The Presence of the Future: The Eschatology of Biblical Realism* (Grand Rapids, MI: Eerdmans, 1974).

LaHurd, Carol Schersten, 'Re-viewing Luke 15 with Arab Christian Women', in Amy-Jill Levine (ed.), *A Feminist Companion to Luke* (Feminist Companion to the New Testament and Early Christian Writings, 3; London and New York: Continuum, 2002), 246–68.

Levine, Amy-Jill, 'Second Temple Judaism, Jesus and Women: Yeast of Eden', *Biblical Interpretation* 2.1 (1994): 8–33.

—'Jesus, Divorce, and Sexuality: A Jewish Critique', in L.J. Greenspoon, D. Hamm and B.F. Le Beau (eds.), *The Historical Jesus through Catholic and Jewish Eyes* (Harrisburg, PA: Trinity Press International, 2000), 113–29.

—'Lilies of the Field and Wandering Jews: Biblical Scholarship, Women's Roles, and Social Location', in Ingrid Rosa Kitzberger (ed.), *Transformative Encounters: Jesus and Women Re-Viewed* (Leiden: E.J. Brill, 2000), 329–52.

—'Matthew, Mark, and Luke: Good News or Bad?' in Paula Fredriksen and Adele Reinhartz (eds.), *Jesus, Judaism, and Christian Anti-Judaism: Reading the New Testament after the Holocaust* (Louisville, KY and London: Westminster John Knox, 2002), 77–98.

—'The Disease of Postcolonial New Testament Studies and the Hermeneutics of Healing', *Journal of Feminist Studies in Religion* 20.1 (2004): 91–99.

Lincoln, Bruce, *Discourse and the Construction of Society: Comparative Studies of Myth, Ritual, and Classification* (New York and Oxford: Oxford University Press, 1989).

—*Theorizing Myth: Narrative, Ideology, and Scholarship* (Chicago: University of Chicago Press, 1999).

Mack, Burton L., *A Myth of Innocence: Mark and Christian Origins* (Philadelphia: Fortress, 1988).

Malkin, I. (ed.), *Ancient Perceptions of Greek Ethnicity* (Washington, DC: Center for Hellenic Studies, 2001).

Marshall, John W., *Parables of War: Reading John's Jewish Apocalypse* (ESCJ, 10; Waterloo: Wilfrid Laurier University Press, 2001).

McKnight, Scot, *A New Vision for Israel: The Teachings of Jesus in National Context* (Grand Rapids, MI: Eerdmans, 1999).

Meier, John P., *A Marginal Jew: Rethinking the Historical Jesus*. Volume I: *The Roots of the Problem and the Person* (Anchor Bible Reference Library; New York: Doubleday, 1991).

—*A Marginal Jew: Rethinking the Historical Jesus*. Volume II: *Mentor, Message, and Miracles* (Anchor Bible Reference Library; New York: Doubleday, 1994).

—'The Present State of the "Third Quest" for the Historical Jesus: Loss and Gain', *Bib* 80 (1999): 459–86.

—*A Marginal Jew: Rethinking the Historical Jesus*. Volume III: *Companions and Competitors* (Anchor Bible Reference Library; New York: Doubleday, 2001).

Miller, Robert J., 'Can the Historical Jesus be Made Safe for Orthodoxy? A Critique of *The Jesus Quest* by Ben Witherington III', *Journal of Higher Criticism* 4 (1997): 120–37.

—*The Jesus Seminar and Its Critics* (Santa Rosa, CA: Polebridge, 1999).

—'Is the Apocalyptic Jesus History?' in Karen Armstrong, Don Cupitt, Arthur J. Dewey *et. al.*, *The Once & Future Faith* (Santa Rosa, CA: Polebridge Press, 2001), 101–16.

Miller, Robert J. (ed.), *The Complete Gospels: Annotated Scholars Version* (San Francisco: HarperSanFrancisco, rev. and exp. edition, 1994).

—*The Apocalyptic Jesus: A Debate* (Santa Rosa, CA: Polebridge Press, 2001).

Moore, Stephen D., *Literary Criticism and the Gospels: The Theoretical Challenge* (New Haven: Yale University Press, 1989).

Mueller, James R., 'The Temple Scroll and the Gospel Divorce Texts', *RevQ* 10.38 (1980): 247–56.

Newman, Carey C., 'Foreword', in Paula Fredriksen and Adele Reinhartz (eds.), *Jesus, Judaism, and Christian Anti-Judaism: Reading the New Testament after the Holocaust* (Louisville, KY and London: Westminster John Knox, 2002), ix–xi.

Nicklesburg, George W., *1 Enoch: A Commentary on the Book of 1 Enoch* (Hermeneia; Minneapolis: Fortress, 2000).

Nkwoka, A.O., 'Mark 10:13–16: Jesus' Attitude to Children and its Modern Challenges', *African Theological Journal* 14 (1985): 100–110.

Paget, James Carleton, *The Epistle of Barnabas: Outlook and Background* (WUNT, 2/64; Tübingen: J.C.B. Mohr [Paul Siebeck], 1994).

Pannenberg, Wolfhart, *Jesus—God and Man* (Philadelphia: Westminster, 1968).

—'Religious Pluralism and Conflicting Truth Claims: The Problem of a Theology of the World Religions', in Gavin D'Costa (ed.), *Christian Uniqueness Reconsidered: The*

Myth of a Pluralistic Theology of Religions (Maryknoll, NY: Orbis Books, 1990), 96–
106.

Patte, Daniel (ed.), *Kingdom and Children: Aphorism, Chreia, Structure. Semeia* 29 (1983).

Patterson, Stephen J., *The Gospel of Thomas and Jesus* (Sonoma, CA: Polebridge Press, 1993).

—*The God of Jesus* (Harrisburg, PA: Trinity Press International, 1998).

Peabody, Francis Greenwood, 'New Testament Eschatology and New Testament Ethics', in Percy Stafford Allen and John de Monins Johnson (eds.), *Transactions of the Third International Congress for the History of Religions* (Oxford: Clarendon, 1908), II, 305–12.

Pearson, Birger A., 'The Gospel According to the Jesus Seminar', *Religion* 25 (1995): 317–38.

—'The Gospel According to the Jesus Seminar', *Occasional Papers of the Institute for Antiquity and Christianity* 35. Claremont: The Claremont Graduate School, April 1996.

Perrin, Nicholas, *Thomas and Tatian: The Relationship between the Gospel of Thomas and the Diatessaron* (Leiden: E.J. Brill, 2002).

Pitre, Brant, 'Marginal Elites: Matt 19:12 and the Social and Political Dimensions of Becoming Eunuchs for the Sake of the Kingdom'. Unpublished paper presented at the Annual Meeting of the Society of Biblical Literature, Boston, MA, November 1999.

Poole, Matthew, *Synopsis criticorum aliorumque S. Scripturae interpretum* (4 vols. in 5; London: Cornelius Bee, 1667–76).

—*A Commentary on the Holy Bible* (4 vols.; London: Henry G. Bohn, 1846).

Rabin, C., 'Jubilees: Introduction', in H.F.D. Sparks (ed.), *The Apocryphal Old Testament* (Oxford: Oxford University Press, 1984), 1–10.

Rashdall, Hastings, 'The Creeds', *The Modern Churchman* 4 (1914): 204–14.

Relton, Herbert M., *A Study in Christology: The Problem of the Relation of the Two Natures in the Person of Christ* (London: SPCK, 1917).

Sanders, E.P., *Jesus and Judaism* (Philadelphia: Fortress; London: SCM, 1985).

—*The Historical Figure of Jesus* (Harmondsworth, Middlesex: Penguin, 1993).

—'Jesus, Ancient Judaism, and Modern Christianity: The Quest Continues', in Paula Fredriksen and Adele Reinhartz (eds.), *Jesus, Judaism, and Christian Anti-Judaism: Reading the New Testament after the Holocaust* (Louisville, KY and London: Westminster John Knox, 2002), 31–55.

Sawicki, Marianne, *Crossing Galilee: Architectures of Contact in the Occupied Land of Jesus* (Harrisburg, PA: Trinity Press International, 2000).

Schüssler Fiorenza, Elisabeth, *Jesus and the Politics of Interpretation* (New York: Continuum, 2000).

Schweitzer, Albert, *Von Reimarus zu Wrede. Eine Geschichte der Leben Jesu Forschung* (Tübingen: J.C.B. Mohr [Paul Siebeck], 1906).

—*The Quest of the Historical Jesus: A Critical Study of Its Progress from Reimarus to Wrede*, with a preface by F.C. Burkitt (New York: Macmillan, 1910).

—*Geschichte der Leben-Jesu-Forschung.* 2nd edn of *Von Reimarus zu Wrede* (Tübingen: J.C.B. Mohr [Paul Siebeck], 1913).

—*The Mystery of the Kingdom of God: The Secret of Jesus' Messiahship and Passion* (New York: Dodd, Mead, 1914).

—*Christianity and the Religions of the World* (Selly Oak Colleges Publications, 3; London: Allen & Unwin, 1923).

—*Civilization and Ethics*. Vol. II. *The Philosophy of Civilization* (London: A. & C. Black, 1923).

—*Out of My Life and Thought: An Autobiography* (New York: Holt, 1933).

—*Indian Thought and Its Development* (Boston, MA: Beacon, 1936).

—*The Kingdom of God and Primitive Christianity* (ed. Ulrich Neuenschwander; London: A. & C. Black, 1968) [posthumously published].

—*The Quest of the Historical Jesus* (ed. John Bowden; Minneapolis: Fortress, 1st complete edn, 2001).

Scott, Bernard Brandon, *Hear Then the Parable* (Minneapolis: Fortress, 1989).

Scott, E.F., 'The Place of Apocalyptical Conceptions in the Mind of Jesus', *JBL* 41 (1922): 137–42.

Sim, David C., 'What About the Wives and Children of the Disciples? The Cost of Discipleship from Another Perspective', *Heythrop Journal* 35 (1994): 373–90.

Simon, Marcel, *Verus Israel: étude sur les relations entre chrétiens et juifs dans l'Empire romain, AD 135–425* (Paris: Boccard, 1948).

Smith, Jonathan Z., 'Fences and Neighbors: Some Contours of Early Judaism', in *idem*, *Imagining Religion: From Babylon to Jonestown* (Chicago: University of Chicago Press, 1982), 1–18.

—*Imagining Religion: From Babylon to Jonestown* (Chicago: University of Chicago Press, 1982).

—*Map is Not Territory* (SJLA, 23; Leiden: E.J. Brill, 1978).

Sparks, H.F.D. (ed.), *The Apocryphal Old Testament* (Oxford: Oxford University Press, 1984).

Stark, Rodney, *The Rise of Christianity: A Sociologist Reconsiders History* (Princeton, NJ: Princeton University Press, 1996).

Stone, Michael E., *Fourth Ezra: A Commentary on the Book of Fourth Ezra* (Hermeneia; Minneapolis: Fortress, 1990).

Strauss, David Friedrich, *A New Life of Jesus* (London and Edinburgh: Williams & Norgate, 1865).

Taylor, Gary, *Castration: An Abbreviated History of Western Manhood* (London and New York: Routledge, 2000).

Theissen, Gerd, and Annette Merz, *The Historical Jesus: A Comprehensive Guide* (London: SCM; Minneapolis: Fortress, 1998).

Tiller, Patrick A., *A Commentary on the Animal Apocalypse of 1 Enoch* (Early Judaism and its Literature, 4; Atlanta: Scholars Press, 1993).

Tindal, Matthew, *Christianity as Old as the Creation: Or, the Gospel a Republication of the Religion of Nature* (London: n.p., 2nd edn, 1732).

Vaage, Leif E., *Galilean Upstarts: Jesus' First Followers According to Q* (Valley Forge, PA: Trinity Press International, 1994).

Vermès, Géza, *Jesus the Jew: A Historian's Reading of the Gospels* (London: SCM; Philadelphia: Fortress, 2nd edn, 1983 [1973]).

—*The Religion of Jesus the Jew* (Philadelphia: Fortress, 1993).

Weber, Hans-Ruedi, *Jesus and the Children: Biblical Resources for Study and Preaching* (Geneva: World Council of Churches, 1979).

Weiss, Johannes, *Die Predigt Jesu vom Reiche Gottes* (Göttingen: Vandenhoeck & Ruprecht, 1892).

—*Jesus' Proclamation of the Kingdom of God* (ed. and trans. Richard H. Hiers and David Larrimore Holland; Lives of Jesus Series; Philadelphia: Fortress Press, 1971).

Werner, Hermann, *Die psychische Gesundheit Jesu* (Berlin: Edwin Runge, 1909).

Wiedemann, Thomas, *Adults and Children in the Roman Empire* (New Haven: Yale University Press, 1989).

Witherington, Ben, *The Jesus Quest: The Third Search for the Jew of Nazareth* (Downers Grove, IL: InterVarsity, 1995).

Wrede, William, *Das Messiasgeheimnis in den Evangelien* (Göttingen: Vandenhoeck & Ruprecht, 1901).

—*The Messianic Secret*, with a foreword by James M. Robinson (Greenwood, SC: Attic, 1971).

Wright, N.T., 'Taking the Text with Her Pleasure: A Post-Post-Modernist Response to J. Dominic Crossan, *The Historical Jesus: The Life of a Mediterranean Jewish Peasant*', *Theology* 96 (1993): 303–309.

—*Christian Origins and the Question of God. Volume 2: Jesus and the Victory of God* (Minneapolis: Fortress; London: SPCK, 1996).

Young, Frances, 'The Finality of Christ', in Michael Goulder (ed.), *Incarnation and Myth: The Debate Continued* (Grand Rapids, MI: Eerdmans, 1979), 174–86.

Zahn, Paul, *The First Christian: Universal Truth in the Teachings of Jesus* (Grand Rapids, MI: Eerdmans, 2003).

AUTHOR INDEX